We hope you enjoy this book. Please return or renew it by the due date.

You can renew it at www.norfolk.gov.uk/libraries or by using our free library app.

Otherwise you can phone 0344 800 8020 - please have your library card and PIN ready.

You can sign up for email reminders too.

D1470817

30129 084 800 102

NORFOLK COUNTY COUNCIL
LIBRARY AND INFORMATION SERVICE

'Campaign journalism at its most urgent.' *Evening Standard* Book of the Week

'A heartbreaking, shocking and deeply moving book that dares to give voice to the voiceless, say the unsayable, and reminds us, with remarkable power, why journalism truly matters.' The Orwell Prize Judges

'A searing picture ... It's impossible to read her account of the step-by-step betrayal without feeling ashamed that it was done in your name.' Bel Mooney, *Daily Mail*

'A superb first-hand account of the immigration scandal that rocked Britain and shamed Theresa May's Conservative government ... Gentleman's reporting is exhaustive and the human experiences she details are harrowing.' James Maxwell, *Herald*

'Reads like dystopian fiction ... *The Windrush Betrayal* knits together a devastating picture of the human cost of punitive immigration policies.' Reni Eddo-Lodge, *Guardian*

'A timely reminder of why journalism matters and what truly great journalists can achieve. Written with both humanity and humility, it reveals, step-by-step, how one of the most shocking scandals of recent years came about and how it was uncovered while always giving voice to the people who matter most, the victims of the Windrush Scandal themselves.' Professor David Olusoga

'Recounts and exposes some of the most egregious effects of the "hostile environment" approach.' *Financial Times*

'Should be compulsory reading for all Home Office ministers and civil servants. Immigration lawyers and campaigners also have much to learn ... Gentleman writes brilliantly and her very readable book is full of moving portraits of the victims. It is a reminder that Gentleman's ability to collect and then convey these very human and humane stories was absolutely critical to the exposure of the Windrush scandal.' Free Movement

'[Gentleman's] reporting for the *Guardian* on this shameful episode saw her named journalist of the year at the British journalism awards ... Gentleman's book contains valuable lessons.' Sukhdev Sandhu, *Observer* Book of the Week

'Amelia Gentleman is a journalist of the old school: enraged by injustice, dedicated to detail and fully committed to speaking truth to power. Every page is a subject for national shame but the final, terrible lesson is that responsibility for the scandal reaches to the highest levels of Government and has still not been properly accounted or atoned for. This incredible story reminds us that we live in an era where power increasingly refuses to listen. The rest of us must.' James O'Brien

'Gentleman has carefully documented the hell experienced by ordinary citizens caught up in the Tories' "hostile environment" for illegal immigrants – so carefully that you have to believe the unbelievable.' *The Oldie*

'Journalism at its best ... A page-turner with the pace and intrigue of a good novel ... Gentleman's great achievement ... is to recognise that the real heroes of the piece are not the campaigners or journalists who brought the issue into the public consciousness, but these ordinary, flawed but decent people whose lives were shattered.' COMPAS, University of Oxford

AMELIA GENTLEMAN

THE
WINDRUSH
BETRAYAL

Exposing the
Hostile Environment

First published by Guardian Faber in 2019
Guardian Faber is an imprint of Faber & Faber Ltd,
Bloomsbury House, 74–77 Great Russell Street,
London WC1B 3DA

Guardian is a registered trademark of
Guardian News & Media Ltd,
Kings Place, 90 York Way, London N1 9GU

This paperback edition first published in 2020

Typeset by Faber & Faber Ltd
Printed and bound by CPI Group (UK) Ltd, Croydon CR0 4YY

We are grateful to the following for permission to reproduce copyright material:

Extracts from *Windrush: The Irresistible Rise of Multi-Racial Britain* by Mike Phillips
and Trevor Phillips, copyright © Mike Phillips and Trevor Phillips, 1998. Reprinted
by permission of HarperCollins Publishers Ltd; Extracts from *The Lonely Londoners*
by Sam Selvon, Penguin, 2006, copyright © 1956. Reproduced by permission of the
Estate of the author; Extracts from *To Sir, with Love* by E. R. Braithwaite, Vintage
Classics. Reproduced by permission of David Higham Associates; and an extract
from *Small Island* by Andrea Levy, first published in Great Britain by Headline
Publishing Group, copyright © 2004 Andrea Levy. Reproduced by permission of
David Grossman Literary Agency Ltd.

A CIP record for this book
is available from the British Library

ISBN 978–1–78335–185–5

MIX
Paper from
responsible sources
FSC® C020471

2 4 6 8 10 9 7 5 3 1

To Sarah O'Connor
1961–2018

CONTENTS

ILLUSTRATIONS

FOREWORD BY KATHARINE VINER

Towards the end of April 2018 I received a letter from Guy Hewitt, the high commissioner for Barbados to the UK. It was quite an exceptional letter, one which I'll never forget.

'"Never was so much owed by so many to so few",' it began.

This wartime quote by Winston Churchill . . . is to me the most apt way of expressing the gratitude of the Caribbean high commissioners and the West Indian diaspora for the incredible work by Amelia Gentleman on the issues confronting elderly, Caribbean-born, long-term UK residents.

In less than a week, a story that was for too long begging for attention became front-page news and in the process won the hearts of the nation and engaged the mind of a government. I want to recognise the seminal work by Amelia in almost singlehandedly leading the charge.

The Caribbean owes her an immeasurable debt of gratitude, and I commend her for an immense dedication to her craft and outstanding service to the people of the Caribbean.

While we are not there yet, I am now optimistic that soon, in large part because of Amelia's work, those elderly West Indians who lived in fear will be able to embrace their loved ones.

What a beautiful way of expressing the extraordinary impact of Amelia Gentleman's reporting in the *Guardian*.

In October 2017, Amelia had started investigating why law-abiding, pension-age people, who had been born in Commonwealth countries but who had spent much of their childhoods and all their adult lives in Britain, were being classified by the Home Office as illegal immigrants. Some were being detained and threatened with deportation. Others were being sacked from their jobs, losing their homes and being denied NHS treatment. Most had no idea that they had been silently 'illegalised' by changing legislation and they were struggling to obtain the complicated documentation needed to prove they had done nothing wrong.

These were untold stories of institutional cruelty that shocked *Guardian* readers when they were published. The government paid no attention to them. It was clear that officials did not consider those affected to be people who mattered, or imagine that anyone would care about them. Ministers thought this was an issue they could safely ignore.

And for months these stories were highlighted only in the *Guardian*, until in April 2018 the government was finally forced into action. Inspired by Amelia's focused tenacity, and backed by our readers' outrage, the *Guardian*'s editorial team was determined to make sure this issue could no longer be overlooked. For two weeks, we put it on the front page of the *Guardian* every day – both in print and online – and made headlines around the world. We refused to allow the government to bury the scandal that Amelia had exposed.

The impact of this reporting has been extraordinary. In the year since the government was finally forced to acknowledge it had made a mistake and to promise to put things right, more than seven thousand people have called the Home Office hotline asking for help. Thousands of people have been granted citizenship or given paperwork confirming that they are living in this country legally. A compensation scheme has been announced, which could end up paying out as much as £570 million in damages to people who were wrongly deported, detained, made homeless or pushed out of their jobs. No one knows how many people have been affected but Home Office staff believe as many as thirty thousand may apply under the scheme. Aspects of Theresa May's hostile environment have been suspended. The Home Secretary, Amber Rudd, resigned and her successor, Sajid Javid, promised to make Britain's immigration system fairer and more compassionate. We are still waiting for comprehensive reform to happen, but the lives of many caught up in the Windrush scandal have unquestionably changed for the better. Some people have been allowed to return to the UK, years after they were deported. Others have got their jobs back. People who have for years lived unsettled lives, terrified that Immigration Enforcement officers were going to arrive in the night and take them away, say they can now sleep easily.

Before the Windrush revelations, the concept of the hostile environment was unfamiliar to most people. These stories revealed the toxic nature of an immigration policy that humiliates and exhausts applicants into submission, routinely ruining lives so the Home Office can help the government meet its quest to bring down net migration figures. And the scale of the outcry showed, I think, that British people are not quite as racist as their government took them to be.

None of this would have happened without Amelia's reporting. The Home Office mostly responded with cynicism when those affected tried repeatedly to explain that a terrible mistake had been made. But Amelia listened to their stories, really listened, calmly and carefully and empathetically. For many of those interviewed, talking publicly about their immigration difficulties was an act of real bravery. I'm so glad their courage proved worthwhile.

This was one of the most shameful episodes in recent British political history. The hostile environment which drove it has been revealed as a social catastrophe and a moral failure. This was a stunning example of the capacity of journalism to bring about dramatic, positive change. While *Guardian* readers were shocked by what they read, no one in government wanted to listen – but Amelia pressed ahead, defiantly publishing articles that revealed the depth of the scandal. The voices of those affected were finally heard, their stories finally told, and justice, at last, is in sight.

Katharine Viner
Editor-in-chief, *Guardian* News & Media
April 2019

INTRODUCTION

How do you pack for a one-way journey back to a country you left when you were eleven and have not visited for fifty years?

Around lunchtime on 24 October 2017, staff at the Yarl's Wood Immigration Removal Centre in Bedfordshire told sixty-one-year-old Paulette Wilson to gather her belongings and get ready to be taken to another holding centre near Heathrow airport, where she was due to be placed on a plane and sent back to Jamaica. After half a century in Britain, she had been classified as an illegal immigrant and was scheduled for imminent removal. Packing did not take long. The clothes she had been wearing when she was arrested a week earlier had been confiscated, leaving her with nothing she could call her own. She put the detention centre-issue toothbrush and nightclothes into a large plastic laundry bag, along with a towel, some soap and some underwear which had been provided by the guards. She looked at the grey prison tracksuit she had been given and wondered how she would manage in Jamaica with no appropriate clothes and no money. Staff led her to an upstairs room to wait for a van to transfer her to Heathrow.

For a moment Paulette, a cook who had worked in the House of Commons canteen, was quiet, dazed by her own terror. Then she asked if she could call her daughter Natalie. She dialled the number, waited for Natalie to pick up, and began to scream.

'They're taking me away. You have to stop them.'

This was a distressing call for Natalie, at home in Wolverhampton. She barely recognised her mother's voice, which had become distorted by fear, and she had trouble understanding the words.

The only thing that was really clear was a repeated plea: 'Natalie, you have to help me.'

Staff were disgruntled by the noise Paulette was making, and tried to remonstrate with her. She told them she would strip herself naked if they tried to put her on a plane and would try to kill herself. Most officers at Yarl's Wood get rapidly jaded by the daily business of handling distraught detainees; they paid little attention to the threats. 'Calm down, Mrs Wilson,' they told her, as they led her to a prison van. She was driven sixty miles to an airport detention centre and locked on a wing with about eight cells. An official prison inspection report describes the high-security centre as 'gloomy, bleak and in many areas unclean',[1] but Paulette was too alarmed to take in her surroundings. She could hear the roar of aeroplanes taking off from the nearby runways and, somewhere out of sight, the cries of another woman, who she assumed was being taken away for immediate deportation.

From one side of the unit she watched two officers working through a pile of papers, and saw them checking off each person, with the words: 'She's going; she's going; she's going.'

She cried in the shower, imagining her new life in Jamaica, a country where she has no surviving relatives. The last time she had been there, in 1968, she had been wearing white knee-high socks, an orange dress and the matching orange ribbons that her mother had tied in her hair before sending her away. Since then a lifetime had passed, and now she was about to embark on a plane for the return journey, a grey-haired grandmother, wearing prison clothes.

An official had asked her, in an apparent gesture of thoughtfulness, which airport in Jamaica she would like to be returned to. Paulette had explained this was a very peculiar question, pointing out despairingly that she could hardly be expected to have a view on Jamaica's available airport options, since she had not flown there or indeed flown anywhere, or even left England for fifty years. This reply does not seem to have perturbed the official compiling the Return Logistics report, who wrote in the 'Preferred home country airport' box of the questionnaire: 'Cannot provide a response as she has been here so long'. The report, which is littered with typos and bears the signs of having been written in great haste, also noted that the detainee had made no preparations to return home because she 'has been here since arriving at the age of ten to be with grandparents'.

Paulette's immigration file states, under the heading 'Reasons for detention': 'Detention is necessary as there is no evidence of subject's lawful entry into the UK; she claims to have arrived as a 10 year-old;[2] so far she has failed to provide evidence of this . . . therefore detention is proportionate.' Her repeated protestations that she had been in England since childhood do not seem to have triggered any concern in the minds of the many officials who were processing her through the system towards removal.

She was confused. She saw herself as a hard-working, law-abiding citizen. How could someone who had been in England since she was a primary school pupil five decades earlier have been classified as an illegal immigrant?

————

I met Paulette and her daughter Natalie in November 2017 and the publication of her story in the *Guardian* inspired dozens of other people to come forward, gradually, to speak out about how they too were experiencing similarly brutal treatment at the hands of immigration officials.

Very slowly to begin with, and later in a dramatic eruption of anger, more people began to call and email me, describing how they had been detained in immigration removal centres, or been sacked from their jobs, or evicted from their homes, or denied life-saving treatment on the National Health Service, or been prevented from travelling abroad to visit dying relatives. Some had received alarming letters instructing them to take immediate steps to leave the country; others had been told that they were unemployable because they had no papers to prove their right to be here. Initially, neither I nor the people affected understood why they were being targeted in this way. Most assumed that they alone had been caught up in a bureaucratic tangle; few guessed that thousands of others were experiencing the same difficulties. Nobody knew what was behind it. The only thing that united them was that they had all arrived in the United Kingdom as children in the 1950s and 1960s from Commonwealth countries, particularly from Britain's former colonies in the Caribbean. Most had travelled to join their parents who had come here to work, often staffing the new health system or the rapidly expanding transport network, or working on the new construction sites which were popping up all over the country as the devastation wrought by Second World War bombing was gradually repaired.

Most had never had the money to go on holiday, so they had never applied for a passport. Until recently being passportless had posed no problem, but the Conservative-led coalition government which came to power in 2010 had created a deliberately hostile environment for immigrants and suddenly these Commonwealth citizens found themselves routinely required to show they were here legally and prove they were British. For many, the official scepticism about their status set off a devastating existential crisis that punctured any sense of security about their identity and the notions of belonging and home.

In a political climate where the rhetoric on immigration had been steadily hardening for a decade, these people were viewed by officials as acceptable collateral damage. In its haste to implement measures which it hoped would cut stubbornly high net migration figures, the government reclassified a large, wholly legal cohort of long-term residents as illegal immigrants.

This vision of the British state, in a final shrug of post-colonial nonchalance, trying to flick citizens back to the same Caribbean islands where centuries earlier their ancestors had been brought from Africa by British colonisers as slaves, was painful to witness – not least because so many felt they had been encouraged by the British government to leave those islands and travel to the UK to work to rebuild a nation shattered by war. The scandal emerged as the latest chapter in a long, guilty history of colonial occupation and exploitation. The names of many of those affected – Winston, Gladstone, Nelson – speak to their colonial childhoods. The jobs they and their parents took in Britain – as night-shift workers in hospitals and car plants, rail track maintenance workers, traffic wardens, construction workers, healthcare assistants, London underground staff – were vital but low-paid. It was hard to avoid the feeling that officials dismissed them as a group of people who didn't matter, a group who, if nothing else, were sufficiently marginalised that they were unlikely to complain.

These people became known collectively as the Windrush generation. This is a slightly misleading term, suggesting that those affected were the same age as the 492 passengers (and a handful of stowaways), the vast majority from Jamaica, on the *Empire Windrush* ship which arrived at Tilbury Docks in Essex on 22 June 1948. That ship's arrival has come to symbolise the start of Britain's transition to a multicultural nation, and the beginning of black Caribbean immigration to the UK, but those affected by the Windrush scandal tend to be much younger, part of a later wave of immigration from the West Indies that gained pace through the 1950s and 1960s, until the government finally succeeded in stemming its flow with the implementation of the 1971 Immigration Act. This act, long forgotten by everyone except students of migration policy, took on a critical significance in Paulette's case and those of thousands like her, because the Home Office insisted that she and others in her situation provide documentary evidence of their presence in the UK decisively locating them in the country before 1 January 1973 (when the Act came into effect). For many, the enormous quantity of documentary proof required was impossible to gather.

The Windrush scandal revealed a number of unpalatable truths about Britain. It came as the direct result of a government attempt to assuage the anxieties of a nation stoked up into a frenzy about immigration. Years of front-page scare stories incited mistrust by peddling narratives of new arrivals occupying school places, hospital beds, council houses. The leaders of all parties know that immigration is vital for the economy, but polling and the media have kept up pressure for repeated promises that immigration will be cut. Ministers tackled these concerns with a brutality that had devastating consequences for many, and in a manner that ultimately did nothing to calm the anxieties of those they were trying to placate.

The uncovering of the scandal revealed how desensitised and dehumanised the Home Office had become, after several years of budget cuts and shrinking staff numbers. It showed a department operating a system that put targets before humanity. It showed how an anti-immigrant rhetoric infected everything, until blameless grandmothers found themselves being locked up by the state.

This is an important cautionary tale, displaying British government at its worst. This is what happens when ministers pander to a populist thirst for anti-immigrant measures by introducing tough, hostile policies, and steadfastly ignore all the warnings that the wrong people will get hurt. This is what happens when politicians become so disconnected from the world outside Westminster that they become oblivious to the disastrous impact of their policy decisions.

How did it happen that thousands of people who thought they were British were told they were illegal immigrants and no one really noticed? As I spoke to more and more of them about their treatment at the hands of the Home Office, the thing that shocked me most was the complete lack of interest that their difficulties had provoked in those they had contacted in search of help. I was disturbed to see how government policies had catastrophically affected a large group of people that they were not originally designed to target, but I was more dismayed by the fact that nothing had happened in response to their repeated expressions of distress. The most senior civil servant in the Home Office admitted later that perhaps this was because the minds of ministers and officials were elsewhere. But their minds wouldn't have been elsewhere if they hadn't had such scant regard for the people affected. This is a story about who gets listened to in Britain and who gets ignored. It's about race, poverty and marginalisation.

For the most part, local and national media had expressed no interest in the subject. The anguish of those affected was a theme neither picked up by the mainstream nor by the non-mainstream media – there were no Facebook or Twitter appeals for action. For at least four years, politicians of all parties were barely aware that this problem was simmering below the surface. In their new determination to be tough on illegal immigration, officials refused to see what was unfolding in front of them. The few politicians who heard occasional accounts of people having difficulty did not seem inclined to be horrified. To begin with, most immigration lawyers did not notice the emerging pattern. It was a scandal hiding in plain sight.

This book opens a window into the lives of many of the people worst hit by the government's policies. It describes what it feels like to get caught up in the tightening vice of the government's hostile environment measures, based on detailed interviews with more than thirty people who found themselves wrongly targeted by the Home Office. We will hear from a chambermaid at the Ritz forced out from Britain after fifty-three years here, from a special needs teaching assistant sacked from his job, from an ambulance driver made homeless, from a car mechanic denied cancer treatment. We will hear from a man whose children took him to Jamaica for a fiftieth birthday surprise holiday, who wasn't allowed to travel back to Britain for almost two years and was meanwhile left almost destitute in a country he hadn't visited since he was six. Behind their stories is a migration history that should not be sugar-coated – people came as children, faced poverty and racism, gradually built good lives for themselves, and then, after half a century in the UK, found themselves rejected, as a direct result of government policy. In extreme cases they were forced out of their homes to live in sheds, in parks, obliged to beg for money to feed children, pushed into tens of thousands of pounds of debt, locked out of the country they viewed as home.

There are many accounts of lives unravelling here, but they are essential to grasping what it's like to face Home Office cruelty after decades in Britain, to see security disintegrating simply because of the absence of a faded stamp in a passport. Together their stories reveal the bigger picture of what went wrong and why.

Understanding the depth of the injustice meted out to thousands of long-term British residents requires an immersion into the story of the arrival of the Windrush generation and the difficulties they experienced during their first years, before building permanent lives here, so one chapter looks at the difficult history of Caribbean migration that contributed to the unfolding of this scandal. I was struck repeatedly by the accounts I heard of long, happy, productive years spent in Britain, before the government chose to question an individual's right to be in the country and to threaten him or her with removal.

This is also the story of an investigation, an account of the difficult, protracted journalistic process of trying to understand and expose the roots of the Home Office failings. I spent months scratching away at the immigration difficulties being encountered by Paulette and others, convinced that there was something happening on a wider scale, but struggling to understand why the government was mistreating people so harshly. To begin with I felt I was looking at it through fog, fumbling for the shape of the problem, with clarity only emerging later. For a while I was transformed into an immigration case worker, spending all day scouring Home Office letters and files of evidence, learning a whole new vocabulary of complex immigration acronyms, trying not to drown in the confusing nuances of twentieth-century nationality legislation. For a few months, all the cheerful pictures of pets and children on my phone were replaced by photographs of interviewees' immigration enforcement notices and legal case notes. For a time, it became all-consuming. Each case seemed to break a new low threshold of injustice. *Guardian* readers were outraged; ministers and officials were mostly silent, except that again and again I noticed that as soon as I raised a difficult case with the Home Office, it would unexpectedly be expedited and resolved with mysterious speed.

Working to uncover the truth was like being in a slow-moving (unglamorous) detective drama, encountering endless red herrings and failing to see the wood for the trees, until suddenly the denouement came in an explosion of political fury and protestations of government regret. The investigation which followed unleashed one of the most damaging political crises within the British government in recent decades, wounding the prime minister and forcing the Home Secretary to resign, profoundly shaking the debate on immigration in the UK. The Home Secretary admitted that something had gone fundamentally wrong within her department as staff worked to implement the government's newly toughened immigration policy.

Journalists are meant to be cool, neutral and collected. Writing about this issue I found myself often being none of those things, moving over the months from feeling puzzled to confused, then in rapid succession concerned, horrified, angry and finally sad, as the remaining few scales fell from my eyes and I realised what the government was capable of doing.

This became a study of a struggling government department, where staff were placed under immense pressure to push down immigration numbers, working to ambitious targets to remove illegal immigrants from the country. At a time when US President Donald Trump's anti-immigrant policies were being criticised – his lavish plans for a wall, his readiness to hold children in cages at the Mexican border, his desire to impose a travel ban on visitors from majority Muslim countries – this scandal forced sober reflection on our own record, revealing Britain to be a more callous nation than we had realised. As a result of this investigation, people in Britain began to have a much deeper understanding of the nature of the government's hostile environment policies, and were forced to consider whether those policies were something they wanted to continue to support.

The lessons that should be learned from what happened remain acutely relevant, as the same department begins to register over three million Europeans to allow them to remain in the UK after Brexit. In other departments, ministers have promised in the wake of Windrush to be more thoughtful about the impact of policies on individuals, as they push through reforms to benefits and healthcare.

What happened to Paulette Wilson and others like her was terrible, but in some ways this is also an optimistic story. Things went horrifically wrong, but the fury of those people who were mistreated eventually brought about important changes. It transpired that the British public have a more fair-minded approach to immigration than politicians believed. I'm writing this book partly in an attempt to show how journalism, which currently feels much maligned, can be a powerful force for good, a potent medium to expose problems and to shame governments into action.

For some people change came too late, with tragic consequences. I'd like to make sure that we don't forget the extreme suffering inflicted by the British government on thousands of people who were British but unable to prove it. Some people who got caught up in this mess did not survive, and their lives should not be forgotten.

———

None of this was clear to Paulette as she sat in her cell at the airport immigration removal centre, expecting to be escorted on to a flight to Jamaica. That night she made up her bed and tried to sleep but found she was too troubled to rest. She spent much of the night pacing around the unit.

'I was up and down all night, wondering if they were going to put me on a plane tonight or tomorrow morning,' she told me later. 'I've got no clothes, no money. They're going to pick me up from here and put me somewhere I don't even know, a place where I wouldn't know if I was going north, south, east or west. I thought: God, this is really it now.'

A PERSON WITH NO LEAVE TO REMAIN

In August 2015, a little over two years before she was detained, Paulette Wilson had received an extremely worrying letter. 'That was the day my world changed,' she told me later, an unmistakable Midlands lilt in her voice. On a sheet of paper decorated with the Home Office logo and headed with the words 'Notice of Immigration Decision', the letter stated: 'Paulette Wilson. You are a person with no leave to enter or remain in the United Kingdom.'

Paulette was alone at her flat in Wolverhampton when she opened it; she skimmed through the document, which was written in clunky and perplexing officialese, to try to understand why she had been sent such a distressing notification. 'You are specifically considered to be a person who has failed to provide evidence of lawful entry to the United Kingdom,' it announced. 'Therefore you are liable for removal.' This was followed by a warning in alarming capitals: 'LIABILITY FOR REMOVAL'. 'If you do not leave the United Kingdom as required you will be liable to enforced removal to Jamaica.'

'Removal' is the gentler official term for deportation, a word which is technically used only when a criminal is being sent out of the country; but beyond Home Office employees, few people understand the distinction, and most view a forced expulsion from the country, often with handcuffs used, as deportation, regardless of whether this is the correct terminology.

The document upset Paulette profoundly, shaking her sense of who she was. After a lifetime in England, she had always assumed she was British and had never had any reason to question her identity. This sudden official challenge to her status was as horrific as it was surprising. 'It made me feel like I didn't exist.' Uncertain how to respond to the letter, she stuffed it in a drawer so she wouldn't have to look at it, hiding it alongside another mystifying notification she had received the week before from the Department for Work and Pensions which stated that she was no longer entitled to any financial support because her immigration status was unclear. She mentioned the letters to no one. 'I was panicking. I was too scared to tell my daughter. I didn't know why they wanted to get rid of me.'

In the days that followed, Paulette's thirty-nine-year-old daughter Natalie noticed that her mother was behaving extremely oddly. Normally very bubbly and cheerful, Paulette had withdrawn into herself. It was a while before Paulette steeled herself to show Natalie the Home Office letter. Natalie was as confused as her mother had been, and had to read it several times.

You have no lawful basis to remain in the UK and you should leave as soon as possible. By remaining here without lawful basis you may be prosecuted for an offence under the Immigration Act 1971, the penalty for which is a fine and/or up to 6 months imprisonment. You are also liable to be removed from the UK. If you do not leave voluntarily and removal action is required you may face a reentry ban of up to 10 years. If you decide to stay then your life in the UK will become increasingly more difficult.

A list followed explaining that anyone who employed Paulette would face a £20,000 fine, that her landlord would be fined for failing to spot her irregular immigration status, and that she could be charged for NHS treatment.

Natalie knew that her mother had arrived in England as a child and had never left the country, but her first instinct was to feel annoyed with Paulette for having failed to be upfront with her.

'Mum, are you an illegal immigrant?' she asked, aghast and angry. 'All this time, and you haven't told me?'

'I didn't know,' Paulette replied. Her evident distress and

confusion convinced Natalie that this was as shocking and new to Paulette as it was to her.

Natalie, who works part time as a dinner lady at the local primary school, embarked on a heroic but ultimately futile two-year campaign to persuade the Home Office that a bureaucratic error had resulted in her mother being misclassified as something she was not. Anyone who has tried to take on the Home Office will know that it is an unequal battle, with confused and frightened individuals spending hours held in automated telephone queuing systems, waiting to speak to government employees who read from scripts and have scant discretion to listen or to divulge any helpful information.

Initially, all Natalie was able to understand was that Paulette needed to start making regular trips to a Home Office reporting centre twenty-four miles away in Solihull. She had already missed one appointment, after which another terrifying letter arrived informing her that she was 'liable to detention' and that if she failed to report again she would be prosecuted under Section 24 (1) (e) of the Immigration Act 1971, which could lead to a prison sentence or a £5,000 fine, or both.

The Home Office letters were written in deliberately frightening language, and I was startled by their menacing tone when Paulette showed them to me during our first meeting in November 2017. She had been released from Yarl's Wood a few weeks earlier, after a last-minute intervention by her MP, but she had been told that she was still facing deportation. I was shocked by the Home Office's decision to imprison a grandmother who had spent a lifetime in the UK, and to terrify her with such disturbing warnings. From the moment I heard about her treatment it was clear that a terrible mistake had been made, but I struggled to understand how such a serious error could have happened, why Home Office staff were persisting in threatening her with removal, and why no one had bothered to apologise. I sat for several hours with Paulette in Natalie's Wolverhampton flat, listening to Paulette's life story, trying to unravel why she could possibly have been branded an illegal immigrant and scheduled for forced removal from the country she called home.

———

Paulette travelled alone to the UK on a British Overseas Airways Corporation flight from Kingston, Jamaica, some time in 1968. She doesn't know the precise date because all the adults who were responsible for looking after her then are now dead, and there is no one she can ask. She doesn't still have her plane ticket (of course) and doesn't have a diary chronicling this life-changing event (unsurprisingly), and she isn't even entirely sure if she was eleven or possibly twelve when she arrived. She just knows it was winter and extremely cold when she stepped out of the airport, wrapped up in several aeroplane blankets layered over her skimpy orange dress, and saw England for the first time. Fifty years later, the memory of the icy sensation that hit her when the airport door opened still makes her shudder.

She remembers looking down at the pavement, puzzled by the white stuff scattered on the ground. She turned to her grandparents, Isaiah and Zenika James, who had come to collect her at Manchester airport, and asked: 'What is all the salt doing outside?'

'No, Paulette. It's not salt,' her grandmother said, producing a woollen coat and boots for her. 'It's called snow.'

'All of a sudden my body started changing colour. I went purple from head to foot. It was that cold,' she told me.

It had been a confusing twenty-four hours. Her mother had taken her to the airport in Jamaica; she was so overwhelmed by what was happening to her, that she was unable to register fully the significance of the looming permanent separation. Instead she focused on her fear of the beast-like aeroplane that she was going to be travelling on. 'I'd never seen a plane before. I'd heard them and seen them moving in the sky but I'd never seen one close. It looked like a giant truck that was going to have to fly.' She doesn't remember anyone explaining why she was going, she just has a dim recollection that it was accepted unquestioningly that she was leaving her mother in Jamaica so she could have a better life in England.

For much of her early childhood in central Jamaica, Paulette's grandparents had raised her because her mother had only been seventeen when she was born and not ready to look after her. But Isaiah and Zenika had left to work in England when Paulette was seven or eight. Zenika, in particular, had missed Paulette terribly and had sent money for a plane ticket so her granddaughter could join her.

She was looked after by an air hostess on the flight, someone she remembers being very kind. She thinks this was the first white woman she had ever spoken to. Paulette found it hard to understand her strange accent but eventually realised she was being offered something to eat, so she asked for yam dumplings, which she was sorry to discover were not available. She remembers the BOAC woman retying the ribbons in her hair before they landed, and leading her through the airport to find her relatives.

Her grandparents drove her to their home, on a redbrick, two-storeyed terraced street in Wellington in the Midlands. She was appalled by how dark the new country seemed but excited to find that for the first time in her life she had her own room, with a bed, a dressing table and a wardrobe. Downstairs there was a television, which delighted her because there had been no electricity in her village in Jamaica.

Her new life did not go smoothly. She was very homesick and found England cold and unwelcoming. She used to cry for her mother and tell her grandmother she wanted to go back to Jamaica, where her life had been much freer. 'I preferred to be in the trees than being with people. I was always climbing the mango trees, climbing the coconut trees to get the best coconuts. I grew up in a little village, surrounded by orange trees. I liked catching fish down by the river. By the time I was five I was catching fish with my hands and throwing them on to the bank. My mum would pick them up and cook them.'

She found the rules imposed on her constraining and she frequently ran away from her grandparents' house to the woodland nearby. She found school extremely difficult. She hadn't been to school regularly in Jamaica and she struggled with reading and writing; she quickly began to rebel. Her grandmother, who was working long hours as an NHS midwife, felt unable to cope and so Paulette was sent to live with a foster family. It was a tough beginning.

Paulette had moved to an area where racial tension was running high. Four years earlier, in 1964, the nearby town of Smethwick had witnessed the most racist general election campaign in Britain's history, in which the local Conservative candidate, Peter Griffiths, fought and won on the slogan: 'If you want a nigger for a neighbour, vote Liberal or Labour'. The American civil rights activist Malcolm X travelled to the town in 1965, just nine days before he was assassinated, because he had heard disturbing reports of the way black and Asian residents were being treated. He visited one street where some locals were calling on the council to make housing available to white families only.

In 1968, the year Paulette flew to England, the Conservative shadow health minister Enoch Powell delivered his 'Rivers of Blood' speech on 20 April, dwelling in agitated detail on the arrival of West Indian children like her in the constituency of Wolverhampton South, which he represented. 'It almost passes belief that at this moment twenty or thirty additional immigrant children are arriving from overseas in Wolverhampton alone every week,' he said. He claimed that residents had found 'their wives unable to obtain hospital beds in childbirth, their children unable to obtain school places, their homes and neighbourhoods changed beyond recognition, their plans and prospects for the future defeated.'

'Those whom the gods wish to destroy, they first make mad,' he continued. 'We must be mad, literally mad, as a nation to be permitting the annual inflow of some fifty thousand dependents, who are for the most part the material of the future growth of the immigrant-descended population. It is like watching a nation busily engaged in heaping up its own funeral pyre.' He described how his constituents were being followed down the street by immigrant children, 'charming, wide-grinning piccaninnies. They cannot speak English.' An opinion poll conducted by Gallup indicated that 74 per cent of the population supported his repatriation proposals.

Local journalists tried in vain to find the families Powell said had had difficulties getting school places or hospital treatment. The Conservative leader Ted Heath swiftly sacked Powell from his shadow ministerial position, but his words had enormous impact.

Paulette remembers people at school telling her: 'Enoch Powell is the greatest.' There were only two black children at Prince's Street primary school and her skin colour and hair were the subject of enduring interest. Other pupils would occasionally call her names: 'Black sambo – you go back to Africa and swing in the trees, you monkey.' She dealt with it fiercely. 'I punched them,' she said. 'I didn't know who Enoch Powell was. I didn't understand what they were talking about.'

———

Enoch Powell's speech was indirectly the reason I met Paulette. As part of the *Guardian*'s coverage of the May 2015 general election, I went to write about the marginal seat of Wolverhampton South, Powell's constituency, to take a snapshot of how concerned voters were about the issue of immigration. I didn't find much real evidence of voter unease on the subject. Even in the headquarters of the local United Kingdom Independence Party (the party talking most about migrants), the single pledge which had been framed and nailed on to the wall was not about immigration but promised: 'We will work to provide more free parking for the high street.' There was some mild irritation among the residents I spoke to at the failure of recent arrivals from the EU to adhere to the council's recycling policies, but voters seemed much more preoccupied by the economy and jobs and the rise of food bank use in the area. There was no sign of the smouldering funeral pyre Powell had predicted, just a very diverse and peaceful community getting on with their lives. I spent a fascinating hour talking to staff at the local migrant support organisation, the Wolverhampton Refugee and Migrant Centre, listening to their perspective on local attitudes to immigration.

Two and a half years later, at the end of October 2017, I had an unexpected email from the charity headed: 'Urgent: imminent deportation of a lady who has been in UK for 49 years'. The email asked if I could look at 'a very urgent case of a deportation that we are hoping to prevent'. Staff at the Refugee and Migrant Centre had been helping Paulette to unravel why she was being targeted by the Home Office, and had gathered evidence of thirty-four years' worth of National Insurance payments proving she was a long-term legal resident, when unexpectedly she had been arrested and sent to a detention centre. 'Arrangements are going ahead for her to be deported imminently, regardless of the evidence that she has the right to live in the UK. Ms Wilson is now 61, she has never returned to Jamaica and is distraught at the prospect of being separated from her family and sent to a country where she has no connections or support and [which she] has had no contact with for nearly 50 years.'

It seemed odd and I forwarded the email to the team of *Guardian* news editors, suggesting that since I was away for a few days someone else should contact the charity. At the time, the newspaper was publishing a lot of articles about immigration problems, some connected with fears over how EU nationals would be dealt with after Brexit, others about the harsh treatment of asylum seekers fleeing conflict, instability and poverty in countries in the Middle East and Africa. Sometimes it is hard to decide how to handle pleas for publicity for an individual's case; occasionally a newspaper article can help resolve things, if Home Office staff think media coverage might damage the department's reputation. Often the cases are extremely complex and it is hard to justify spending time picking through someone's inevitably complicated immigration dossier unless you suspect that the problems they're experiencing reflect a difficulty that is shared more widely.

But news that a woman who had been living here for half a century, who had attended primary school in Britain in the 1960s, had now been classified as an illegal immigrant and sent to Yarl's Wood, a notoriously unpleasant, four-hundred-bed, women-only immigration detention centre run by the vast private outsourcing firm Serco, was really unusual. I had visited Yarl's Wood in the past and interviewed inmates, many of whom had endured long periods of incarceration, often with no clarity about when they would be either released or removed from the UK. Undercover filming in 2015 caught guards expressing world-weary cynicism about the desperate behaviour of detainees. 'They are all slashing their wrists, apparently. Let them slash their wrists,' one official was recorded telling another in a report for Channel 4. 'It's attention-seeking.'

I assumed a clerical error had been made about Paulette's status. I'd read and written a lot about Home Office mistakes, most of which I guessed were the inevitable result of the workload placed on this huge, understaffed bureaucracy, combined with the political requirement to bring about a drastic reduction in immigration figures.

Back at work a week later, I was curious about what had happened. The editors had asked a reporter to look into the email; she had spent time talking to a case worker at the charity, but before anything was published she'd had a call to say that Paulette had been freed at the last minute, after her MP, Labour's Emma Reynolds, had contacted the Home Office. It wasn't clear why Paulette had been detained in the first place but my colleague thought it might have been something to do with an application form that had not been submitted correctly. I felt it was an extreme response to lock someone up for a week because they had been a bit chaotic with their admin, and was sure the subject was worth revisiting.

Persuading people to talk about their immigration problems is difficult in a climate where the Home Office's whole ethos is based on its tough approach to illegal immigrants. It's a lot to ask people to lay bare all of their difficulties to be set out in print next to their photograph. Paulette was still feeling traumatised and was initially uncertain about whether she wanted to be interviewed, but her daughter Natalie, was so angry that she encouraged her to talk to me.

We met at Natalie's flat on the second floor of a long, brown-brick, low-rise apartment block, a fifteen-minute walk from Wolverhampton station. The flat's entrance was accessed along an external balcony corridor. A demolition vehicle was attacking a walkway that linked her building and the adjoining one (to prevent teenagers from running away from the police, Natalie said). A thoughtful young immigration adviser from the Refugee and Migrant Centre, Daniel Ashwell, came to help explain what seemed to have happened.

I was struck by how supportive Natalie was of her mother, totally on top of the paperwork, efficiently answering all my questions. Taller and wirier than her mother, her hair pulled tightly back, Natalie was wearing a sharply ironed shirt and trousers; she exuded a quiet determination, ready to expose the shameful treatment her mother had experienced. Paulette, in a long turquoise and black tie-dyed dress, was quieter and more withdrawn, very upset and confused by the Home Office's decision to target her. Natalie's brusquely efficient manner instantly disappeared when she looked at her mother struggling to explain her situation, and a gentle sympathy transformed her face as she listened and encouraged Paulette to go on.

Paulette had been so young when she arrived that she had never thought about the issue of citizenship or her immigration status, and neither her grandparents nor the council officials responsible for her care ever discussed the process of naturalisation with her. In her late teens, she went a bit off the rails for a while, perhaps in reaction to the shock of such a disrupted childhood; she only really settled down after she gave birth to Natalie when she was twenty-two. They moved to London, where Paulette worked for years in hotel kitchens and in a Chinese restaurant. At some point, amid the various house moves, she misplaced the Jamaican passport she arrived on as a child, which would have had a stamp recording the date of her entry into the UK and granting her indefinite leave to remain. She had no reason to suspect that the loss of an out-of-date passport would be such a life-changing event.

When she applied for a job at the House of Commons canteen, she provided the National Insurance card that she had been issued with when she turned sixteen; no one questioned her immigration status. She enjoyed working there. She remembers that Mikhail Gorbachev visited while she was there in 1984, and dimly recalls House of Commons staff being made to line up outside to meet him.

As she grew older, she began to think about visiting her mother in Jamaica, but she had no money and no passport. She applied for a passport in 2005 when she heard her mother had been diagnosed with polio; the application was rejected – she's not sure why. 'I was so upset. I hadn't seen my mum since I was a little girl.' Her mother died in 2010 before Paulette had a chance to see her again. Paulette had moved back to Wolverhampton to be closer to Natalie, who had settled there with her own daughter. She found a job working nights as a chef at a large casino in the centre of town, and later took up voluntary jobs, cooking for the local church and helping make meals in a soup kitchen for the homeless community.

She led a reasonably happy and stable life, until the Home Office notice dropped through her letterbox. With nowhere to turn for advice, Paulette had no option but to follow the requirement to start making regular visits to the Home Office reporting centre in Solihull.

The first time Natalie and Paulette went to the ugly 1980s red-brick building, a complicated hour and a half's journey by train involving multiple changes, they were hopeful that this would be an opportunity to untangle the confusion. Natalie thought she would just need to explain that her mother had been in Britain since 1968 and viewed herself as British, and that officials would adjust the files accordingly. But the Home Office reporting centres have a different function. They are there to monitor the movements and the compliance of people whose immigration status is uncertain. They are not there to listen.

Paulette found even the walk to the centre upsetting. 'There were Somalis, Jamaicans, Africans. Everyone looks miserable. We are all following each other from the train station, we start lining up outside the building. There's always a big queue. Everyone feels not very happy about being there.' Inside visitors have to go through security scanners and hand in their watches, belts and mobile phones. Natalie was conscious of a strange and upsetting smell of sweat and fear inside the building.

'I felt sad for myself and for some of the people I saw in there . . . women with two or three kids, their babies crying,' Paulette said.

On arrival, people take a ticket from the machine, then sit, on metal benches which have been screwed to the floor, and wait for anything between thirty and ninety minutes. Natalie hoped that they would eventually be able to have a conversation with someone about what had gone wrong. Instead they were called up to a counter, to speak to an unnamed official sitting on the other side of a thick sheet of Perspex. The official told them that Paulette had six months to leave the country because she had been classified as an illegal immigrant.

'But my mum has been here since the 1960s,' Natalie protested. This response left the official unmoved. They needed to start gathering evidence to prove that Paulette was not here illegally, the official said.

'What evidence?' Natalie asked.

'All we can say is that your next appointment is booked in for two weeks' time.'

The meeting lasted less than five minutes, and subsequent reporting sessions were much shorter. Every fortnight Paulette and Natalie had to make the journey from Wolverhampton to Solihull. Paulette was sent a letter with a black-and-white passport-size photo of her printed on the front, which she was advised to carry with her at all times, and which had to be handed in to a Home Office administrator at every appointment. She felt there was something humiliating about the document – something about it made her feel like a criminal.

'They'd just go tap, tap, tap on the computer,' Paulette said, dropping her eyes to the ground to mimic the officials' refusal to make any eye contact. 'Tick, tick, tick. They turn the letter over, write another date on it, hand it back. That was it. They say nothing to you at all – not a word.'

Once Paulette had lost her state benefits and was no longer allowed to work in the UK, Natalie had to pay for her to rent a spare room in a neighbour's flat. Natalie was also buying her mother's food and other things she needed, which was difficult because her own job as a dinner lady was part-time and not particularly well paid and she was a single mother, bringing up a teenage daughter who needed dance lessons and school trips. For the two and a half years when they were trying to sort out Paulette's problems, Natalie stopped buying clothes for herself. 'There were times when I went without eating,' Natalie said. 'My mum wasn't eating properly. Sometimes she went for days without eating.' The train tickets to Solihull cost £8.80 each, which was another chunk out of Natalie's income. Paulette felt unhappy at having to rely on her daughter for help. 'I didn't like asking her. Sometimes I'd say: "Babes, I'm hungry," and she would be cross that I hadn't asked before. I thought: I can't keep asking her for money.'

The more Paulette told me, the more I felt troubled by her treatment. What was particularly upsetting was the unflinching refusal of immigration staff to believe her consistent account that she had been in the UK for a lifetime.

Paulette began to eat meals at the same homeless shelter where she was still volunteering and cooking food. Once a week she would go to the food bank at the New Testament Church of God around the corner from her flat. Paulette discovered she felt quite cheerful about picking up tins and packets of pasta alongside her more vulnerable neighbours – some of whom were drug addicts, but most of whom were families having problems with their benefits. The staff at the centre were concerned for her. 'They kept saying: "I'll pray for you."'

For months Paulette and Natalie tried to work out how to extract themselves from this mess. They contacted their MP, Emma Reynolds, who wrote a letter on Paulette's behalf to the

Home Office, explaining that she had been in England for almost fifty years and asking for some kind of documentary confirmation. A Home Office official wrote back with an unsettling reply, a version of which would be sent to hundreds of others affected by Windrush problems: 'I have been unable to locate any record of Ms Wilson's current immigration status in our records.'

The official advised the MP to tell Paulette to gather a file of evidence proving that she was telling the truth, and that she had been here since 1968. She began to collect statements from relatives and from the manager of the soup kitchen, who described her as a 'kind-hearted and generous person'. A Home Office letter was sent to Paulette advising her to apply formally for the right to remain in the UK. She did not understand the letter. In any case, there was a £279 fee for the application, which she did not have. They were unable to afford a lawyer. Legal aid for most immigration cases had been stopped in a round of government cuts a few years earlier.

Natalie eventually became annoyed with the time-consuming and endlessly stressful reporting sessions. On one occasion, she was told she would no longer be allowed to accompany Paulette into the centre because staff had become very fed up with her questioning.

'I got banned from the Home Office for all my questions, telling them that my mum was a British citizen and she's not illegal. For doing that they banned me. They told me they can't answer any questions through the screens. They said you have to speak to your case worker.' Natalie found that piece of advice funny in a bleak way, because the notion of a case worker you could actually speak to had taken on a mythical status. Natalie had never come across one. She couldn't decide if they really even existed. Paulette had never been allocated one, as far as she knew. 'I never met a case worker in two and a half years,' she told me later.

When the security guards at the entrance to the building told Natalie she was not allowed inside, she lost her temper. An official noted in Paulette's records, coyly sprinkling the update with asterisks, that Natalie had 'been demanding to come in with her mother, swearing at security and causing a disturbance until she was allowed in. I advised her mother that her daughter would not be allowed into the building in future. The daughter started to swear stating "You are a f*****g b**** you can p*** **f it's my mum."'

Natalie isn't someone who sits back and allows life's problems to envelop her. (Daniel, the charity's immigration adviser, says the Home Office chose the wrong person to pick on when they tried to bully Natalie into accepting the way Paulette was being treated.)

'I have a mouth on me; don't get me wrong,' she told a committee of MPs in the House of Commons some months later, explaining how she responded to another member of staff. 'I swore at him. I said to him: "Can you prove to me that you are English right now? Prove it. Take something out of your pocket to prove to me that you are British. How do I know that you're British and not from a different country?" He swore at me and then I got banned. They banned me from there, because they said that I was causing a disturbance when I was going there, because I was trying to fight for my mum.'

The official printed out a new reporting form for Paulette marked 'Applicant Only', so that in future Natalie would no longer be allowed inside with her. 'To which the daughter started to swear again,' the official noted in the internal report, until staff said they would call the police.

Given that all Natalie was doing was trying to explain that her mother was not an illegal immigrant and that a mistake had been made, threatening to call the police was another inexplicably shabby move by the reporting centre staff. I was beginning to get a clear sense of the bewildering deadlock. This was how it felt to be made powerless, caught in the iron grip of the Home Office.

There was no opportunity for any genuine interaction with officials. Years later in 2019, as politicians assessed the sequence of errors which had led to Paulette's detention, the Home Affairs Select Committee described the absence of 'face to face contact between immigration decision makers and the detainee' as 'shocking'. Their report continues:

We believe this contributes to the cavalier attitude towards detention decisions. Had decision-makers ever met Paulette Wilson before deciding that she should be detained, it might have made them more likely to spot the injustice in her case . . . It is a basic tenet of our legal system that when judges take the decision to detain, that person is brought before the court. Therefore it is extremely troubling that in the immigration and asylum system people can be deprived of their liberty through an entirely paper-based exercise by officials where no one involved in the decision ever interviews the potential detainee.[1]

Natalie was forced to wait outside the reporting centre, but (as she pointed out in a frustrated email to the Immigration Enforcement team) Paulette was becoming very absent-minded and had often forgotten what the officials inside the building had told her by the time she emerged. In September 2016, Natalie sent a desperate email to staff, explaining (again) that her mother had no home to go to in Jamaica and was confused about why she was being threatened with removal. She said they had sent off the relevant documents. 'Please get back to me,' she wrote. 'We are scared.'

A month later, a member of the ominously titled Immigration Enforcement: Returns Preparation Team emailed back suggesting that Natalie should seek legal advice. Natalie made some inquiries, and was given a quote suggesting that legal assistance might cost as much as £5,000. There was no way that a family of three, surviving on a part-time school dinner supervisor's wages, could contemplate paying that much. Natalie began to think that Paulette might die as a result of the mounting stress. It was only then that Paulette was told by a neighbour to seek free advice from the Refugee and Migrant Centre.

By 18 July 2017, the tone of the internal Home Office messages in Paulette's files was becoming more urgent. Paulette had now acquired a note by her name, classifying her as 'Removable to Jamaica'.

Paulette sent a three-page handwritten account of her life to the Home Office, dictated by her and written out by a friend. 'I know nothing but my life in England. I have no memories of Jamaica,' it reads. 'I'm not a bad person. My daughter works part-time in a school so she's saving up to get me a lawyer if possible. I don't know what would happen to me if you send me back. I have nothing and no one in Jamaica. Please don't send me back. My life is in England.' Another desperate note sent to officials said: 'Please help me. This is my home.'

On 26 July 2017 her file was still classified as 'Low Risk', but an official appears to have decided it was time to take action, writing: 'I authorise detention in the interests of effective immigration control and to facilitate removal from the UK'.

Dozens of people are removed from Britain every day by the immigration system; at that time, about twelve thousand people a year were being ejected. Removal is the final stage of a protracted process, orchestrated by teams of Home Office employees who work tirelessly to round up, detain and expel anyone they judge not to have the right to live in the UK.

It emerged later, once the Windrush scandal erupted on the political horizon, that at the time when officials were processing Paulette's case, the Home Office had an annual enforced returns target of 12,800, which was broken down into weekly targets of between 230 and 250. Teams of immigration enforcement staff around the country had posters of these targets on their walls. Sometimes the targets were referred to as 'objectives' or 'business goals' or 'levels of ambition', but regardless of the precise vocabulary used, end-of-year bonuses were available for good work, some of which was related to removals; some staff were set 'personal objectives' on which bonus payments were made, 'linked to targets to achieve enforced removals'.[2] In 2016–17, 23 per cent of people working in immigration enforcement received an end-of-year bonus. It was hard to avoid seeing a link between the determined attempts by officials to remove Paulette, despite her repeated protestations that a mistake had been made, and the existence of these targets.

The process of forcing people on to aeroplanes is messy and often upsets fellow passengers; this aspect of the deportation machine is usually subcontracted out by the government to private firms. At least two people have died during the removal process,[3] resisting to the end as guards have pressed on with the challenging exercise of expelling an unwanted immigrant. It is unusual for the subject of the removal action to agree with the decision to deport them; many continue arguing vigorously that they should be allowed to stay, right up until the moment that the plane takes off. Staff who work in the Home Office's immigration centres become desensitised to protests. For years, critics of the department's performance have highlighted the 'culture of disbelief' that is ingrained in a system run by weary officials who assume that the people they encounter are usually lying.

It wasn't long after Natalie was banned from the reporting centre that Paulette was detained for the first time, in August 2017. She was held only for a few hours, until officials realised they had no available bed in a women's detention centre to accommodate her, at which point she was released. In the weeks which followed, without her knowing, officials in the Detention, Progression and

Returns Command, a subsection of Immigration Enforcement made elaborate preparations for a second attempt to detain and remove her from the UK. On 18 October 2017, when she went to report in Solihull, she was arrested for the second time.

Daniel Ashwell at the Refugee and Migrant Centre was horrified when Natalie told him what had happened. Staff at the charity had been working on her case for a few months and thought that they were finally making progress. For most of the week that Paulette was in Yarl's Wood, he dropped all his other cases and tried to intervene. 'You never speak to the person who is making the decision on the case,' he told me later. Messages would just get passed up an invisible internal Home Office chain. Daniel asked repeatedly if officials were planning to remove Paulette. 'They say: "I can't tell you that."'

Paulette was carrying all her documents with her, the entire file of evidence she had gathered to prove she had spent a lifetime in Britain – letters from relatives, from Natalie's godmother, references, documents from her GP attesting that she had been in the country for decades, tax and National Insurance records, and, crucially, copies of archive records from Shropshire Council showing that she had been in care in 1971. She had everything ready to submit an application to naturalise in the UK, but was waiting for Natalie to be paid in order to have the necessary £279 fee. 'I told them the money would be with them on Wednesday,' Paulette said. No one wanted to look at the form or the documents.

She was taken to a van, with darkened windows, covered with the branding for Serco, the private company to which the government outsources some of its immigration work. 'I couldn't see any buildings, just flashes of trees as we drove through the countryside.'

When she got to Yarl's Wood, her eyes were scanned, her fingerprints were taken and she underwent a full body search. She had to hand in her bag containing all her papers and to remove her jeans and red anorak so she could change into a prison-issue grey track-suit. A photograph of her looking unhappy and startled without her glasses was taken and attached to her forms.

She was led to a two-bed cell. Her room-mate, a kind but very devout Christian woman from Africa, had invited a group of women to come and pray with her that night. Every bit of the room seemed to be full of women, praying to be released. 'These women were getting on my nerves.' Paulette was left looking out at the view of a huge barbed-wire fence. She went to sleep to the noise of prayers, but during the night she was woken several times by screaming in the corridors. 'It sounded like people were getting taken away at all different hours of the night. It was horrible.'

Jim Wilson, a Birmingham-based lawyer who does pro bono voluntary work for the Refugee and Migrant Centre, stepping into the gap left by cuts to legal aid, prepared to lodge a judicial review – an appeal designed to get the removal decision overturned. He was scathing about the handling of her case. 'It seems to me that the people who have been dealing with this case in the Home Office have not known what they were doing. Their approach has been: Let's take action first and ask questions later.' His outline case against the Home Office pointed out that there was no legal requirement for Paulette to regularise her immigration status because it was already assured by virtue of the fact that she had been in the country before the crucial cut-off date of 1 January 1973 and had never left the UK since.

But the wheels of the machine continued to turn; Paulette was transferred to Heathrow.

At this point, the Refugee Migrant Centre decided to go to the media to protest at her treatment, and staff emailed me and a local BBC reporter. Paulette's MP, Emma Reynolds, had broken off from maternity leave to make urgent applications to the Home Office. Finally this forced officials to reconsider.

'23 October: Call received from Emma Reynolds MP advising that Refugee Migrant Centre have gone to the press with this case,' a note in her Home Office file states. The prospect of negative media coverage seems to have prompted officials to pause and consider whether they should really go ahead with the removal. Belatedly they looked at Paulette's files and saw the evidence she had provided to demonstrate long residence. 'Records show she has 34 qualifying years up to 5 April 2017. Due to her potential length of residence, I therefore propose that Ms Wilson is released from detention and her case forwarded for further investigation and consideration.'

The speed and ease with which her situation was reassessed, as soon as officials learned that the media had been tipped off, were galling. Paulette and Natalie had been consistently telling officials they were wrong for over two years; no one had thought their protestations were worthy of attention. This was possibly the most enraging detail in her story.

The morning after her arrival at Heathrow, Paulette was released. She was given some train tickets, let out of the detention centre and left by the roadside. She remembers putting her hands over her ears to protect them from the thunderous noise of planes taking off overhead.

——

When we met in 2017 Paulette took several hours to give a detailed account of everything that had happened to her. Towards the end, the *Guardian* photographer Fabio de Paola arrived to take pictures, and I sat in the kitchen of Natalie's flat, talking to Daniel, trying to understand what might have gone wrong. He said his job gave him daily insights into the cruel consequences of Home Office decisions. 'You see people facing injustice from the Home Office all the time. The way they make decisions seems sometimes to be about grinding people down, making them give up.'

He had never previously come across anyone in this category who had been detained, but he and his colleagues had recently encountered a number of people of around the same age, born in the Caribbean, who were experiencing difficulties because they had no papers. He wasn't sure how many, but it was something that was beginning to trouble the staff at the charity. They were at a loss as to how to make their concerns known to officials. 'There's no channel to get to the Home Office to say: "Your policies are having this impact." You might as well throw your letter in the bin,' he said.

I was dismayed. It appeared that Paulette's only crime was that she hadn't filled in the correct form from the Home Office, and even then it wasn't entirely clear that she needed to fill in any Home Office form at all, given that she had been granted the right to remain when she came as a child. For that non-offence she had been detained twice and held in a removal centre for seven days. Besides being extremely cruel, it seemed like a huge waste of public resources.

Paulette told us that she was still having trouble sleeping, and would occasionally walk from the flat where she was staying to Natalie's home in the middle of the night, calling through the letter box to be let in, so she could get in her bed to sleep next to her. 'I'm still having nightmares,' Paulette said, apologetically. 'I'm wondering, is it going to happen again? Are they going to take me away?'

A Home Office response to inquiries from Emma Reynolds MP had not ruled out the possibility that Paulette could be arrested and detained again; the threat of being sent back to Jamaica remained current. 'It may help to explain,' the response began, with careful courtesy, 'that Ms Wilson currently has no legal basis of stay within the UK and is liable to detention or removal.' There was something that upset me about this formality, something blood-freezing about the way the official composed this sentence – the brutality, cloaked in passive-aggressive politeness ('it may help to explain'), and the total failure to offer any hint that anyone understood how utterly Paulette's life was being torn apart by the department's decisions. The Home Office had mistakenly and needlessly locked up a vulnerable woman, after subjecting her to two years of torment, and they were persisting in asserting that she was at fault.

Before I left I asked Paulette if she felt British. She looked affronted by the question. 'I don't feel British. I am British. I've been raised here, all I know is Britain. What the hell can I call myself except British? I'm still angry that I have to prove it. I feel angry that I have to go through this.'

―――

Writing about Paulette Wilson's treatment was simple. I came back from Wolverhampton and typed out an article about her very quickly, fuelled by a sense of pure outrage. Officials were preparing to remove a former House of Commons canteen worker who was spending her retirement years volunteering in a food bank, to send her back to a country she had left when she was eleven, almost fifty years earlier. It made no sense.

When the article appeared, the response from readers took me by surprise. Dozens of people offered to pay any further Home Office application fees or contribute to the cost of legal advice. Mostly people wanted to send messages of support to the family. The extraordinarily cruel treatment she had received spoke for itself, but the large photograph of Paulette, looking worried and vulnerable, printed on the front of the features section of the newspaper, made readers want to reach out to support her.

One reader emailed to say: 'Paulette Wilson should never have been treated this way. It makes me ashamed of the country she and I both rightly call home.' Another described her experience as 'heartbreaking and cruel beyond words'.

There was silence from the Home Office and the government.

Because of the amount of interest Paulette's story had triggered, I was asked during the newspaper's 10 a.m. meeting (attended by journalists and editors, setting out priorities for the next day) to explain why the Home Office had treated her so badly. About forty people in the crowded conference room waited for an answer, and I had to admit that I wasn't entirely sure. The government's attempts to bring down migration numbers appeared to be catching the wrong people, I said. I had a sense that Paulette was not the only one suffering this treatment, but no evidence.

Later that morning, as I sat at my desk reading through the emails of support and forwarding messages to Natalie, I received a call from a man who said I needed to speak to his father, Anthony Bryan. Anthony had lived in Britain almost all of his life. He had just been released after five weeks in immigration detention, and was facing deportation to Jamaica, a country he left when he was eight and had not visited for fifty years.

FIVE WEEKS' DETENTION AND
A TICKET TO JAMAICA

Weekend mornings on Anthony Bryan's quiet North London street are usually very tranquil, so he was alarmed to hear a huge commotion outside his home at around nine o'clock on a Sunday in early September 2016. Confused by the noise, he came to the front window in his dressing gown, peered through the curtains and saw a flash of police officers, running past. 'I thought it was for next door. The people there drink a lot.' He went back to the kitchen stove, where he was frying himself two eggs for breakfast. 'I thought nothing of it.'

Suddenly people were banging on the front door and windows. He put down the pan and opened the front door to find seven officers, six men and a woman, getting ready to smash their way into the house. One of them had a battering ram, another was carrying a shield. 'Something like a Viking might carry, but made of plastic.'

Anthony is a quiet, courteous man, who was then in his late fifties. He politely indicated that there was no need to kick the door in and asked them inside.

With hindsight, Anthony can see there had been a few warnings that the Home Office might be getting ready to pounce. Earlier that week, he had noticed a large white van, marked 'Immigration Unit', frequently parked up the road from his house; every time he caught a glimpse of it, he felt momentarily uneasy, but reassured himself, telling himself they were probably there for another Jamaican family, newly arrived in the area. 'I thought maybe they were watching them. It was very unusual to see a van like that in the street. You couldn't mistake it – it's got the logo on the side.'

That Wednesday his girlfriend, Janet, had arrived home from

her job as a respite care worker helping families with autistic children, to find the same van parked a few doors along, on the opposite side of the road. As she got out of her car, she saw a smaller van, also branded with Immigration Enforcement logos, driving down the road. It circled the block once, pausing by the house, then left, followed by the larger van. 'My heart stopped,' Janet said. Anthony had unresolved issues with the Home Office that had been troubling him for almost a year; she began to wonder if the vans might be coming for him.

But they didn't discuss the vans that week. It was a difficult time because Anthony had just buried one of his sons, who had died at the age of thirty-two from a rare neurological condition, and he was distracted by grief. Janet couldn't really persuade herself that Anthony – a reliable, calm presence in her life – could actually be the target of such sinister immigration intelligence manoeuvres. She swept the thought under the carpet. That Sunday morning she had already left to get to work.

Extensive police records from the raid give an insight into how Britain's immigration enforcement machine relentlessly grinds forward, sweeping up suspects without ever stopping to listen to what they have to say. The arresting officer's notes offer a staccato account of what was a heavy-handed, excessively staffed Sunday morning arrest of a mild-mannered painter-decorator.

'At 09.25, officers arrived on scene', the Immigration Compliance and Enforcement Officer's report states. 'At 09.26 a warrant was executed on a man known to be Anthony Bryan (Jamaica, 28 May 1957)'.

The account of the interrogation which follows reeks of lip-curled scepticism – 'the subject claims to have lived in the UK for over 52 years'; 'the subject claims his mum, who worked as a machinist, sent for him and his brother to come from Jamaica'; 'he claimed that he worked as a painter decorator'; he 'claims to have lived in the UK since 1965'. The word 'claims' seems to be an official shorthand indicating: 'this is what the suspect is saying but we're not in the least inclined to believe him'; its repeated use conjures a vision of the immigration officer holding out something distasteful for inspection, eyebrows raised in contemptuous disbelief.

The questioning does not seem to have been very extensive because a few minutes later, the officer noted he was 'satisfied that the subject is a person liable to be detained' and arrested Anthony.

'Given the fact that the subject has not provided satisfactory answers to Immigration Officers' enquiries, at 09.38 hours, I recommended for the subject to be detained. I then allowed the subject to change his clothes and pack a bag.'

Anthony's clothes were searched before he put them on, to check whether he was hiding anything that he could use to make an escape or harm the immigration team – he wasn't. 'The subject was allowed to use the toilet and wash.' Then there was a brief discussion about what to do about the family's cat, during which the immigration officer's all-pervasive cynicism made him doubtful even about whether Anthony was telling the truth when he said he had already given the cat its food. 'The subject had a pet cat in the premises which he claimed was fed earlier,' he noted with pointed mistrust.

Anthony's memory of the raid is mainly of how bemused and sad he felt. He thinks there were seven officers, some of them police and some of them immigration employees – an overwhelming group to be confronted with at the doorway to his small flat, and a strange number to send to the home of someone so unthreatening. He asked if he could make a phone call and was told that was not allowed. He remembers the officer saying: 'Get some clothes together because you're not coming back.' He did nothing to resist the arrest or protest, and went quietly to the waiting immigration van. 'Handcuffs were not used as the subject had been fully compliant,' the Immigration Enforcement Officer wrote.

'They said they had a warrant for my arrest. I said: "Warrant for my arrest??"' Anthony told me when we first met, remembering his incredulous reaction. 'I had to comply because there were police there with the immigration officers. You don't want to do anything silly so you just follow what they say. I thought they had just made a mistake.'

He felt so ashamed as he was led out from the house that he thought for a moment he should put a towel over his head. 'But then I told myself, why would I do that? I'm not guilty of anything.'

A friend from across the road was watching as he was put into the van. 'Where are you going with him?' he shouted. Anthony wanted the pavement to split open so he could fall inside and disappear. He had told his neighbours that he had lived in England since he was eight. 'They must have thought I was lying.'

He was driven to a Home Office immigration office in central London, where the same officer conducted an 'in-depth interview regarding his long claimed residency in the UK'. 'During this interview he continued to claim that he entered the UK with his brother on his brother's passport.' The record lists eighteen bullet-pointed bits of evidence Anthony provided to help explain that he had lived in the UK all his life – from the name of the head teacher of his primary school, to the place where he met his first girlfriend, to the names and ages of his children, all born in London, and details of the companies he had worked for. The list reads like a fairly comprehensive account of a lifetime spent in the UK – and yet the officer persists with his scepticism, concluding (incredibly, given the amount of information listed): 'All the details above do not produce satisfactory evidence to prove his long residence.'

If anyone had taken ten minutes to listen to him talking in detail, in calmer circumstances, about life in London they would have been left with little doubt that he was telling the truth. It's not a very forensic test, but Anthony only has to open his mouth and say a few sentences to persuade you that he is someone who has lived in North London for a lifetime. But judging by the police and Home Office records, in most of the interviews with Anthony officials were more absorbed with process, ticking boxes to ensure the arrest was done correctly.

So the questions shifted quickly to other issues. 'Is there a history of a threat of Violence; Disruptive behaviour, self-harm/attempted suicide/food refusal/fluid refusal; Escape attempts; Psychiatric disorder; Medical problems/concerns; Vulnerable adult (eg due to learning difficulties); Currently pregnant or claims to be pregnant; Religious extremism; Racism; Abuse of women/children; Known associates a risk; Is there a history of Homophobia or transphobia?' A capital N is marked next to each box. Perhaps if officers had chosen instead to have a more normal, human conversation, and encouraged Anthony to describe how it felt to come from Jamaica as an eight-year-old child, to rejoin a mother he had not seen for five years, and to start school in an unfamiliar country during an era of high racial tension, they might have paused before despatching him to detention.

Initially police officers seemed dubious about Anthony's account of how he had come to England and chose to describe his elder brother Desmond, with jaundiced mistrust, as his 'claimed brother'. But once they checked on their computer database and realised there was a brother registered, who was also having problems proving his immigration status, they noted: 'No evidence is found on any of our systems to show that either of them ever entered the UK lawfully.'

'I was naïve,' Anthony told me. 'I thought: as long as I tell them where I went to school, and my National Insurance number, and that I paid my taxes . . . I thought all of that would have been enough. But it wasn't.'

Anthony was refused bail and driven 143 miles to the Verne

Prison, on the Isle of Portland, off the south coast of England, a vast immigration removal centre in a converted Victorian fort with room for 580 inmates. There is no time limit for immigration detention and Anthony was dismayed to discover that some of his fellow detainees had already been held there for more than fourteen months, waiting to be freed or deported.

'How did it feel? It felt like you were deeply in trouble, I didn't know how I was going to get out of it.'

———

It was 1 December 2017 and unusually cold, with a few occasional flakes of snow falling as I made my way to Antony and Janet's new home in a terraced street in Edmonton, North London.

Janet, friendly and welcoming but very worried, made me tea, and I sat on the brown leather sofa in their open-plan ground-floor room. I spent the morning talking to them, looking at photographs of Anthony's life in England, and reading through letters from the Home Office and correspondence from lawyers. When I listen back to the recording of our conversation, I can hear the cat miaowing at my ankles and my own voice, steadily more and more amazed and disturbed by what they were telling me.

Anthony had been released from a second stint in immigration detention just a few days earlier, and had only narrowly avoided being deported on a plane back to Jamaica (thanks to Janet's success in finding several thousand pounds to pay a lawyer to challenge the removal). He was happy to talk to me, relieved that someone was finally taking an interest in what had happened to him. Soft-spoken and quiet, Anthony was more incredulous about his treatment than angry, but he was so absolutely sure that a terrible mistake had been made that he had resolved to be calm about having the details of his life extracted and laid out for newspaper readers. 'I don't mind what you ask me. I've got nothing to hide,' he told me.

We spent a long time talking about his childhood in Jamaica and London; he revealed details that I knew would never make it into a newspaper article, but which were so fascinating that we kept getting sidetracked into questions of what it was like to travel from his grandmother's yellow house in a small village in the mountains of central Jamaica to live in rooms in a shared house in North London in September 1965.

He doesn't remember being told much about the trip in advance. 'It wasn't discussed with us before. We were only told when it was finally set: tomorrow you are going to England.'

His mother, Lucille Thompson, had left five years earlier to try to earn money in London, to support her three children. She had struggled to make a living as a single mother in Kingston, so she decided to sell her best furniture, a chest and a glass-fronted cabinet, bought herself a £70 plane ticket and carried out what must have been an unusually brave plan in the conservative mid-1960s, to travel alone to London. She had an aunt who had moved there a few years earlier. ('She told me to bring warm clothes or my bottom will freeze off,' Lucille told me later.) The aunt helped her find somewhere to stay, lent her an umbrella and helped her look for work. She quickly found a job in a factory, stitching mattresses.

When Lucille left, Anthony and his elder siblings, Desmond and Vi, became what were later known in the Caribbean as 'barrel children' – those who received regular care packages in large cardboard barrels, shipped to them by parents who had gone to seek work in the US or the UK. Anthony remembers getting shoes and condensed milk when the barrel was delivered from London. 'It was exciting, like Christmas when it arrived. Everyone would have something in it – clothes, toothpaste, money. We were the only ones with shoes like that where we lived. We'd be so happy. We used to idolise English stuff.'

The barrels did not come often because Lucille's wages were low and she was trying to pay rent and also save money so she could buy plane tickets for her children. Her daughter came first but it took her about five years before she was in a position to send for Desmond, who was then eleven, and Anthony, who was eight. Anthony travelled on his brother's Jamaican passport, he thinks because it was cheaper to apply for one document.

He hadn't wanted to leave his grandmother. 'I was crying; I used to call her mum. She said: "You're going to see your mum" – which was puzzling.' He was scared on the plane, but remembers looking around and seeing how calm the rest of the passengers were. 'Once you realised that everyone else is relaxed then you relax.' But he had a shock at the airport, when a strange woman tried to take him away. 'I said: "You're not my mum." That really upset her. My brother said: "Come on, this is Mum."'

He arrived in a country he found unexpectedly bright. 'There were so many lights; Jamaica is a dark place. I remember I thought all the houses were factories because they had chimneys on the top, smoke coming out like mad. Houses in Jamaica didn't have chimneys like that.' I noted this down with particular interest as a curious detail, but over the following months I heard this story of mistaking the houses for factories repeated over and over by Jamaican interviewees. It conjures up the common experience of dislocation and culture shock for those arriving from the Caribbean.

Anthony is not sure how much he had attended school in Jamaica and he was behind when he got to primary school in England. He liked school but he never really caught up, and his difficulty with reading and writing gave him (like Paulette) a lifelong aversion to filling in forms, which was at the root of many of his immigration problems. He found it very taxing to register at a GP's surgery, and he never opened a bank account because the papers he needed to complete gave him a headache.

They moved a lot when he was a child. It was stressful for his mum sharing houses with other families; sometimes rows would break out and she would have to set off again to find new rooms, always leaving the children at home, because landlords were never keen to rent to people with children. Anthony thinks it was hard for her to find people happy to rent to Jamaicans. 'She got a lot of racist abuse. We were all getting it.'

His primary school was small and friendly, but at secondary school he found he had to be very careful to escape getting into fights. He had to make sure he was on a bus going back from his school in Shoreditch (a mainly white area in East London) to Stoke Newington (a much more mixed area in North London) before evening set in if he wanted to avoid getting beaten up.

This was the late 1960s and racial tensions were surging across Britain. Although he has no memory of hearing about Enoch Powell's speech, in retrospect he thinks that this might have been behind some of the hatred he faced. 'When I look back, I think those white kids at school, they must have heard the speech. They were looking at me like they wanted to kill me. There was a lot of "you black bastard, you wog, you nigger". There were pubs I had to avoid walking past because those people would drink there and I would get attacked.'

He left school at sixteen and started work on an assembly line making wardrobes, dressing tables, sideboard cabinets. Later he moved into painting and decorating, sometimes self-employed, sometimes working for bigger building firms. He worked as a caretaker for Edmonton Council for a couple of years. He made over thirty years' worth of National Insurance contributions and never claimed benefits. For fifty years he led a full and busy life, helped bring up seven children, and had been living happily with Janet for around seven years when they decided it was time to visit his mother, who had returned to Jamaica over a decade before. Lucille was approaching ninety, sometimes unwell, and no longer able to fly to England.

Janet, who is incredibly organised, offered to help fill in a passport application form so Anthony could take the first holiday of his life abroad. Janet's parents were also from Jamaica, but she was born in England, and was puzzled by his situation. She quickly realised it was going to be hard to resolve because he had none of the right papers, so she took on the challenge of sorting it out in her spare time. It proved unexpectedly complicated. His elder brother's passport that he had travelled on had gone missing somewhere in the intervening fifty years. Anthony had had a hint that there might be a problem with his documents in 2005, when he was briefly out of work and decided to apply for unemployment benefits, but he found he was unable to because he had no acceptable papers – no passport, no driving licence, only a copy of his Jamaican birth certificate. He shrugged it off, found a new job and forgot about it. It had never occurred to him that there might be anything wrong with his immigration status.

It wasn't possible to apply for a passport without first applying to regularise his immigration position, so Janet sent off a 'leave to remain' application. They didn't realise that this well-intentioned move would trigger an unstoppable bureaucratic process to eject him from the country. He gathered together bits and pieces of evidence that showed he had been here since childhood, producing National Insurance records and a letter from the mother of his first three children, who stated that she had known Anthony for the past forty years and that he had never left the UK, and described him as 'dependable, honest, reliable and hardworking'. Somehow that was not enough.

As soon as the application was refused Anthony began to get calls and letters about his status from a company contracted by the Home Office to round up irregular migrants. 'They said: "We are coming to lock you up and deport you because you are an illegal immigrant,"' Anthony remembers. He couldn't decide whether to laugh or to be horrified. 'The first phone call from them made me so irate. I was telling them they had made a mistake. I didn't like the arrogant way the man was talking to me. I said: "Come and get me then."' He put the phone down and felt his heart beating faster with fear. 'I was shocked that they could just say they were going to come and lock me up. I was upset. They were saying they had a removal team on me, to make me go back.'

Again and again he protested that he had been in the UK since he was a child. 'I told them I haven't been to Jamaica since I was eight but they didn't believe me and they said that was nothing to do with them. They said they were coming to get me and I would have to sort all that out when they'd brought me to wherever I was to go.'

He found the Verne immigration detention centre 'a nightmare, like a castle on an island', violent and very noisy. An inspection report found levels of violence at the centre were 'too high', and criticised the excessively long periods for which immigration detainees were held there, waiting for removal. 'One man had been there for five years – one of the worst cases of prolonged detention we have seen,' an inspector noted.[1] Anthony tried repeatedly to tell officials that a mistake had been made, but they did not want to listen. Every night he was locked in his cell and left to reflect on why, as a peaceful, law-abiding person, he was being treated like a dangerous criminal by the state. He couldn't understand why officials thought he posed such a risk to society that he had to be locked up while they investigated his situation further. He had a stable address, which was known to the police. 'I've no prison record, I've not killed anyone.' Describing his confusion, later he said: 'You are not a criminal, yet they nick you and bring you 150-odd miles from your house. Now, what is that all about?'

It is a peculiar sensation, telling the truth repeatedly and being repeatedly told you are lying. After a while Anthony found it was driving him a bit mad. Occasionally he began to wonder if he perhaps was actually lying. 'They were telling me I could not have been here in 1965. I could not have come on my brother's passport. I was even questioning myself. I was thinking: You couldn't have come here at that time.' When I asked him to describe how it felt to find that no one believes you when you tell them the basic facts of your life history, he stopped talking for a while, put the tips of his fingers to his eyes and rested his head on them, remembering the painful experience. 'You feel like you are going crazy. I don't know what this has done to me, I'm not a doctor. But it was very stressful. I isolated myself.'

An official called him in for an interview after two days at the Verne; Anthony explained (again) that he was not an illegal immigrant but had lived in the UK continuously since he was eight years old. 'He didn't believe me. I did feel angry then because I'm locked up and nobody is listening to me.'

Another guard told him: 'Yes, yes, yes. We hear you, but we can't help you.' This is an ongoing theme, a constant in the Home Office treatment of Anthony and others in his position. No one was listening, or if they did take the time to listen they simply did not believe him. 'I tried to tell people all the time. All they wanted to know was: what is your name, and are you the right person to put in this cell.'

After two weeks he was released anyway. Anthony isn't quite sure why. When a fellow inmate read his files for him, they said there appeared to have been a mix-up of identities, because the name on the file wasn't quite right, and officers seemed to have muddled him up with an entirely different prisoner who had a long history of gun offences. Another recurrent issue that became clear through the months, as I heard dozens of stories of Home Office cruelty, was that the desire to classify people as illegal immigrants and remove them from Britain was frequently tempered by official incompetence which meant that threatened removals did not happen. Short-staffed and overworked Home Office employees make stupid mistakes that sometimes have disastrous effects on people's lives. Frequently, on the letters sent to him Anthony Bryan is referred to as Anthony Byron. When Janet visited him in the Verne, prison officers brought out someone quite different with a similar name, and it took a while to persuade staff that this was not the person she had come to see.

Shortly after he was released from detention for the first time, Anthony was sacked by the man who had employed him for years as a painter and decorator. His boss was very apologetic when he told him in December 2016. They had become friends, and he respected Anthony as a dependable and efficient worker. But since the fines for employing illegal immigrants had recently doubled to £20,000, he felt he had no choice; a fine of that level would push a small firm into bankruptcy. With characteristic thoughtfulness, Anthony said he quite understood. He was at pains to make his boss feel better about the decision – he told him he didn't blame him and that he would have done the same if he had been in his position.

Although he had been freed from detention, he was still under Home Office scrutiny and was told to go fortnightly to register at the Home Office reporting centre at London Bridge, south of the river. Like Paulette, he quickly found that there isn't much of an opportunity to put your case at the reporting centre. Occasionally he tried to make his position understood through the holes in the plastic barrier, but he was unimpressed by the young staff who were processing him. 'I would say: "I came here on my brother's passport in 1965." They would tell me: "You couldn't possibly have come on your brother's passport." They're too inexperienced to know that that's how things were done in the 1960s. I would mention the 1973 Immigration Act to them.[2] They don't know what I'm talking about. I'd think: what kind of immigration people are you if you don't know these things?'

Once, one of the officials asked him why he didn't just go back to his country. 'He was a young man, not even thirty. I'm sixty – I've been here since before he's even born. That upset me.' That man told him: 'Go back and then you can appeal from there.' Home Office letters to Anthony from around this time say that he has been given (as if it were a great favour) an 'out of country appeal right'. He was wise enough to understand that this would be a fatal move. 'I knew that no one would listen to me from Jamaica.'

He and Janet continued to try to unravel all the problems associated with his unclear immigration status, but the steady turning of Home Office bureaucratic cogs proved too much for them. His formal appeal was refused and officials advised him to seek advice from a solicitor. Since Anthony had been prevented from working for the past year (and since, as we've seen, legal aid for immigration cases had been largely abolished), he knew this was going to be hard to afford. Janet pulled together all the money she could find, and found another solicitor. 'The solicitor was worried,' Janet remembers. 'She said: "I can't stop this. I don't know how to stop this."'

On 13 October 2017 he was arrested at the Home Office reporting centre and taken to Campsfield House, another immigration removal centre, ahead of a planned deportation to Jamaica. Anthony found the atmosphere inside hard to bear. A lot of the inmates had been taken there after stretches in prison, and were awaiting deportation to different countries all over the world – China, Vietnam, Poland; some of them had lived in Britain for as long as twenty years, but no one had been here as long as Anthony. Most of the inmates were desperate and angry. 'It felt a bit rough because of this tension. Some people know they can't get out; you have a lot of arguing.'

Janet was increasingly worried about his state of mind. 'He called me one night to say he couldn't take it any more because people were fighting. He said people stayed up late, banging the doors; he couldn't sleep,' she said.

This time the Home Office bought a ticket for him to return to Jamaica. Officials asked him, just as they had asked Paulette, which airport he would like to fly to and he told them with some impatience that he had no idea because he hadn't visited the country in half a century. Anthony was given a letter informing him, helpfully: 'Your expected time of arrival in Kingston will be 17.15 hours.'

A cursory risk assessment of the possible difficulties Anthony might experience after deportation notes with confidence: 'It is considered that you would be returning to a country where you have social, cultural and lingual ties, having resided there for the majority of your life.'

In the letter finally informing him that his application to stay in the UK had been unsuccessful, immigration officer P Davey, RCC T6, Sheffield, sets out fifty-three numbered reasons why his case has been refused. Some of the arguments wheeled out are grimly funny, as the official makes a risible effort to bamboozle Anthony with ruthless circular logic. Point 39 states: 'You have confirmed that you have worked within the United Kingdom whilst having no authority to. It is also noted that you have not been issued with any leave to enter or remain which gives permission to work within the United Kingdom. As such, you have been working within the United Kingdom illegally.' The official then compliments Anthony for his talent at being a successful illegal immigrant. 'You have therefore shown that you are resourceful, supporting and making an independent life for yourself in a foreign country. The skills and experience you have gained whilst working in the United Kingdom should stand you in good stead for obtaining gainful employment on your return to Jamaica.' So, because Anthony has thrived as a so-called illegal immigrant in the UK, he should be well equipped to thrive in the difficult circumstances of his new home. The fact that he is not an illegal immigrant, and has been working quite legally for decades, slightly diminishes the potency of the argument, but the officer ploughs on with this bureaucratic demolition job, determined to expose Anthony's life story as a tissue of lies.

Point 40 adds: 'You state that you have developed relationships with family and friends in the United Kingdom. However it is considered that the relationships described could continue from overseas via other methods of communication.' The Home Office apparently expected Anthony to leave his home of fifty years, his partner, his children and grandchildren, fly 4,700 miles to Jamaica, and happily continue a relationship with them by Skype, email and text messages.

Janet was frustrated by the inaccuracies in the Home Office responses. Part of the problem was the official refusal to talk to Anthony in detail about his situation. 'Every point they've made is wrong, but if they haven't seen us to ask us, they haven't interviewed any of the witnesses . . .' Officials had chosen to be sceptical about whether Anthony was really the father of his children and about whether he was really in a relationship with her. Every reference to Janet in Anthony's files is prefaced with 'claimed partner'. 'They think I'm lying about that. They basically think I'm lying about everything,' Anthony said.

After we had been talking for an hour, Anthony's son Sean arrived, still in his uniform after a night shift working for the food delivery firm Ocado. He told me that he had noticed, a few days into the second spell in detention, that his father was beginning to abandon hope.

Janet scraped more money together and paid her lawyer £1,350 to get an injunction stopping the flight. Her finances were now in such a dire state that she was unable to pay two parking fines (which led to her car being impounded) or to collect her glasses from the menders, but she got Anthony released from detention for a second time. By the time we met she estimated they had spent over £5,000 on legal fees – which, given that Anthony had been banned from working, had not been easy.

The Home Office released him on Monday 28 November, two days before I met him; no one had explained why. 'They don't tell you why they're holding you and they don't tell you why they're letting you out.' After five weeks in detention, in two separate stints, his situation was no clearer. He remained classified as an illegal immigrant, required to report to the Home Office weekly, still facing the threat of deportation.

When the *Guardian*'s photographer arrived to take pictures of Janet and Anthony, wrapped up warm against the wind, in their back garden, Sean explained to me how badly hit his father had been.

'He has really kind of given up. I know he cares, but he has lost the will to fight for whatever rights he has. He has kids, grandkids, he is an integral part of the family. To tell someone that you are going to take them away from all that and ship them to somewhere they haven't been for over fifty years is quite ludicrous. It's been traumatic really.'

Besides feeling traumatised, Sean was perplexed by what was happening to his father. 'It doesn't make any sense,' he kept repeating. I was equally puzzled.

'I can understand where there has to be a certain amount of prying and a certain amount of investigation that has to be done,' Sean said. 'But to say that this man doesn't have any family, has no ties to this country? They just scoop him up and say they're going to throw him on a plane within two days. How would anyone feel? It's like losing your dad. You don't know when you're going to see them again.'

Anthony's entire family was struggling to cope with the uncertainty unleashed by what they saw as a campaign of Home Office persecution. Sean continued: 'My daughters are worried. I can't tell them it's going to be OK, because I don't know myself that it will.

Who says who can stay and who says who can't?'

All the way through our conversation, I was struggling to answer the same questions. Why would the Home Office treat a long-term resident, near retirement age, in such a callous way? Why were officials ignoring Anthony's repeated insistence that he was British, and the piles of evidence he provided to prove he had lived here continuously for fifty-two years?

'They're saying: "It doesn't matter how long you've been here. Piss off out of my country,"' Anthony said, summing up his frustration.

Somehow he seemed less incensed than I was, and something about his world-weary approach to his situation made me feel that he found my outrage slightly naïve.

'I know quite a few people in the same position,' he said, 'quite a few people who are stuck like this. They'll never leave the country because they are frightened to apply for papers. I know lots of people who are too frightened to go to the Home Office.'

'How many?'

'I've still got friends who I went to secondary school with who are frightened to get passports. They all know about my detention. Once they apply for any documents to leave the country, the same thing is going to happen to them.'

He counted through the school friends he knew were caught up in a similar mess – Hubert, Tyrone and Jeffrey. Then there was his elder brother, who had also had such difficulties with his immigration status that he had chosen to avoid all contact with the state; all of them had arrived in the UK from the Caribbean as children around fifty years earlier.

If Anthony could quickly think of four people who were encountering similar problems, I began to realise this could be happening on a bigger and much more serious scale. What I couldn't understand was why it wasn't headline news.

HIDDEN LIVES

For a while I worried that I had misunderstood something about Anthony's case. I couldn't understand why teams of Home Office officials had bulldozed ahead for so many months, going to great lengths and expense to lock him up twice. How could someone live here for fifty years without a passport and without a bank account? Could there be something more to the situation that I was unaware of?

I often find my job quite stressful. Writing articles where you showcase people's life stories, illustrated with big pictures of them in a newspaper, is a sensitive business. I don't often interview celebrities who are more practised in talking to journalists and who have teams of press people to protect them. For years my job has been mainly about examining the consequences of government policies on the people affected by them. It works best when you travel as far away as possible from Westminster and the people who designed the legislation to talk to those feeling the impact. Sometimes people are delighted to be able to speak about why they feel something has gone wrong, and can be very open about their lives and their problems, in a selfless attempt to show why things might not be working. But it is hard to predict how you're going to feel about seeing your life summed up in a few newspaper paragraphs, your problems foregrounded, until the article is published. The *Guardian*'s huge online readership guarantees powerful impact, but it also means that stories are widely shared on Facebook and Twitter and once the information is out there is no pulling it back, no escaping from the exposure. Now that articles exist forever online, the notion that yesterday's news is just fish-and-chip paper is no longer a reassuring source of comfort to those made unhappy by a story about their life.

I'm anxious to make sure the representation of the people I've interviewed is fair and won't upset them. At the same time I'm endlessly worrying about making mistakes. All journalists have these misgivings, working fast against immovable deadlines, but some wear their concerns more lightly; if there is a spectrum of worrying I am at the ulcerous end. I'm usually in a state of controlled anxiety, which I've learned mainly to channel towards constructive ends.

My uncertainty about Anthony's case was only momentary, part of the process of going through a mental checklist before committing something to print. I asked a colleague in the *Guardian*'s personal finance department if it was odd for a sixty-year-old not to have a bank account, and he said it was unusual but not unheard of; another colleague explained that around 17 per cent of UK residents do not have a passport, around nine million people. By the time I had gone through the documents that Janet had let me photograph, I had no doubt about Anthony's account. He and Janet had compiled a handwritten summary of every year since 1973, noting what he had been doing and what paperwork they could provide to prove it. There were one or two gaps where documentation had gone missing over the decades, but the evidence was persuasive.

When I spoke to Anthony's MP, Kate Osamor, the Labour representative for Edmonton, she was unsurprised. She described his case as the 'tip of the iceberg', estimating that she had dealt with at least ten similar instances of older people being sent to detention after decades in Britain. 'They often get a knock on their door on a Sunday. They try to catch people when they are at their most relaxed.'

She was very familiar with the issue. 'Many arrived here as children and have been settled for over fifty years. These are people who have worked hard and contributed, with no criminal record, no blemish. They find that when they apply for a passport, the authorities come down heavily on them and write back to notify them that they are not welcome here,' she said. 'People are left wondering: how can someone who has done so much for the community be treated like a piece of rubbish? It is barbaric. Why send people to detention when they have done nothing wrong?'

I emailed details of Anthony's case to the Home Office press office. After some delay, an official responded with a bald statement: 'Mr Bryan is not currently subject to removal action. Over the last three years we have had ongoing enquiries with Mr Bryan about how he can regularise his immigration status. These enquiries did not lead to him providing the necessary evidence to show a lawful right to remain here.' I wondered what necessary evidence officials had in mind; the piles of paper Janet had shown me seemed very comprehensive.

Anthony's account didn't make the front page, but there was a long piece about him in the newspaper on a Saturday, the day the *Guardian* has the largest newspaper sales. It didn't trigger any political unease or much wider reaction. His case just appeared to be another peculiar and sad mistake made by the Home Office.

I was sure that there was something deeper going wrong, and set about trying to expose the scale of the problem, but for weeks I seemed to hit obstacles.

I arranged to meet Kate Osamor towards the end of the day in Portcullis House, the modern extension of parliament, across the road from the House of Commons. Here politicians see constituents and journalists, or just pause to drink coffee with colleagues at tables in the glass-roofed atrium in the shade of two rows of beautiful but high-maintenance indoor trees. We met in a noisy side room. I was hoping that she could give me more details of the cases similar to Anthony's that she had dealt with, and ideally put me in touch with other people who had been detained or experienced similar maltreatment at the hands of the Home Office.

She was helpful but distracted; the Labour party was in the throes of a prolonged leadership crisis and there was a lot on her plate. Her constituency caseload was overflowing with complicated immigration issues. She said she would ask her constituency case worker to see if any of the people she had helped would be willing to talk to me, and would put out feelers to other Labour MPs to see if they had handled comparable cases. She also recommended trying church groups. A few weeks later her assistant emailed to say that unfortunately none of the affected constituents wanted to be contacted, and that they had heard nothing from any other MPs.

A lawyer in South London sent me a very informative email explaining that he was dealing with a number of cases like this, including one person who had been refused cancer treatment because he was told he was an illegal immigrant and therefore not eligible, despite insisting that he had lived here a lifetime. I wondered if I could speak to this client or write about his situation. The lawyer thought that would not be constructive while the case was still being prepared, and besides, his client was not feeling well.

I tried calling other law centres to see if they were handling cases of pension-age, Caribbean-born, long-term residents who had been told to leave the country, despite having lived here for half a century. I realised that the drastic legal aid cuts that had kicked in around 2013 not only meant that fewer people were getting the help they needed, but also made it harder for lawyers to raise the alarm about problems they were seeing. These already overstretched law centres were often at breaking point, and none of them had dedicated people able to deal with questions from journalists. I emailed the Immigration Lawyers' Practitioners Association to see if they could put out a request to all their members; they said this was not something they could do.

I asked Tottenham MP David Lammy's office if they had seen cases like this. They checked their files and said not as far as they could see. I asked staff in the office of shadow home secretary Diane Abbott if they could help; they said they had recently had a switch-over of constituency case workers and it was not a request they could manage. I rang homelessness charities without any success. I called the charity Praxis, which helps refugees in East London, but they were in the process of recruiting a new press officer and were unable to help. I tried to contact the Jamaican High Commission repeatedly, requesting an interview with the High Commissioner or someone else there, and people kept promising to pass on messages, but I heard nothing. I know phone calls from journalists are often time-consuming and an unwelcome additional burden, and am trained to be persistent. Everyone was busy, and I made no progress.

I sat, despondent, at my desk in the *Guardian*'s large open-plan newsroom, writing long lists of potential contacts on an A4 note-pad, crossing them off when I'd phoned them.

Sometimes when I bring visitors into the office, I try to see the room where we sit through fresh eyes, stretching it into a glossier film-set version of the newsroom. The rows of desks and screens lose their call-centre banality and are transformed into an exhil-arating hub of rolling news. The design of the building does have some touches of real Hollywood newspaper glamour – clashing pink and yellow armchairs where we meet to discuss projects, a pol-ished silver-and-glass stairwell dropping between floors, ceiling-height windows with views stretching over the new King's Cross development with its railway sheds converted into art schools and restaurants, the horizon outside constantly shifting and rising with the arrival of more expensive apartment blocks. The glamour is pretty illusory, undercut by the reality of desks piled high with grimy newspapers, often more than six months old, unwanted books, half-eaten sandwiches, abandoned cups of coffee, the froth solidified into undrinkable sludge, and the occasional glimpse of exhausted reporters resting on the sofas. The office is a nicer place to work than when I was first hired as a trainee in the late 1990s, when most of the older (male) reporters smoked at their desks, their keyboards yellowed with nicotine and dotted with black spots of melted plastic from the falling ash; back then my friend cried in the loos when she got pregnant because she was worried about the effect that weeks spent inhaling the newsroom smog would have on her baby. It is cleaner today and the atmosphere, now that no one has the time or desire to go to the pub in their lunch break, is less endlessly hungover, but with its life-shortening strip lighting it still lacks a certain sheen.

In the afternoons in the office, everyone is on the phone, typing as they talk, racing to hit deadlines, but for me this was a disheartening time, and I spent much of it staring absently across the room, chewing my biros, wandering up and down the stairs to the canteen for tea and crisps, trying to find new people who might help me, but getting nowhere. I tried to get a sense of the scale of the problem by finding out the number of people held in the UK's immigration removal centres who were over fifty and had been born in Commonwealth countries, but the data was not available in the correct form.

I was also working on other projects and couldn't focus exclusively on this odd and tortuous immigration issue, but I kept coming back to it because it seemed so worrying that people who had been at primary and secondary school here should, after half a century in the UK, suddenly be told that they were illegal immigrants and required to leave the country. Obsessiveness is helpful as a reporter. It would have been easier to shove my notebooks to the side and focus on something less elusive, but it kept nagging at me. I knew something very problematic was unfolding, and I couldn't work out why no one else was making any noise about it.

I asked Janet if I could speak to Anthony's school friends. For a while I heard nothing more from her. She and Anthony were busy with the continuing legal battle to prevent him from being detained again, so it wasn't until late January 2018 that I had a call saying Hubert Howard was happy to meet.

———

While Anthony was quietly resigned about his problems and Paulette was bewildered, Hubert was furious about the Home Office's treatment of him. He had arrived in England when he was three, and had never left the country since, but found himself classified as an illegal immigrant and rejected by the state as he neared pension age. He had lost his job as a caretaker with the Peabody housing association, then been refused unemployment benefits. Perhaps most upsetting, he was prevented from travelling to Jamaica to visit his mother before she died. He had spent the last six years attempting and failing to get someone to help him, or at least to listen. The relief at finally talking about it meant his words fell out, fast and angry, and I had to keep asking him to slow down so I could keep up with my notes. I sat on a stool in his ground-floor kitchen in North London, typing, with my computer balanced on my knee as he talked.

Hubert has no memories at all of Kingston, Jamaica, where he was born; not even the faintest of recollections warped into exotic nostalgia – the heat, the rain, the sea, the palm trees – nothing. All his consciousness is here, in the dirty streets of North London where he has been knocking about for over half a century – Euston, Clapton, Dalston. So to be told, quite suddenly when he was in his late fifties, that he had no right to be living in the UK was life-shattering.

Hubert's parents brought him to London in 1960, hoping for a better life. He travelled by plane with his mother, his name added in beautiful official copperplate beneath hers in her passport. This was two years before Jamaica gained independence, so the navy blue passport issued to Hubert's mother describes the bearer as:

'British subject: Citizen of the United Kingdom and Colonies', and is identical to one which would have been issued in the UK. Before independence, travelling from Jamaica to London was effectively considered an internal journey from one bit of the British Empire to another – in theory equivalent to going from Glasgow to London. There were no immigration restrictions on people travelling from colonies, no visa was required, and arrivals were classed as 'freely landed'. If you lived anywhere in the shrinking British Empire you had the right to live and work anywhere within the territories of the United Kingdom and colonies. The notion of nationality or citizenship would not have been discussed. His mother's passport was stamped with a blurry triangle in dark purple ink and the date of arrival, 15.11.60, added in biro.

When he tried to make a return journey half a century later, to see his dying mother who had retired to Jamaica, Hubert was told he needed to be naturalised as a British citizen before he could get a passport. After a lifetime in Britain he was amazed at the requirements involved. 'I thought they were being kind of racist because I had to do a course called "English as another language". So I'm saying: "What are you talking about? What language do Jamaicans speak?"'

A letter from the UK Border Agency confirmed that if he wanted to naturalise it would cost him £780 and that applicants had 'to demonstrate that they have sufficient knowledge of Life in the United Kingdom and of the English language'. He needed to take a test or successfully complete a course of study in English for Speakers of Other Languages. Hubert believed he already was British, and found these requirements absurd and humiliating. Wearily he decided to go ahead, but the place running the course suddenly closed. His attempts to explain this to Home Office staff were futile, because no one ever answered his numerous calls to a helpline. He estimates he made over fifty fruitless calls to the Home Office in the course of five years.

Being classified as illegal affected everything. He was informed bluntly by a Jobcentre official that he was not eligible for unemployment benefits; he went into debt; he was unable to get a mobile phone contract. He was so short of money that his friends were buying his clothes. He became too stressed and too ill to go on trying to persuade officials that a mistake had been made. 'My health deteriorated. I had to completely drop the Home Office thing.'

In 2015, he received a letter informing him that he needed to leave the country because he had no right to be here.

In the internal notes about Hubert's case made by Capita, a private company contracted by the Home Office, staff refer to him as 'Migrant' rather than 'Mr Howard'. 'Migrant advises he should have leave to remain in the UK based upon a law passed in the 1970s. Could the migrant be referring to the Immigration Act 1971?' Checks are made and the officials finally decide that Hubert is right, and that he is here legally, but they persist in referring to a man who has lived in London for fifty-eight years in this weirdly hostile (and wholly inappropriate) way.

'Migrant has valid leave. Attempted to contact Migrant via telephone to confirm unfortunately i got no response.' It's worth noting that migrant is not a neutral word. Words like émigré, migrant and expat all mean the same thing but in the modern British lexicon, migrant carries the heavy weight of something unwanted and unwelcome, and to use it against a sixty-one-year-old man who has been living in London since he was three is insulting as well as inaccurate.

The Home Office later casually acknowledged over the phone that it seemed he did after all have 'settled status' allowing him to reside legally in the UK. However, this was never confirmed in writing. Hubert remembered feeling shocked at the ease with which they adjusted their position, years after he had lost his job because of this mistake.

When we met, he was still very worried that the lack of clarity meant he was vulnerable to renewed attempts to force him to leave. Outrage was burning in his voice as he spoke. 'They basically messed up my life,' he said. 'They took my job away, stating quite clearly I had no status in this country. It broke my heart losing my job as a caretaker. It was the best job I was ever in. When my mum passed away, I wasn't there, and I still have not been at her graveside. Since November 1960 I've never left this country. Never. I haven't even been to France. I haven't even been to Ireland.'

Hubert had over thirty years of tax and National Insurance records. 'The people they have targeted have all worked and contributed. I've paid my tax and insurance. The Home Office should know that,' he said. Hubert knew a handful of people similarly affected. While it was barely understood elsewhere, this Home Office mistreatment of a cohort of long-term residents was an open secret among his group of friends. 'The whole system stinks because there is no one to help us. That's what is hurting me most. When I started this, I was entitled to legal aid, but they took it away. I've got no one to turn to . . . No one helped me. Not Labour, not the Conservatives.'

———

That week I also met Jeffrey, who started at the same primary school as Anthony, aged nine, in the winter of 1966, shortly after he arrived from Grenada to join his parents who were working in London. Like Anthony, he had travelled with his elder brother, on his brother's passport.

Jeffrey had lived a stable, conventional life: worked, married, had a baby and bought a house. When his marriage broke up after twenty-two years, he moved to live by himself in Hackney. When he lost his job in 2012, he was unable to get a new one, finding himself repeatedly refused jobs which he had successfully interviewed for because he had no papers. He had heard what had happened to Anthony and was becoming increasingly unsettled. He wanted to visit Grenada, a country he hadn't been to since leaving as a child, to see land left to him by a grandfather, but he was too scared to apply for a British passport in case he found himself, like Anthony, added to an official list of illegals. He decided to retreat to a life in hiding.

I was puzzled. I couldn't understand how a man who had had a mortgage for years and decades of employment records could possibly get into such difficulties. I wondered if he was overreacting a bit to his situation.

'Probably you'd be OK if you applied, wouldn't you?' I said, with the casual confidence of someone who has never been kept awake at night worrying about deportation. I feel cross with myself as I listen back to the dictaphone recording; I can hear myself cheerfully crunching on a rich tea biscuit and sipping my tea.

'As soon as I apply the red flag will go up,' he said.

Then he began to describe the level of his fear. For several years he had been avoiding walking down the nearby high street because he was frightened of the Immigration Enforcement teams who frequently waited there. 'You see immigration vans – they are often parked up the back streets here, and you think they might be after you. It is always at the back of your mind. You feel very uneasy. I've heard about people who've been put straight on a plane.' It was affecting how he slept. If a car pulled up outside the house at night, he would get up to peer out of the window to see if it was a Border Force van coming to pick him up. He was worried about what it would like to be deported. He was not planning to claim a pension for fear of being identified as an illegal immigrant. He had deliberately stopped having any interaction with official bodies. 'You avoid confrontation, like the plague, in case the Bill get involved.' He had been living in hiding for years.

Friends had told him about people disappearing, having travelled to the Caribbean for funerals or holidays and subsequently been prevented from re-entering the country. 'You hear someone's auntie's gone . . . his friend's gone. It's not nice.'

I had spent weeks looking for people who had been detained, like Paulette and Anthony, but as I spoke to Hubert and Jeffrey I began to realise that this problem was not just about being wrongly locked up and threatened with deportation. It was about a much wider issue of fear and humiliation, losing jobs, losing homes, being refused the right to visit family, denied the chance to see dying parents, having your identity ripped away from you by brutal, invisible bureaucratic processes.

———

Gradually more people emerged wanting to talk about how they had been targeted by the Home Office. I met Judy Griffith, aged sixty-three, who had worked for the Metropolitan Police and Camden Council, and who had been horrified to hear from a Jobcentre employee: 'As far as we're concerned you're an illegal immigrant.'

She had been living in Britain since she was nine, when she flew from Barbados in 1963 to join her parents, who had been persuaded to emigrate here by a recruitment appeal for workers to drive buses. Her passport had been lost in the post a decade ago. She had been rejected from jobs because of her undocumented status, and prevented from travelling back to Barbados to see her mother before she died. Because she had been barred from working, she had accrued thousands of pounds' worth of debt. 'I feel a sense of anger because of the humiliation I've had to go through. I don't think the Home Office realise how much I've suffered.'

I spoke to sixty-four-year-old Renford McIntyre, who had arrived in the UK from Jamaica in 1968 at the age of fourteen to join his mother, who had come over to work as a nurse, and his father, who was working as a crane driver. Renford had worked constantly, latterly as an NHS driver, and had been meticulously paying tax for decades but in 2014, a routine request from his employers for updated paperwork revealed that he didn't have a passport and had never naturalised in the UK. He was sacked. Unable to find new work without papers, he became depressed, and then homeless. The local council said he was not eligible for emergency housing because he had no right to be in the country. Similarly, he had been told he was not allowed to sign on for benefits. He gathered together paperwork showing thirty-five years of National Insurance contributions, but the Home Office had returned the application, requesting further evidence. 'It makes me so angry. I've always worked. I'm a grafter. I can't explain how bad it makes me feel,' he said.

He was sleeping in an unheated industrial unit in Dudley, in the Midlands. The space had no shower and nowhere to cook, and he had to visit friends when he wanted to eat hot food or wash. 'It's an appalling place to live. I'm a proud man; I'm embarrassed at my age to be living like this,' he said. A *Guardian* photographer took pictures of the place where he was living. It was a very sad scene, with Renford wrapped in several layers of clothes, two jackets and a woolly hat to keep warm, sitting on a greying mattress, heaped with old bedding, in a room decorated with health and safety posters on the walls instructing visitors that safety footwear must be worn. The door had fallen off its hinges; Renford managed to put on a bravely smiling face for the camera.

By now I was no longer in any doubt that there was something seriously bad going on. It was impossible not to see a pattern. But I was still puzzled about why no one was raising the alarm. How could this be happening to so many people without anyone noticing?

I wrote a long article about Hubert, Jeffrey, Judy and Renford, and hoped the severity of their experiences might finally spark some political response, but somehow the story got rather lost.

Something very significant had happened to the *Guardian* during the weeks that I had been struggling with this. The size of the paper had shrunk to a tabloid, as part of an ongoing cost-cutting drive to reduce the huge losses that the business was facing. A new digital editorial tool, Ophan, now allowed everyone in the building to see instantly how many thousand people had clicked on an article online, and precisely how long they had continued to read it before they drifted away. It was sobering information for journalists because we could see how rapidly attention dissipated, and it increased the pressure to keep articles short.

I wrote something for the features section, worried there wouldn't be enough space in the smaller news pages to explain the complicated issue, but it ended up being pushed from the front by an article about hamburger restaurants (a much less gruelling read). Daily newspaper journalism can be a messy process, as reporters and editors feel their way towards working out where to point readers' attention, trying to get things right.

At the time we were publishing daily articles about immigration-related problems – about the harsh treatment of refugees from Syria, about thousands of people dying in the Mediterranean as they battled to get to the UK, and about official hostility towards asylum seekers from Calais. I had struggled to make clear that this was a different issue, an unjustified persecution of a whole generation of people by the government. But the problem was complicated to explain, and required a clunky introduction describing those affected as a group of retirement-age, Commonwealth-born, long-term UK residents with immigration problems. It did not make an easy headline.

The article did not provoke the outrage it should have triggered. There was no comment from Home Secretary Amber Rudd or from any politician. I felt responsible.

£54,000

The Royal Marsden Hospital in Chelsea specialises in cancer treatment and its doctors have an excellent reputation worldwide. Its website announces with pride: 'We deal with cancer every day so we understand how valuable life is. And when people entrust their lives to us, they have the right to demand the very best.'

When Sylvester Marshall was referred to the hospital by his GP for a twelve-week course of daily radiotherapy sessions, as the second stage of his prostate cancer treatment, he wasn't planning to demand the very best. It's not really his style to go around demanding things and in any case, he had no reason to doubt that he would get the vital treatment his doctor had arranged. He arrived at the red-brick Victorian building in South Kensington to start the first session on a cold morning in early November 2017, went to the front desk to register and was told to wait because someone needed to talk to him about his documents. After a while a woman in her late thirties came to find him, took him to stand in a corridor outside the waiting room and told him that unless he could provide a British passport he would have to pay £54,000 for his treatment.

Sylvester was stunned. 'The lady wasn't at all polite,' he remembers. 'I didn't like the tone of her voice, she sounded a bit aggressive . . . it was sort of rough, the way she spoke to me. First she said it would be £53,000 and then she said it would cost £54,000. I said: "Oh my God, I don't have fifty-four pence, let alone £54,000."'

He left the hospital in shock. After forty-four years in Britain and over three decades paying tax and National Insurance, he was devastated to be told he was not eligible for the cancer treatment he had been prescribed. 'I went home with a broken heart. I couldn't believe that after working here for so many years, they would just close the door on me. That afternoon I locked myself away in my room, very depressed, knowing that I had no money for the treatment.'

'Where am I going to get £54,000 from?' Sylvester asked me when I met him at a charity-run hostel for homeless people in Brixton. 'I've got no savings. Since I stopped work when I got ill, I've just been living from day to day.' Four and a half months after he had been turned away from the hospital, he was still not receiving radiotherapy and he was feeling so concerned about whether the cancer was silently growing somewhere inside him that he found it hard to think about anything else.

'I can't sleep at night. It takes a lot out of me . . . I am stressed, depressed . . . It feels like they don't care any more, like they are leaving me to die.'

His small room on the first floor of the hostel was mainly taken up by his single bed and a desk which doubled as a kitchen (with a toasted sandwich maker, a jar of Tesco Everyday Value instant hot chocolate, and a tidily washed-up stack of one plate, one bowl, one saucepan and sieve on the bookshelf by a small fridge). There was no space to sit down, so we crowded into a cramped, narrow basement room at the back of the hostel. His case worker from the homelessness charity St Mungo's had come to support him, as had Laura Stahnke from the migration charity Praxis which had been helping him with his legal situation.

Quietly spoken and unsettled at the prospect of speaking to a journalist about his immigration problems and his health, Sylvester had nevertheless steeled himself to go ahead, hopeful that publicity might persuade the hospital that a terrible mistake had been made and prompt them to start treating him as an NHS patient. It was obvious from his uneasy laughter that he wasn't much looking forward to the process of talking about himself. His lawyers had asked that he should not be named in print while they were preparing his papers to submit to the Home Office in an attempt to resolve his immigration status, so together we chose the neutral-sounding name Albert Thompson.

Sylvester was born in Clarendon province, central Jamaica, in a small village in the hills. His mother and father left for England in 1960 when he was six, in search of work. For most of his childhood he and his younger sister were brought up by their grandparents. There was no telephone, so communication with his parents and the two younger siblings who were born in London was very limited. He would send them a letter every month or so and occasionally he received parcels from London containing smart brown leather lace-up shoes or Wrangler jeans; once they sent him a portable record player and he remembers the excitement of walking with it around the yard in front of the house, next to the small plantation where his grandparents grew bananas, oranges, tangerines and pears, his reggae music playing. 'It was brown, I think. You slid the records in. Everyone loved it and wanted to know where I got it from. I felt like a king.' He was the only person in the village who had anything like it, but it didn't compensate for his parents' absence, which nagged at him throughout his childhood. 'Whenever I cried and asked where they were, my grandmother would say: "They've gone to the shop to buy sweets and they will be back soon."'

A decade after they left, his parents (who had found jobs as a nurse and a roadworker) managed to save enough money to send for their two older children. Sylvester flew to London in December 1973.

He thinks he was wearing a suit and a bow tie for the journey. 'I wanted to look smart.' He was carrying a small grey suitcase made of a hard cardboard material, containing very little, just a few things to wear, because he had been told he would need to buy more suitable clothes in England. He has a clear mental picture of the reunion at the airport with his parents and siblings as he walked out from passport control. 'They lifted their hands up and shouted my name. There were big hugs and kisses.' They drove to Battersea, where his parents had bought a house. 'It felt like they were rich. The house felt very big inside. Everything was different; I had my own room, with wallpaper, carpet, extra bits of furniture which we didn't have in Jamaica.' His room in his grandmother's house had been very bare, with white walls, just a bed and a table. Electricity hadn't reached his village in Clarendon so the house there was lit by oil lanterns; in London there were electric lights with switches on the wall. 'I think I was a bit in shock.' Mostly, though, he found London ugly and gloomy and was depressed by the dirty remnants of snow melting into ice. 'There was smoke and soot in the air. At the beginning I wanted to go back.'

His parents tried hard to make him feel at home. They took him to Madame Tussaud's, but every time he went outside he struggled with the cold, and feared the ice on the pavements which made him lose control of his feet, occasionally flipping him over. The family went on an outing to Brighton, where the sight of the murky brown water, so different from the sparkling Caribbean sea, horrified him. 'I didn't like it. I wouldn't go in the water at all.'

A few weeks after his arrival he went with his mother to the Home Office to sort out his papers. He was nineteen and still finding his way around a new country so he let his mother handle the process. 'I didn't know anything. My mum did everything to arrange my stay in the country, sorted out whatever paperwork was needed,' he said. He has never managed to find out what forms his mother filled out for him, but he had no reason to doubt that things were in order. 'She made sure I was legal from day one.'

Both his parents were working hard, often at night. His father was working on the roads, laying tarmac and repairing holes; his mother did four night shifts a week as a nurse at the Royal Hospital and Home for Incurables in Putney, from seven or eight in the evening until seven or eight in the morning.

Remembering how hard his mother worked upsets Sylvester. He had watched her give up her life in Jamaica to travel across the world to take up a job with the National Health Service, where she worked long hours, for decades taking the unpopular night shifts that the other workers did not want to do, which made family life in London complicated. She died in 2006 and Sylvester was glad she wasn't around to witness him being rejected by the service to which she had dedicated her life. He gently articulated the injustice of the situation. 'She would have been angry. It does seem unfair, knowing that she worked for them for so long.'

Sylvester helped look after his younger siblings, and managed to get a job as an apprentice mechanic in Camberwell, mending black taxis. He remembers this was the time of the National Front. He once strayed into one of their pubs in Battersea with his uncle, and had to leave rapidly. 'Those National Front people – they were something else,' he said. The KBW ('Keep Britain White') slogan was still visible painted across brick walls in London in the 1970s. Sylvester hated confrontation and tried to keep himself to himself. He heard about the Brixton riots from the radio and television but stayed well away.

He married, had two sons, and later a daughter. In time the marriage failed and he moved out. After the breakup, he stored a lot of his belongings with a friend, but one day she got fed up with the sight of them and called him to tell him that he needed to come and move his bags. 'That woman had a screw loose. She chucked everything away,' he said. 'By the time I arrived she had put it all by the rubbish chute and the council had taken it away.' As well as his clothes and pictures of his family, he also lost the

Jamaican passport he had arrived on; it had expired, but the document contained the crucial indefinite leave to remain stamp that proved his right to be in the UK. This happened around 2005, at a time when a passport was only needed as a travel document; there was no need to produce one in order to get a job or healthcare. Sylvester had no plans to go travelling, so he was annoyed but not distraught at the loss of his papers. It wasn't immediately clear to him how significant it would be.

Having worked constantly since he was nineteen, latterly as an MOT test mechanic, in his mid-fifties Sylvester got ill with lymphoma and had to stop work. He was evicted by his landlord in 2013 because he was no longer able to afford the rising rent. The council housed him in a hostel in a Victorian terraced house, with eight rooms for homeless single people and families; each room had a stove, but the bathrooms were shared.

He was told he was categorised as high priority for a council flat because of his cancer, but council staff began to ask questions about his passport and so the move never happened. In January 2017 he had an operation to remove some of his prostate cancer; over the next few months, while he was convalescing, the questions about his passport and his immigration status began to become more insistent.

On 11 May 2017, a Lambeth Council official wrote to Sylvester to say that an investigation had concluded that he was not eligible for publicly funded housing assistance. The letter was written in a confusingly impenetrable official style, but the final paragraph was very clear: 'Because we do not have a duty to house you, you will be required to leave your temporary accommodation. A separate notice to quit will be sent to you, so I expect that your current accommodation will end soon.'

Still feeling unwell in the wake of the operation, he tried to find out how he could prove that he had a right to live here. He visited

Lunar House, the huge immigration headquarters in Croydon, to see if they could help him to find a record of the paperwork that his mother had completed on his behalf. They said there was no trace of him. He began to worry that he might be deported. 'I'd seen television programmes about it; they pick you up, take you to a detention centre, hold you there until you get a flight back home. I felt so tormented I couldn't sleep. I'd go walking in the night to try to calm myself down. I'd walk through the streets, sometimes to the park, until I felt I could sleep. But when I woke up the worry would get to me again.'

Sylvester tried repeatedly to explain that a mistake had been made, but he got no help from the council, and one morning while he was in the shower, the manager of the hostel changed the locks on his room, so he was unable to get back inside. 'All my medication was inside the room. She refused to get it out for me. I didn't have anything. The woman said she would call the police if I didn't leave the building. I rang the council and told them I would be sleeping on the streets that night, that I was a cancer patient. They didn't listen.' Council officials packed up his belongings and stored them in the basement in plastic bags; it was six months before he got his things back and in the meantime some of them had been lost or thrown away. He feels a weary anger towards the council. 'I told them loads of times that there must be a mistake. They wouldn't take my word for it. They wanted to see the proof in black and white.'

That night he stayed with a friend, but after that he had to sleep outside – in bushes, shop fronts, parks. He knew nothing about how to sleep rough, having lived a stable life for the previous sixty-three years. 'I'd never done it before. It's a bit frightening when you're not used to things like that. When you fall asleep, you don't know who is going to come. You worry about being attacked.' He had to decide whether it was better to sleep in the open, protected by the presence of passers-by, or hidden in the back streets, away from people's gaze. 'You feel a bit better in the open, safer, but there's the question of pride.' He was desperate to avoid being seen by anyone he knew, so he decided the park was a better bet. He didn't know where the local soup kitchens were, and was alarmed by how much food costs when you have nowhere to cook and you're just buying things as you go along. He lost his appetite. 'I was more worried about getting my medication.'

Things only improved when a friend suggested he go to the homelessness charity St Mungo's to ask for help; they rehoused him in a new hostel and referred him to the migrant support charity Praxis (even though he didn't view himself as a migrant). He was beginning to feel he could begin to think about rebuilding his life when he visited the Royal Marsden in November and was denied treatment.

A letter from the hospital stated that unless Sylvester could provide documents to prove that he was 'ordinarily resident and legally entitled to live in the UK', he would be required to pay for treatment 'in full, in advance'. It went on, 'Mr Marshall has been seen by one of our consultants who considers that his treatment is not urgent or immediately necessary, and as such Mr Marshall would not be eligible for NHS treatment prior to payment being received.'

The letter made no sense to Sylvester. After forty-four years in London, how could anyone suggest he was not 'ordinarily resident'?

———

In October 2017, a month before Sylvester went for his hospital appointment, the Department of Health published new guidelines outlining NHS trusts' legal responsibility for charging overseas visitors.[1] In an introduction to the NHS Visitor and Migrant

Cost Recovery Programme, Jeremy Hunt, who was then Health Secretary, wrote: 'Our NHS is the envy of the world and we have no problem with overseas visitors using it – as long as they make a fair contribution, just as the British taxpayer does. My ambition is that by 2020 no one will get NHS care for free if they should be paying.'[2] The foreword is illustrated with a smiling picture of Hunt, looking earnest and cheerful about the new policy. 'We will ensure that for the first time it becomes a legal obligation to pay upfront and in full for any non-urgent treatment on the NHS.'

Described in carefully neutral terms as a policy for charging people who aren't 'ordinarily resident' in the UK, it was nevertheless obvious that this was part of a new government campaign to make life harder for immigrants who were unable to prove they were here legally. 'The NHS should never withhold potentially life-saving treatment from overseas visitors or migrants because of their inability to pay. But it is right that people who are not resident here make a fair contribution to the cost of their NHS care.' The stated goal was to raise £500 million a year from patients who were ineligible for free treatment. GP treatment would remain free, but patients who were charged for non-urgent hospital care would be made to pay an elevated price, set at 150 per cent of the normal tariff.

The policy caused considerable unease among doctors, who wondered how they could possibly know who to charge. They were uncomfortable with the role of border guard that seemed to be implicit in the new requirement to check eligibility. The rules were complicated – urgent and immediately necessary care was still to be provided to everyone, but everything else was to be withheld from anyone unable to prove their immigration status. Hunt had said everyone should occasionally expect to be asked questions about eligibility for free healthcare, but the new policy obliged busy hospital staff to make swift decisions on the immigration status of patients. In the absence of training or experience in immigration law there was a strong risk that they would rely on dubious shortcuts when choosing who to question.

Satbir Singh, who heads the Joint Council for the Welfare of Immigrants, summarised the problem: 'Nurses and hospital administrators are being asked to carry out the functions of an entry clearance officer as well as their own duties, without the expertise. It's a horrible situation to put them in; they have to use some sort of proxy. Typically those proxies will be your name, your skin colour, your accent.'

Ministers were aware that taking tough action on health tourism was a very popular initiative, but there remains some uncertainty about how much it was actually costing the NHS, and whether the relatively small amount of money clawed back by these checks justified the tough and controversial measures.

As a result of the new guidelines, patients have to complete a form headed with an alarming set of warnings:

This hospital may need to ask the Home Office to confirm your immigration status to help us decide if you are eligible for free NHS hospital treatment. In this case, your personal, non-clinical information will be sent to the Home Office. The information provided may be used and retained by the Home Office for its functions, which include enforcing immigration controls . . . If you are chargeable but fail to pay for NHS treatment for which you have been billed, it may result in a future immigration application to enter or remain in the UK being denied.

Many medical staff hated these forms. 'We don't want to be immigration enforcement officers,' a hospital doctor (who didn't want to be named) told me. 'We're annoyed that there is a legal requirement to check people's status and an outsourcing of this responsibility to doctors. It fundamentally goes against why I became a doctor. I signed up to become a doctor to provide care based on need – not on ability to pay, certainly not based on the colour of their skin or their immigration status.'

As well as the ethical questions around the inherently discriminatory nature of the policy, there were practical concerns about how to decide whether someone's care was urgently necessary or slightly less than urgently necessary. Determining that is really challenging, the doctor told me. There's no good guidance on it and there are a lot of grey areas. 'Where does the buck stop? Does it stop with me? Because I'm not prepared to have someone's health deteriorate on my watch,' the hospital doctor said. Conditions fluctuate and what might seem non-urgent one day could quickly develop into an urgent case. 'There's a conflict between what is a medical assessment and what is an assessment of chargeability.'

Another doctor, Kitty Worthing, a member of Docs Not Cops, the campaign group set up to oppose the changes, wrote in a powerful piece in the *Guardian*: 'These crucial decisions are being made in response to ill-thought out, politically motivated policy that has nothing to do with clinical judgment.'

The requirement for hospitals to share data with the Home Office had the potential to make anyone with irregular immigration status very nervous about seeking medical help, she explained. 'Data sharing and charging have a cumulative effect: they deter patients from seeking and receiving potentially life-saving treatment, and ultimately, people die.'

'It is clear that these callous policies are ideologically motivated,' she concluded. Healthcare was being used 'to scapegoat migrants for the underfunding and privatisation of our NHS. As an NHS doctor, I believe denying anyone access to healthcare on the basis of their ability to pay is fundamentally inhumane. Healthcare workers have a primary duty of care to our patients, which we cannot fulfil if we are policing the UK's borders too.'[3]

This was the context in which Sylvester had been told he had to pay for his treatment, but Hunt's justification of the policy on the grounds that it was important to be fair to British taxpayers made no sense since Sylvester was himself a British taxpayer.

His case worker, Chloe Robinson, at Praxis had helped gather an extensive set of documents to offer evidence of his long residency in the UK – tax records going back to the early 1970s, GP records stretching back almost as far, and papers from the Department for Work and Pensions. The lawyer working with the charity passed this evidence on to the hospital, but it was not enough to persuade the eligibility team to revise their opinion. 'We sent them medical records, National Insurance letters – unequivocal evidence that he had been in the UK for decades,' the lawyer, Jeremy Bloom, said. The one thing they couldn't send was proof that he had indefinite leave to remain because that proof had disappeared down a South London rubbish chute some years earlier.

The hospital did attempt to get information from the Home Office as they tried to assess whether Sylvester was 'ordinarily resident'. 'Unfortunately the Home Office had no trace of Mr Marshall in their records.' This lack of record-keeping within the Home Office was to become a recurrent and very significant problem.

The people at St Mungo's liked working with Sylvester because he was always joky and made an effort to be friendly, but they were noticing a dip in his mood as his private fears about his health intensified. 'Every pain he felt made him worried. He was beginning to worry that he was going to die.'

'I'm not a stowaway,' he said, despairing at the difficulty he had had trying to get someone to listen to him. 'I'm here legally.' It seemed so peculiar and wrong that he was still struggling four months later to get the treatment restarted, or indeed to get anyone official to listen to him.

Sylvester's lawyer was adamant that as well as changing his name for the article, we should not reveal his real name to the Home Office in case it complicated matters while the legal case was being prepared. I felt this was problematic, because it meant that I couldn't ask the Home Office for a response and explanation, but the lawyer was insistent that this was an important protective measure for Sylvester, so I agreed. Instead I gave the Home Office a summary of the situation, to see if they could comment. They were extremely annoyed, and called the news editor to demand that the article should not be published since they were unable to respond to the detail of the case.

I was becoming quite familiar with all the different people in the Home Office press office, and was spending too long listening to their clunky and ugly hold music. My family were getting used to press officers calling back in the evening when I was making supper, or at the weekend. Sometimes the officials were helpful, usually they were reasonably friendly, but lately I had been getting the sense that they were annoyed with the increasing number of requests I was making about individuals' immigration cases. Sometimes I felt like I was being told off for asking inconvenient questions; this time I felt bullied.

We went ahead anyway, without their input, but I carried the worry around with me for days – what if I'd got something wrong? What if I'd neglected to ask the right questions that would explain the hospital's decision? What if somehow the publication of the piece made Sylvester's situation worse, not better? Worrying about an imminent article as you imagine hot newspaper presses printing hundreds of thousands of copies, spewing them out on to looping conveyor belts to dry before folding them and packaging them up for distribution, is a useless but strangely acute emotion that has the capacity to eat at you for hours. I still find it hard to be philosophical about it; it can manifest itself as anything from a physical feeling of mild nausea to a general mood-dampening presence at the back of your mind.

The response when the article appeared online on Saturday morning was enormous and instantaneous. About half a million people read about Sylvester's case on the *Guardian* website. Our readers were outraged and this time, finally, politicians began to ask questions.

'I read the story of denial of care and other problems for "Albert Thompson" with great sadness, as yet another example of the persecution of people who came to this country with their parents many years ago, but who do not apparently have the documentation to prove this,' a retired NHS director wrote. 'I am appalled that the Royal Marsden Hospital has become so tainted by a combination of the Home Office's culture of hostility and "austerity" that it has refused to take this man's word or to treat him. I am old enough to have encountered and appreciated the contributions made by the likes of "Albert's" parents when they came to the UK in the 1950s and helped to keep our public services and industries going, and to have known children of my age who may now, after years of residence, be facing this Government-inspired witch hunt.'

My inbox was quickly filling up with messages from dozens of people offering to raise money towards paying the £54,000 for treatment. While I was thrilled that they wanted to help, I felt it was really the NHS that needed to pay, not individual donors.

I rang Sylvester to ask how he was. Laura Stahnke from Praxis had gone to his home that morning to show him the article and to explain that it was causing a lot of online noise. He was subdued – unsettled to see his life story in print, focusing narrowly on the problems he was experiencing, uneasy at his picture being circulated on Facebook, but hopeful that perhaps something might now change.

Although I wouldn't have said so to him, I was reasonably confident that the situation would instantly be seen as the result of a crazy error and that things would be swiftly resolved. However, that didn't happen.

On Monday the Royal Marsden Hospital gave a very cautious half-apology. 'We are very sorry that Mr Thompson has suffered distress and uncertainty.' It was a carefully worded statement expressing sorrow at his distress but not admitting any responsibility for that distress.

As well as the hospital's doubt about Sylvester's right to be in the UK, there was a secondary issue about whether or not the cancer treatment he was due to receive should be described as 'urgent' or 'immediately necessary'. A hospital spokesperson said: 'Following a clinical assessment, a urology consultant categorised the treatment need in Mr Thompson's case as non-urgent.' There was evident unease at the negative attention the case had attracted. 'We are working hard to try to resolve this as quickly as possible.'

A Department of Health and Social Care spokesperson gave a statement which bounced the responsibility for the decision back to the hospital: 'Our guidance makes clear that urgent and immediately necessary care should never be withheld or delayed, but the classification of urgent care is one that only local clinicians can make, and can only be done on a case-by-case basis.'

We went around in circles trying to understand how it was possible to have cancer treatment prescribed by a doctor and then have it refused by a hospital administrator on the grounds that it was not urgent or immediately necessary. Surely once a cancer treatment has been prescribed, it is by definition necessary and there is an urgent need for it to be carried out?

Sylvester's lawyer, Jeremy Bloom, with the law firm Duncan Lewis, was also focused on this point, which he said highlighted the irrationality of the entire policy. 'It forces people to get sicker so that their treatment becomes urgent. How is this going to save the NHS money? In the end you're going to have to treat people with more serious conditions.' Bloom had been waiting for weeks for a decision on whether or not exceptional legal aid funding could be granted so he could pursue Sylvester's case. In the wake of legal aid cuts, a complicated and time-consuming application process had been introduced to access emergency funding for extreme cases, adding an extra layer of delay to the process. This funding was unexpectedly granted on the Monday morning after the article appeared about Sylvester, six weeks after it was applied for. The lawyer felt that the timing was not a coincidence. Over the months of reporting on this issue a pattern emerged of long-delayed decisions being made suddenly after media exposure. It was a positive reflection of the power of the media, but it sometimes felt a bit depressing to see so clearly that this was how things got done.

Sylvester's case was seized on by Labour as powerful ammunition to be used against the government. The shadow health secretary, Jon Ashworth, said: 'I think it is utterly shameful that a man who has been a UK resident for forty-four years, who came as a teenager because his mum came to work as a nurse to care for our sick, who has lived here all his life, paid his taxes, should be denied cancer treatment in this way. We warned that these new regulations could prohibit UK residents from getting treatment and increase bureaucracy in the NHS.' Labour's shadow home secretary, Diane Abbott, said the case was 'inhumane'. The Labour MP for Tottenham, David Lammy, described it as 'horrendous'.

But the outrage went much wider. The Conservative MP, and former GP, Sarah Wollaston said she was 'very concerned'. 'The right thing to do is to start the treatment and then sort out why this case has arisen, in my view,' she said. The head of the British Medical Association, Dr Chaand Nagpaul, described the decision as 'morally indefensible'.

I was with Sylvester again the following Wednesday with the *Guardian*'s film team, sitting in a hall at the East London headquarters of Praxis, when I got a text from colleagues in the parliamentary office saying that the Labour leader Jeremy Corbyn was raising his case with Theresa May at prime minister's question time.

'If we believe in universal healthcare, how can it be possible for someone to live and work in this country and pay their taxes, and then be denied access to the NHS and life-saving cancer treatment? Can the prime minister explain?' Corbyn asked May. It was obvious that she had no idea what he was talking about and had not read or been briefed by aides about Sylvester.

I thought it was odd that no one in May's team had anticipated that this question might arise during the most high-profile parliamentary encounter of the week. It showed how unimportant the government considered the issue to be.

Sylvester really just wanted the radiotherapy to begin and was less interested in being on the news. He felt uneasy about being used as a political football. He had hoped that the publicity around his case would persuade the hospital to rethink its decision, and would also help him get his immigration status resolved, but neither of these things had happened.

Later that week Jeremy Corbyn wrote to the prime minister about Sylvester's case, warning that the new charging regulations meant many undocumented British citizens were being denied NHS treatment and 'that the principle of the universal NHS, free at the point of need, is being eroded'. Corbyn called on the government to suspend the new eligibility rules. 'The government runs the very real risk of allowing a patient to die because they are unable to prove their immigration status,' he said.

Theresa May's response was very tough. She stood firm, taking the Home Office position. 'The decision on whether his treatment is urgent or immediately necessary must rightly be made by the clinicians treating him,' she wrote. 'While I sympathise with . . . the worries he will be facing given his condition, we encourage him to make the appropriate application in order to seek leave to remain or otherwise evidence his settled status here.'

The prime minister's insistence that all Sylvester needed to do was to prove his eligibility for treatment revealed no understanding of the fundamental difficulty of satisfying the Home Office's requests for proof. Officials were still not listening and the explanation of what was going wrong had still not been passed up the chain to ministers, let alone the prime minister.

If the government was holding fast, readers were horrified. Over four hundred thousand people signed an online petition calling on the government to pay for his treatment.

I was surprised at the lack of reassurance coming from the hospital. Sylvester had been taking hormone tablets since the prostate operation to lower the risk of the cancer returning, as an alternative to radiotherapy, but no one had taken the time to reassure him that this would be adequate treatment until his immigration status was resolved. Without that information being clearly spelled out by a medical expert, he felt intensely worried about the impact of the cancellation of radiotherapy. 'My body is full of pain at times,' he said. 'As far as I understand it, if I had the radiotherapy I could live a bit longer; if I don't then my life span is a bit shorter.'

The hospital was adamant that it was not able to exercise discretion in Sylvester's case. 'It is a legal requirement to identify and charge patients who are not eligible for free NHS treatment,' they said, and it would be inappropriate for staff to try to make their own 'ethical and moral judgements on a case by case basis'. They stressed that a clinical decision had been made that his treatment was not urgent. They explained they had a duty to check eligibility, and that they risked bad publicity about the prevalence of 'health tourists' if they gave treatment to people who were ineligible.

Sylvester was left in his room in his homeless hostel waiting for someone in the government to change their mind. With his customary understatement, he would only say that it was disappointing.

———

For weeks I'd been searching for more conclusive evidence that this was a widespread problem and for some sense of how many people could be affected. Bethan Lant, one of the senior case workers at Praxis who was helping Sylvester, gave me a powerful anecdotal snapshot. Until 2015 Praxis did not monitor undocumented people as a category because they had so few clients in this situation. In 2015 they created a new classification because they had seen twenty cases. In 2016 they saw thirty-nine. In 2017 they saw fifty-four. In 2018, she said, the numbers were 'galloping up and up'. 'These people have done nothing wrong. The legal environment has changed around them leaving them in an impossible situation.'

The most forensic response came from an academic unit specialising in immigration, the Oxford Migration Observatory. Prompted by the *Guardian*'s articles, they had researched the numbers of people who arrived in the UK before 1971 who had not taken steps to naturalise and become British citizens. They estimated that of around 524,000 people from Commonwealth countries who arrived before 1973 (and were thus eligible for citizenship, provided they filled in a form), around fifty-seven thousand had not formally naturalised. Madeleine Sumption was very cautious about the findings, making it clear that this was an upper limit, and that many might have other ways of proving their immigration status – their original Commonwealth passports bearing arrival stamps, for example. 'It won't be the case that all fifty-seven thousand don't have legal status,' she said. 'We don't know what share of them have problems with their paperwork and what proportion have everything in order. This is the population who are potentially at risk.'

This first clear indication of the potential scale of the problem suggested it could stretch far wider than anyone had anticipated. And yet the government still seemed very reluctant to pay any attention.

WE ARE HERE BECAUSE YOU WERE THERE

Much of the pain expressed by the people I was talking to was tied up with a powerful sense of betrayal. Their parents had come to Britain as young adults and spent most of their lives helping rebuild the country in the wake of the devastation of the Second World War. Some had responded to official government recruitment drives and had taken jobs as nurses in the new National Health Service, or as labourers on the thousands of construction sites repairing the wartime bomb damage, or staffing the expanding transport system. But most had made the brave decision to travel across the world to the UK to start building better futures for their families without a firm job offer in hand.

Many of those now afflicted with passport problems had been left behind with relatives in the Caribbean for chunks of their childhood, as their parents tried to put by enough money to bring them over to join them. Because wages were low and West Indian workers were forced to pay disproportionately high rents by exploitative landlords, their parents found that it was difficult to save quickly, so the separation often stretched on for far longer than intended. It is hard to imagine the unhappiness those separations must have caused. In the 1950s and 1960s there were no phones to keep in touch, just letters and the occasional barrelful of presents, clothes, money and food.

Often the reconciliation in the UK was awkward, to such an extent that some children, like Paulette, ended up for a while in care, struggling to forge relationships with families they barely remembered. Others found that they had left the security of their homes in the Caribbean to settle in a new country that turned out to be decidedly unwelcoming – from racist landlords and employers to colour bars and race riots, sus laws[1] and racist killings.

It was clear that the roots of the predicament of the people I had spoken to went much deeper than the present day, stretching back to the arrival of the first wave of post-war Commonwealth migrants in 1948.

———

An uncertainty about how enthusiastically to welcome people from the Caribbean predated the arrival of the *Empire Windrush* in June 1948. Over ten thousand West Indian men and women had volunteered to serve in the Second World War, in a spirit of patriotism towards a nation they had been encouraged to view as the Mother Country. Many signed up for the RAF, where their contribution was greatly valued (particularly after the decimation of pilots in the Battle of Britain). But their presence, alongside black American GIs, caused a degree of unease in rural parts of the country and some British people found it necessary to set out rules for appropriate behaviour. The wife of a vicar in the village of Worle, near Weston-super-Mare, drew up a six-point code offering guidance in case of contact between white women and black soldiers. Mrs May's advice began: '1: If a local woman keeps a shop and a coloured soldier enters, she must serve him, but she must do it as quickly as possible and indicate as quickly that she does not desire him to come there again. 2: If she is in a cinema and notices a coloured soldier next to her, she moves to another seat immediately,' etc. In *Black and British*, the historian David Olusoga notes that her rules were mostly met with distaste by both the local women and the national press;[2] many of the black men and women who served with the British forces in the Second World War received a warm welcome.

Once demobilised, the majority of West Indian troops returned to the Caribbean after the war, but the economy there was faltering. A huge hurricane had caused horrific damage to sugar cane farms, fruit trees had been destroyed, buildings ruined and unemployment was rising. Having seen life in the UK, many felt ambivalent about returning to live in a colony. When a Jamaican newspaper, the *Gleaner*, advertised tickets for the *Empire Windrush*, a refitted and renamed Nazi troop carrier, there was a rush to secure places. Tickets cost £28.10, around half the usual fare (but still equivalent to about six months' average wages in Jamaica, or the proceeds of selling three cows).

Alford Gardner was one of those who managed to get a ticket. He was ninety-two when I met him at his home in Leeds, to hear about his decision to emigrate, the journey and the mixed welcome he received in the UK. Alford, like about half the West Indian *Windrush* passengers, had served in the RAF in Britain during the war before returning to Jamaica to spend some time with his parents, where he had quickly decided that life would be better for him back in England.

Just twenty-two and with no money, he asked his father, a policeman, to lend him the cost of the fare, and got ready to travel with his elder brother Gladstone. 'There were more people who wanted to go on the ship than there were places. There was a long queue, lots of people hustling and bustling to get tickets, offering to pay more – but my name was on the list,' he said. Passengers treated the journey like a holiday. When the weather was fine, Alford would take his food out to eat on deck. A handful of musicians who would later become famous in London, including the Trinidadian calypso singers Aldwyn Roberts and Egbert Moore, who went by the names of Lord Kitchener and Lord Beginner, formed an impromptu band. 'Anything that moved, they could sing about it.'

The ship stopped for a few days in Bermuda, where Alford encountered segregation. 'That was the first time I saw a sign saying "No blacks".'

While the ship made its way across the Atlantic, the Labour government in London was alarmed to hear that around five hundred West Indian migrants were on their way. On Tuesday 8 June, the *Daily Express* warned that a 'shipload of worry'[3] for the Minister of Labour, George Isaacs, would be landing in less than a fortnight. The matter was debated in parliament, with one Conservative MP asking Isaacs to find out who was 'responsible for this extraordinary action'. Isaacs told colleagues that the men would be met at the ship and given information on how to register for unemployment support, but indicated that he hoped this would not be the first of many such arrivals. 'The arrival of these substantial numbers of men under no organised arrangements is bound to result in difficulty and disappointment. I have no knowledge of their qualifications or capacity, and can give no assurance that they can be found suitable work. I hope no encouragement will be given to others to follow them.'

There had already been a flurry of concerned correspondence between civil servants in London and Jamaica. A telegram sent by the Acting Governor in Jamaica to the Secretary of State for the Colonies on 11 May said:

I regret to inform you that more than 350 troop-deck passengers by Empire Windrush have been booked by men who hope to find employment in the United Kingdom and that it is likely that this number will be increased by another 100 before the vessel leaves. Most of them have no particular skill and few will have more than a few pounds on their arrival. Public announcements on the difficulty of obtaining work here have not discouraged these bookings.[4]

On 29 May a letter from the Colonial Secretary's Office in Jamaica to the Colonial Office in London, took the same abjectly apologetic tone:

We are very sorry indeed that you and your staff will be put to all the trouble which the arrival of this large number, who are mostly unskilled and who will have little money with them, will involve. It is an appalling thing with which to be saddled, but, as you know it has been quite impossible to prevent their going, which is symptomatic of the conditions here. I hope that you will be able to cope with them without too much trouble.[5]

The tone is odd when you consider that Britain had a severe post-war labour shortage and was desperate for workers from abroad to come and help rebuild the country. The explanation is that officials were mostly hoping for white Europeans, and were much less comfortable with the idea of black West Indian labourers. In 1946 the government had estimated that the country needed an extra 1,346,000 workers. With government assistance, more than one hundred thousand members of the Polish armed forces who had fought against the Germans were given permission to settle with their families in the UK and another eighty thousand Ukrainians, Latvians and Poles were recruited under the European Voluntary Workers scheme.[6] Between 1946 and 1962, around fifty thousand Irish labourers made their way to England every year,[7] prompting almost no discussion about the potential social consequences of the influx. In 1949 around 6,500 Italians arrived, and in each year of the next decade around another eight thousand were made welcome.[8]

But there was such unease at the idea that West Indians might also step forward to help that officials had been taking active steps to discourage them. In 1947 the Colonial Office had sent an official to Jamaica to dissuade people from coming, attempting to suggest that there were not actually many jobs available. 'One glaring problem with this strategy was that the newsagents of the islands stocked copies of British newspapers like the *South London Daily Press*, and West Indians were able to see for themselves the pages of classified advertisements for positions in British firms. Incredulous local governors and journalists were informed that these were not real openings but "paper vacancies",' Olusoga writes in *Black and British.* In parallel, Ministry of Labour officials commissioned an evaluation of the potential of 'surplus male West Indians'. The report suggested that black West Indians would be 'unsuitable for outdoor work in winter owing to their susceptibility to colds and more serious chest and lung ailments'; it also stated that West Indians (despite their familiarity with tropical heat) would not be suited to working in British coal mines, where they would find temperatures 'too hot'.[9] The Ministry of Labour was not commissioned to analyse the capabilities of white, European workers.

Some politicians were more realistic. Colonial Secretary Arthur Creech Jones told colleagues:

West Indians are well aware of the labour shortage in Great Britain, and it is known to them that it is proposed to employ thousands of [European] Displaced Persons . . . In these circumstances there has been a natural and immediate demand for the employment of British West Indians, who are British subjects and many of whom have had experience of work in Britain during the war years, to relieve the labour shortage in Britain.[10]

And there was a general recognition by politicians that there was no way of stopping people in the West Indies from coming to Britain, as subjects of the British Empire. There was a principle of freedom of movement and freedom of settlement between all countries within the empire. Someone born in a British colony had the same status and rights as someone born in Herefordshire. An internal memo from a Ministry of Labour civil servant, despatched two days before the ship arrived, noted: 'There is no logical ground for treating a British subject who comes of his own accord from Jamaica to Great Britain differently from another who comes to London on his own account from Scotland.'[11] Creech Jones told parliament: 'These people have British passports and they must be allowed to land.'[12]

On the day the ship arrived, newspapers took markedly different positions. While the *Standard*'s headline read: 'Welcome Home', the *Daily Express*'s headline warned 'Empire men flee no jobs land' and its article described how five hundred 'unwanted' people had come from a country with large-scale unemployment. 'Many of them recognise the futility of their life at home.'[13]

The passengers' optimism is palpable in the now familiar but still very moving footage of smiling *Windrush* passengers, smartly dressed in ties, fedoras and waistcoats, walking down the ship's gangplank. A Pathé newsreel described them as 'citizens of the British Empire coming to the mother country with good intent', and captured Lord Kitchener, still on the ship, spontaneously performing a song he had composed for the moment – 'London is the place to be'. 'London is the place for me; London, that lovely city.'

But the London that they encountered was not lovely in the least. Panicking officials were scrabbling about for a plan to house the arrivals. The only place they managed to come up with was the Clapham Deep Shelter, a lateral extension tunnel running off Clapham South tube station, created as a wartime air-raid refuge; around two hundred *Windrush* passengers spent their first few weeks on bunks in this dank subterranean cavern. Photographs show three-tier bunk beds crammed into a low tunnel, with smart suits hanging from ceiling pipes.[14]

It was a bleak reception. Those who had not been in England before were shocked by its greyness and the harsh post-war mood of austerity – with rationing of sugar, bread, bacon, tea and jam. The official uncertainty about how welcome they were continued. On the day the ship reached England, eleven Labour MPs had sent a letter to Prime Minister Clement Attlee proposing controls on black immigration. The British people were, they wrote, 'blessed by the absence of a colour racial problem . . . An influx of coloured people domiciled here is likely to impair the harmony, strength and cohesion of our people and social life and cause discord and unhappiness among all concerned.'[15] The government should introduce legislation to 'control immigration in the political, social, economic and fiscal interests of our people'.

It is hard to see anything other than racist discomfort behind their anxieties. Britain had accommodated 120,000 Poles and tens of thousands of workers from Italy and Ireland, barely batting an eyelid, but the arrival of just a few hundred men from the West Indies triggered for some an existential crisis. Now familiar debates on immigration were beginning, centring on the question 'How many is too many?'

Alford remembered sensing a change in attitudes when he returned to the UK on the *Empire Windrush*. The contribution made by the West Indian RAF recruits had been swiftly forgotten. During his time with the RAF he had had no problems finding housing but when he and his brother returned to Leeds, hoping to settle at the same hostel where they had lived previously, they were turned away. He spent the first few nights back in England sleeping upright on a chair, until he and four friends found a room to share. When they found somewhere more permanent, the landlord charged higher than average rents, aware of the difficulties West Indians had finding accommodation. 'He saw that there was money to be made.'

Looking for work, Alford encountered the same problem. The clerk at the local labour exchange was quietly hostile. 'I went to the labour exchange every day; the old man would look up from his desk and say: "Sorry, son, nothing for you." I heard that time and again. I'm sure he was racist,' he said.

The political fallout from the *Empire Windrush*'s arrival continued for weeks. Paradoxically, while the post-war Attlee government had been sent into an undignified panic by the few hundred West Indians on the *Windrush*, with MPs of all parties voicing unease, politicians were also in the process of finalising the 1948 British Nationality Act, an incredibly liberal piece of legislation for the time, which inadvertently opened the door to mass migration of non-white Commonwealth residents. (See the Notes section for a fuller explanation of the 1948 and subsequent immigration Acts.)

The 1948 Act, which received Royal Assent the month after the ship arrived, upgraded the status of the people of the empire, who were previously known as British subjects, to Commonwealth Citizens – granting them all the right to travel to and settle in Britain. During a debate on the Act in the Commons, a fortnight after the *Windrush* docked, the Home Secretary, James Chuter Ede, said:

I know there are also some who feel it is wrong to have a citizenship of the United Kingdom and Colonies. Some people feel it would be a bad thing to give the coloured races of the Empire the idea that, in some way or other, they are the equals of people in this country. The Government do not subscribe to that view . . . We believe wholeheartedly that the common citizenship of the United Kingdom and Colonies is an essential part of the development of the relationship between this Mother Country and the Colonies . . . We believe and we hope it will be understood that citizenship of the United Kingdom and the Colonies means that when we talk, for example, of the development of the Colonies, etc., we recognise the right of the colonial peoples to be treated as men and brothers with the people of this country.[16]

This was an extraordinarily significant official summary of the government's attitude towards hundreds of millions of people living in British colonies, but the generosity behind this description of brotherly relationships was never fully matched by reality. Successive governments spent the next forty years drafting new legislation that limited the scope of the Act's open-door policy, and restricted the rights of residents of former British colonies. Most politicians did not expect the 1948 legislation to trigger a large wave of migration from the West Indies, confident that 'poverty and the high cost of international travel would keep poor black and brown people far from Britain's shores', as Olusoga writes; they thought instead that it would allow movement between Britain and the 'old Commonwealth' nations of Canada, South Africa, Australia and New Zealand, whose populations were described euphemistically as coming from 'British stock'. These 'old Commonwealth' nations were sometimes known as the 'white dominions'. Officials had not bargained for the speed with which the cost of international travel would fall or the growing desire of people living in the colonies to come in search of new opportunities.

In the years that immediately followed, migration from the Caribbean was relatively small. Between 1948 and 1952 the number of West Indians arriving in Britain each year hovered between one thousand and two thousand. In 1953 the number increased to three thousand, in 1954 it jumped to ten thousand and in 1955 quadrupled to over forty thousand,[17] before dropping to thirty thousand in 1958 and to twenty-two thousand in 1959. By 1958 the Home Office estimated that around 115,000 people, mostly single men, had arrived in London from the West Indies in the past decade. Winston Churchill was hostile to the arrivals; his colleague Harold Macmillan noted in 1955: 'PM thinks "Keep England White" a good slogan'.[18] A number of government studies were commissioned by both Labour and the Conservatives on how to respond to the 'continuing influx', focusing again on suitability for employment. Official malevolence seeps through the language of a cross-departmental study which alleged that 'coloured workers' found jobs difficult to obtain because of their 'low output . . . high rate of turnover . . . irresponsibility, quarrelsomeness and lack of discipline'.[19]

But the actions of employers suggest this was simply not true. Official caution about actively recruiting black workers from the West Indies was abandoned once the country's labour shortage intensified in the mid-1950s. In 1956 London Transport and the British Transport Commission sent officials to Barbados to recruit workers. By 1958 there were over eight thousand black workers on

London's tubes and buses.[20] Hotels were recruiting chambermaids, kitchen workers and porters from Barbados, and hospitals were employing Barbadian and Jamaican nurses and cleaning staff.

The arrivals came with blue-black British passports describing each as a 'British subject: Citizen of the United Kingdom and Colonies', with a printed message on the first page that stated that the colonial governor 'requests and requires in the Name of Her Majesty all those whom it may concern to allow the bearer to pass freely without let or hindrance and to afford him/her every assistance and protection of which he/she may stand in need'.

They were met with reactions that mostly ranged from cautious neutrality to blatant hostility. Tryphena Anderson, who came to Nottingham from Jamaica in 1952 to work as a nurse, said: 'You're not thinking of your skin, but you feel other people are thinking of it . . . Some people ask you where you came from. Jamaica. And you could have come from the moon. They don't know where it is and you have to tell them, you know, it's in the Caribbean. And a lot of them would talk behind your back. Darkies, you know. You weren't a person, you were a darkie.'[21]

'Listen, children. If you want to know how it felt to be where we were in that time, think about suitcases,' Charlie Phillips, father of the writer Mike Phillips and his brother, the former head of the Equality and Human Rights Commission, Trevor Phillips, recounts for their book *Windrush: The Irresistible Rise of Multi-racial Britain*. 'You used to see black families walking, humping these dirty great old suitcases with all their belongings, moving with all their belongings, or looking for a place to stay. Moving, always moving . . . I can still remember in my palms and my fingers the agony of the weight, pulling along this suitcase nearly as big as me.'

The Trinidadian writer Sam Selvon, in his 1956 novel *The Lonely Londoners*, describes the arrival of a generation of West Indian men in an unfriendly city and captures the mystifying English politeness that shrouded a seething hostility. He notes the surprise felt by Caribbean arrivals at the ease with which white newcomers from Europe were accepted and found work, Polish restaurateurs for example, in hurtful contrast to the troubles faced by black West Indian men despite the fact that they were British passport holders. The history of Britain's efficient economic exploitation of its colonies made this even more painful. 'In fact, we is British subjects, and he is a foreigner, we have more right than any people from the damn continent to live and work in this country, and enjoy what this country have because is we who bleed to make this country prosperous.'

A new arrival from Trinidad asks Moses, the book's hero, whether people in Britain are as racist as they are in America and is told: 'English people don't like the boys coming to England to work and live . . . They just don't like black people, and don't ask me why, because that is a question that bigger brains than mine trying to find out from way back.' But there is a crucial difference between attitudes in the USA and England, Moses adds.

The thing is, in America they don't like you, and they tell you so straight, so that you know how you stand. Over here is the old English diplomacy: 'thank you sir,' and 'how do you do' and that sort of thing. In America you see a sign telling you to keep off, but over here you don't see any, but when you go to the hotel or the restaurant they will politely tell you to haul – or else give you the cold treatment.[22]

All the books written by Windrush-era arrivals capture the same disappointment. The Guyana-born poet E. R. Braithwaite, another ex-RAF pilot, returned to study physics at Cambridge, but on graduating found he was unable to get work. He writes: 'I was forced to confront the fact that relieved of the threat of German invasion, the British had abandoned all pretence of hand-in-hand brotherliness and had reverted to type, demonstrating the same racism they had so roundly condemned in the Germans.'[23] In his novel *To Sir, with Love,* an account of becoming a school teacher in East London, Braithwaite records the difficulties he encountered searching for work and the initial hostility he met from pupils and fellow staff members who had a very limited understanding about his background. 'Their idea of the Negro was largely conditioned by the familiar caricature in books and films – a shiftless and indolent character, living either in a primitive mud hut or in the more deplorable shanty town, and meeting all life's problems with a flashing smile, a sinuous dance, and a drum-assisted song.'[24] Braithwaite also identifies the polite British prejudice as more hurtful and confusing than American segregation, where the rules were at least clear. 'I have yet to meet a single English person who has actually admitted anti-Negro prejudice; it is even generally believed that no such thing exists here,' he wrote in 1959.

A Negro is free to board any bus or train and sit anywhere, provided he has paid the appropriate fare; the fact that many people might pointedly avoid sitting near to him is casually overlooked. He is free to seek accommodation in any licensed hotel or boarding house – the courteous refusal which frequently follows is never ascribed to prejudice. The betrayal I now felt was greater because it had been perpetrated with the greatest of charm and courtesy.[25]

The West Indians were surprised to be asked repeatedly where they had learned to speak such good English. Most of them had received a colonial education which closely mirrored the British system. Those who had completed their schooling had read Shakespeare, Keats and Wordsworth and studied Latin using Kennedy's primer; the public examinations they sat were set by the Cambridge examination boards. Teachers in rural Jamaica made their pupils learn the names of the English counties and rivers.

Ivan Anglin (who would be deported from Britain in the late 1990s, after thirty-five years' residence) described to me how at his village primary school in Jamaica in the 1930s and 40s, he would sing 'God Save the King' and later 'God Save the Queen', and occasionally 'Rule, Britannia!' with the line: 'Britons never will be slaves.' Given Britain's centuries-long enslavement of Jamaica's plantation workers, it was a peculiar thing to make the children sing, but the strangeness of it only occurred to Ivan in later life, watching television documentaries about slavery. 'We had to sing all these patriotic songs. We had no choice, you just do as you are told by the teacher,' he said. 'We were taught England was the Mother Country; we didn't know what that meant.'

During the war, his teacher asked all the children at the small rural school, which had no electricity and no running water, to ask their parents for money for the British war effort. 'So that we could send contributions to England to buy bomber planes for a squadron. My parents didn't have much money. My mother was a dressmaker, my father was a carpenter.' Despite the pupils' poverty, more extreme than that of their counterparts in wartime Britain, no one thought it odd in the least that they should be invited to send charitable donations to the richer nation that had colonised them. 'We didn't think it was strange to be asked. I think I gave my teacher two shillings.'

Vince Reid, who arrived on the *Windrush* when he was thirteen, said:

I knew more about England than I did about Jamaica . . . Of course, I was also taught that the person who freed the slaves was a white man called Wilberforce, so that one was always encouraged to believe that one must be beholden to white people for whatever happened. Whatever you became, it was due to the benevolence and goodwill of white people . . . the whole imperialistic thing was drilled into you . . . I didn't feel particularly Jamaican because you had no sense of what Jamaica was.[26]

In Andrea Levy's novel *Small Island*, the RAF man Gilbert recalls being indoctrinated during his Jamaican childhood about the charms of the Mother Country, 'a beautiful woman – refined, mannerly and cultured', who 'thinks of you as her children' and 'takes care of you from afar'. He describes the powerful disappointment on arrival when he discovers that the Mother Country is a 'stinking, cantankerous hag' who 'offers you no comfort after your journey. No smile. No welcome. Yet she looks down at you through lordly eyes and says, "Who the bloody hell are you?"'

Gilbert describes his pride in his ability to recite the canals of England, and his feeling of hurt that British people thought Jamaica was in Africa and knew nothing about the country that had for centuries given them coffee, tobacco, sugar, cocoa and rum. 'It was inconceivable that we Jamaicans, we West Indians, we members of the British Empire would not fly to the Mother Country's defence when there was threat. But, tell me, if Jamaica was in trouble, is there any major, any general, any sergeant who would have been able to find that dear island?' he asks. 'Give me that map, blindfold me, spin me round three times and I, dizzy and dazed, would still place my finger squarely on the Mother Country.'[27] Gilbert is troubled by one question: 'How come England did not know me?'

Surprised to be questioned about why they had come to Britain, the *Windrush* arrivals tried to get locals to understand the fundamental truth that their presence was the direct consequence of the country's colonial past: 'We are here because you were there.'

After the shock of the arrival, things got much worse for most West Indian émigrés. Britain was a tough place to be living in the era of post-war depression, and a number of Britons were themselves deciding to emigrate in search of better lives; between 1947 and 1950 720,000 left for Australia, Canada and South Africa.

New arrivals were constantly struggling with the difficulty of renting; because choices were so restricted, people were forced to accept shocking accommodation. Sybil Phoenix, who came from Guyana in 1956, and was later awarded an MBE for her services as a community leader, remembers discovering the flat she had been rented was a converted coal cellar (she hadn't realised initially because she was unfamiliar with the concept). The place was so damp she had to spend her first Christmas cooking underneath an umbrella because water was streaming down the walls. NHS worker Connie Mark, who arrived from Jamaica in 1954, described the inflated rents black tenants were obliged to pay, in an era when Peter Rachman began to profit from a lucrative business renting to desperate West Indians. 'Say you were a white person, you would get a whole flat for £1.25 a week, a whole flat, and some of them got front and back gardens, if you're lucky enough to get a ground floor. But we were obliged to pay £3 and £3.50 for one room. And at that you had to cook outside.'[28] She described her disappointment at how quickly the West Indian contribution to the war was forgotten. She had been 'brought up to love the King, love the Queen, to love England and to respect England. Then when you come here after the war, what do you see? You see a sign saying "No Blacks, no Irish, no dogs, no children". That hurt, that really used to hurt.'[29]

Many experienced an unexpected downward social mobility. Despite politicians' repeated assertion that most of the new arrivals would be unqualified, of the West Indians who came in the 1950s, only 22 per cent had worked in unskilled or semi-skilled jobs in the Caribbean. Because of their difficulties in finding work in Britain, that figure rose to 63 per cent after they settled here. Twenty-four per cent of the men and 50 per cent of the women had left skilled or professional jobs in the West Indies, but only 6 per cent of men and 23 per cent of women found equivalent work in Britain.[30]

In 1958 there were race riots in Nottingham and Notting Hill (although the term 'riots' is now generally accepted to be inappropriate, since these were mainly attacks by white residents on their black neighbours).[31] In 1959, Kelso Cochrane, a carpenter from

Antigua who had been in the UK for five years, was stabbed and killed as he walked back from a hospital in Paddington where he had sought treatment for a broken thumb; his murder was unsolved. Oswald Mosley, who had been imprisoned during the war for his support of Hitler and for his creation of the British Union of Fascists, which encouraged harassment of Jews in London's East End, saw his popularity rise again as his Union Movement turned its energies towards Britain's new black communities, which he claimed were spreading vice and disease. His leaflets had pictures of black people with spears entering parliament, and urged: 'Protect Your Jobs . . . Stop Coloured Immigration . . . Houses for White People . . . People of Kensington, Act Now.'[32] He proposed repatriation.

In 1962, amid growing concern about the scale of the arrivals, the new Commonwealth Act restricted the ease with which residents of the former empire could settle in the UK. Although ministers were at pains to avoid explicitly discriminating on the basis of colour, there was a widespread understanding that the new immigration law was racist. It slashed unskilled migration from Asia and the West Indies, but did nothing to prevent Irish unskilled workers from continuing to come; white immigrants from the old dominions (Canada, Australia, New Zealand) were broadly unaffected. The Labour opposition leader Hugh Gaitskell described the Act as 'cruel and brutal anti-colour legislation'.[33]

'It was obvious that this was not an attempt to stop immigration per se, but to halt black immigration,' Robert Winder writes in *Bloody Foreigners: The Story of Immigration to Britain*. 'The small print exempted the Irish – an independent nation – from restrictions that were imposed on West Indians, many of whom were still British subjects.'[34]

The announcement of new restrictions triggered a rush of pre-emptive immigration, with most people coming by plane rather than ship. While the Pathé footage of the *Empire Windrush* is now very familiar, there are no images of the newer generation landing at airports – many of them children travelling alone and being awkwardly reunited with parents after several years apart. This is the era when most of those affected by the Windrush scandal began to arrive.

When I asked him how acutely he had felt these tensions, having lived through them for almost seven decades, Alford Gardner said he had had plenty of personal encounters with racism: the inexplicable unfriendliness from the father of his Yorkshire-born wife (whom he met at the Mecca dance hall in Leeds), union officials who refused to let him join, jobs he couldn't apply for because he wasn't in the union, years of ignoring 'black this, black that' comments behind his back. He remembered the anger he felt when, setting up a Caribbean cricket club in Leeds, he was confronted by an unexpected decision by the man in the sports hire shop not to give him and his fellow team members the equipment they had already paid to hire. 'Everything was arranged; it must have been racism. We didn't get angry; we put our money together slowly and bought some more gear each week. After a few weeks we had enough.' The Leeds Caribbean cricket club is still thriving.

His general approach was resolutely glass-half-full. Instead of complaining about the pubs he was never allowed into, he would shrug and conclude that these would not in all probability be tremendously relaxing places to hang out. 'We thought, ignore them. Get away from them; find another place where you can enjoy yourself. If you know they don't want you then why would you want to be there?' He was unwilling to focus on those difficulties, determined to highlight the positive. 'It never bothered me,' he kept saying. 'It stopped me from getting work in the early years, but it never bothered me. We didn't have time to get angry. As long as we got a job, whatever job.' He had had a wonderful life in Britain, he said; he had eight children, sixteen grandchildren, twenty-one great-grandchildren, most of them living nearby in Leeds.

I felt he was disappointed by my irritating journalistic desire to dwell on the negative aspects of life, when he had chosen not to complain about the obstacles he had faced. As journalists we spend more time scrutinising problems than celebrating things that have gone well, but when we review our own lives, instinctively we gloss over the downsides and focus on the happier moments. 'I never said a word about it; I didn't tell the kids about it – they knew there were nasty people around. I thought: treat everyone respectfully and you will be treated respectfully,' he said. 'I have absolutely no regrets about anything. If I could start over I would do everything the same.'

But he was unsettled by the emerging news of problems with documents and immigration status affecting his generation and the people who followed. 'I was disgusted. I never thought such things would happen. It is a disgrace – to think of the hard work we put in to get things as they are in England today,' he said.

A friend had warned him in the 1980s that he should get a passport because otherwise he risked being thrown out of the country, so he travelled to London to make an application. 'If he hadn't told me, this might have happened to me. It shouldn't be happening at all. It's definitely racism. They haven't been throwing out Poles or any Europeans in that way. It's not right. We worked so hard.'

———

It was clear how closely connected this history was to the problems being experienced by Paulette, Anthony and others. The discrimination against immigrants from the Caribbean in the 1950s and 1960s led directly to their later vulnerability to being caught out by the Home Office. Because employers discriminated against them, they tended to be in lower-paid jobs. Black British people earned less, so were less able to save money, buy their own homes or travel overseas. 'Not only could they not afford to travel and so had little need for a passport, but they were less likely to establish the other forms of documentation – financial records of savings accounts or mortgages that are more likely to be formally kept and satisfy the Home Office's identity requirement,' states an analysis by the race equality think-tank the Runnymede Trust.

Britain's role in the transatlantic slave trade stands behind all of this. '"Black Caribbean" people are in Britain not only because the ship *Empire Windrush* arrived in June 1948. There are only "Black Caribbean" people because British slave ships transported people from Africa to the Caribbean. Even after the slave trade was abolished, millions of black people in the Empire had fewer political rights, and worse life outcomes,' the Runnymede Trust analysis continues. The economic decline which followed the abolition of slavery in the Caribbean pushed people to search for new opportunities in Britain.

The peculiar concept of the Mother Country cast a long shadow. 'Black slavery is the wider context of any book which lingers over the history of the Windrush generation, as it is the reason why people like my ancestors wound up bent-back toiling in the plantations owned by white men, already once removed from their real mother countries in Africa,' Charlie Brinkhurst-Cuff writes in *Mother Country*. 'That the UK was seen by the descendants of so many of these same people to be akin to their homeland, 400 years on from the beginning of the trade in the 15th century, is an abhorrent marker of the nature of subservience-inducing colonialism.'

In part because of this notion of Britain as the Mother Country, arrivals from the Caribbean felt British. They had been born British, and assumed that this would endure. They felt no need to get a document as supporting evidence of their status.

Britain became rich on the backs of those who produced coffee, tobacco, gold and diamonds in its colonies, but over the past decade ministers in charge of immigration policy have displayed a total amnesia about Britain's colonial past. Centuries of exploitation of the Caribbean islands, first by British slave owners and later by colonial businesses, were conveniently forgotten and the complicated circumstances in which people had migrated to the UK throughout the twentieth century were ignored. This legacy of empire was overlooked as an inconsequential detail. As it became politically expedient to toughen up their anti-immigrant stance, Conservative politicians paid no attention to the complexities of this migration history – rushing to implement policies without considering that those who were meant to have been welcomed here might find themselves ensnared.

A HOSTILE ENVIRONMENT

Two Conservative party political pledges, made casually during media interviews, sit at the roots of all the Windrush suffering.

The first, a Conservative party manifesto commitment to reduce net migration to the tens of thousands, was an arbitrary target, an aspiration plucked apparently out of the blue by David Cameron during a Sunday morning television interview, a few months before he became prime minister in 2010. Sitting calmly in the studio armchair, his waxlike brow unlined, he promised: 'We would like to see net immigration in the tens of thousands rather than the hundreds of thousands. I don't think that's unrealistic; that's the sort of figure it was in the 1990s and I think we should see that again.'

The second promise was made by Theresa May, then Home Secretary, in May 2012, in an interview with the *Daily Telegraph*. 'The aim is to create here in Britain a really hostile environment for illegal migration,' she announced.

Those two pledges worked together to forge the Conservative party's approach to immigration policy throughout its time in office, inculcating a culture of bureaucratic cruelty which culminated in the Windrush crisis.

May's commitment was a fleeting line, barely remarked upon at the time, but one which would acquire huge historical significance. The *Telegraph*'s interviewer noticed the Home Secretary's unease when she was asked about the government's failure to make any progress towards fulfilling the manifesto commitment to reduce net migration to the tens of thousands. Whenever she is asked a difficult question, the reporter noted, May's 'eyes narrow briefly: catlike and wary'. Challenged about the latest figures which showed that net immigration was running at about 250,000 a year (far above the target), May revealed her solution: creating the hostile environment. Work was already underway, she revealed, to deny illegal immigrants access to work, housing, services and bank accounts.

The policies which she introduced over the following four years transformed Britain's immigration system, creating a climate of fear and expanding the border control network far beyond ports and airports, introducing checks in hospitals, council offices and letting agencies. Private citizens, entirely untrained, found themselves required to conduct immigration controls. Unless you were well off it became extremely hard for a spouse born abroad to join you in the UK or to have a visit from a grandparent from a non-EU country. The fines imposed on businesses that hired illegal immigrants doubled, and prison sentences were introduced for employers who took on people without papers. Vans branded with the words 'Immigration Enforcement' patrolled in areas of high migration. Government-funded legal aid for assistance with immigration problems was cut to almost nothing, while application fees to regularise status soared. Immigration policies were distilled into tough, catchy slogans: 'Deport first. Appeal later.'

Deporting people is expensive and difficult; the new policies were aiming instead to hound people out of the country by making it impossible for them to work or get state help. The government aimed to harass people, making life intolerable until they left, pushing them to consent to 'voluntary removal' (a departure which could hardly be described as voluntary, but which was agreed to because there was simply no alternative option). Officials hoped to get people who were unable to prove their right to be in the UK to 'self-deport' – a cheaper, more efficient alternative to forced deportation.

Whether any of this had a discernible impact on immigration

numbers, or indeed the numbers forced to leave the country, is disputed, but it successfully unleashed alarm among everyone with uncertain paperwork, and it fulfilled a critical political function in showcasing the Conservatives as a party ready to stand firm on immigration.

———

The hostile environment policies were incubated in the Home Office, but delivered by the prime minister. The relationship between Cameron and May was at times fractious, with Number 10 resenting the carefully guarded autonomy of the Home Office, but on this issue they were in harmony, nurturing the policy, tending to it as co-parents. They had a shared interest in being able to tell voters that the Conservative party was in control of immigration.

The notion of controlling net migration figures was meant to be a calmer, more neutral way to speak about the subject, stepping away from the emotionally charged, inflammatory debate about clamping down on immigration. Just trying to balance the numbers coming in and those going out – it suggested a precision and manageability that sounded efficient and reassuring, hiding a much messier reality.

In 2012 May was a relatively obscure figure to anyone outside the Westminster bubble, still most famous for declaring in 2002 that the Conservatives needed to be careful about their reputation as 'the nasty party', and for her shoes, which were endlessly analysed by the overwhelmingly male network of political correspondents. But inside Westminster she was already highly regarded as an effective operator. She was acutely aware of the political need to respond to concerns about net migration and her key party conference speeches reliably featured sections on the importance of protecting Britain's borders and controlling immigration.

'Between 1997 and 2009, net migration to Britain totalled more than 2.2 million people. That is more than twice the population of Birmingham. Of course, Britain has benefited from immigration, but if we are going to continue to do so, it needs to be controlled,' she told the Conservative party conference in 2010, a few months after taking up her job as Home Secretary. 'That is why we'll bring annual net migration down to the levels of the 1990s – to the tens of thousands – as David Cameron has promised.'

In 2011 she repeated the pledge. 'We've made it our aim to get net migration back down to the tens of thousands. Cutting immigration is not as simple as turning off a tap – it's a complex and litigious system – and so it will take time. But we're taking action on every route to the UK – and the numbers will soon start to come down.'

In the same speech to the party conference, May poured scorn on the human rights-based appeals that she believed were complicating the deportation process, claiming that in one case an illegal immigrant could not be deported 'because – and I am not making this up – he had a pet cat'.

The claim swiftly unravelled; a spokesman at the Royal Courts of Justice said the claimant's pet cat had 'had nothing to do with' the judgement allowing the man to stay. It quickly emerged that the same case had previously been cited by United Kingdom Independence Party leader Nigel Farage in a speech on immigration. One of May's cabinet colleagues, Justice Secretary Kenneth Clarke, described the claim as 'laughable' and 'complete nonsense'.[1] (The incident was named Catgate by gleeful reporters.)

But the influence of the United Kingdom Independence Party on her speech is significant. Conservatives were watching with growing nervousness the steadily rising popularity of UKIP, which was campaigning noisily about the negative impact of immigration, and there was a growing consensus within the Conservative party that a tougher position was urgently needed. During the 2010 general election, at a time when David Cameron was at pains to downplay the Conservatives' old image as the anti-immigrant, nasty party, UKIP had seized an opening and presented itself as 'the party that can talk about immigration'. Farage was promising an annual limit of fifty thousand migrants, a threefold increase in border staff, the expulsion of illegal migrants and an end to the 'active promotion of multiculturalism' by all publicly funded bodies. UKIP's leaflets were punchy: '5,000 immigrants arrive here every week: stop mass immigration'.

Cameron had described UKIP in 2006 as a bunch of 'fruitcakes, loonies and closet racists'; by 2012 he was feeling less inclined to be so dismissive. But coalition with the pro-immigration Liberal Democrats hampered the Conservatives' ability to act, and after two years in office the Conservative–Liberal Democrat coalition government did not seem any closer to meeting the entirely unrealistic manifesto pledge to reduce the net figure to the tens of thousands.

Officials had advised the prime minister to ditch the commitment. 'We told them it was a ridiculous target,' said Bob Kerslake, who was head of the UK civil service. 'I cannot emphasise too strongly how intense the political pressure was on this issue. They were under attack from UKIP. They were vulnerable because they had made a promise they couldn't deliver. All the polling was saying that migration was top of the agenda for the public.'

It became clear that rules on free movement of EU citizens would make it impossible to meet the target of reducing net migration. A new approach was needed. May started to devise policies which in time would strategically enhance the party's nasty reputation. The plan was to restrict access to visas for non-EU migrants and, in addition, to make Britain as unpalatable as possible for new arrivals who lacked the correct paperwork and for all those here illegally. The government hoped new rules on access to services would 'reduce the factors which draw people to the UK'. Net migration targets were about controlling people who were entering the country legally. Since this was a hard thing to restrict (largely because of EU free movement), they turned their focus instead to illegal immigration.

Focusing on illegal immigration was also more palatable with the Liberal Democrats, who judged this to be the least controversial way to talk about immigration. As a party they were more committed to a pro-immigration stance, although they felt they had lost votes in the 2010 election because of their proposed amnesty for illegal immigrants, which polling suggested had not been popular. No one in the government could disagree with a focus on controlling illegal immigration, because this simply meant controlling something that was by definition against the law.

In 2012 the Hostile Environment ministerial working group was set up (its mundanely businesslike title masking the brutality of its intention), which required ministers from across government to think about how to make immigrants' lives more difficult by increasing the number of checks they encountered every day. Initially this working group was intended to be a small, low-profile event attended by junior ministers, but David Cameron seized on the initiative and decided to chair it. On 1 January 2014, restrictions on Romanians and Bulgarians working in the UK were due to be lifted and there was intense nervousness in the Conservative party about how the arrival of new migrants from these countries would impact on immigration numbers.

'It was something he wanted to be personally associated with. This was Cameron at his worst, saying: "Oh my God, we have to do something about this, we have to have a headline in one of the right-wing newspapers by next week,"' David Laws, the Liberal Democrat minister of state in the Cabinet Office, told me.

The list of attendees to the working group gives an idea of how all-pervasive the new immigration policy was designed to be. Ministers for Immigration, Care Services, Employment, Government Policy, Housing and Local Government, Schools, Foreign and Commonwealth Affairs, Universities and Science, and Justice, as well as the Secretary to the Treasury and Under-Secretaries of State for Health and Transport were there, alongside some of the cabinet's most senior figures: the Liberal Democrat leader Vince Cable, Secretary of State for Work and Pensions Iain Duncan Smith, Cabinet Office Minister Oliver Letwin, Health Secretary Jeremy Hunt and Home Secretary Theresa May. According to Laws, the prime minister set the tone by asking colleagues: 'What are you going to do that will give me a good policy on the doorstep that will make it look like we are addressing the immigration issue?'

Sarah Teather, a Liberal Democrat minister who was present as the Hostile Environment committee was first conceived (before losing her job in a reshuffle), said there was such unease among Liberal Democrats at the committee's title that the working group quickly became known by the acronym MATBAPS: Migrants' Access to Benefits and Public Services. ('You can always trust the civil service to come up with a boring acronym for a malicious and inhumane set of policies,' a senior Lib Dem aide told me.)

George Osborne, who was then chancellor and Cameron's closest ally, said he did not attend the meetings. 'I had a pact with Theresa May and Cameron, where I said: "I don't really like any of this immigration stuff. It is not my responsibility, I'm not going to be part of it; I won't speak out against it but I'm not going to help."'

The Treasury was much more positive about benefits of immigration than the Home Office. Ahead of the 2010 election Osborne had advised Cameron against taking a harsh line on the subject, and for the first two years of Cameron's leadership it had barely been mentioned. However by 2012, even Osborne recognised that it was no longer possible to avoid the issue.

'Two years into the government, the obvious failure to meet the target and with the rise of UKIP – not talking about immigration was not really an option any more.' But he left it up to May and Cameron to take the lead. Cameron's argument was that failure to address immigration concerns was ruthlessly exploited by UKIP and may have led to the referendum outcome.

The starting point at the MATBAPS meetings was that illegal migrants should have no access to benefits and public services, or that access should at least be severely restricted. The difficulty was in working out how. How could the government increase the pressure on illegal immigrants at a time when the global financial crisis had triggered an austerity drive across the public sector that was leading to dramatic funding reductions and job cuts in all government departments, the Home Office among them? The government had an inspired new approach – outsourcing immigration checks to a whole new range of people who would be required to work as amateur, unpaid immigration officers. Landlords, doctors, teachers, hospital staff, DVLA employees and council workers would have to check immigration status before delivering services. Migrants would have to prove their right to be here repeatedly. The occasions on which it would be necessary to produce a passport were set to multiply.

'The logic of it was that you can't arrest and detain and deport your way out of the problem of illegal immigration. The idea that most illegal immigration is made up of clandestines clinging to articulated lorries or Eurostars is just silly. Most illegal immigration is believed to be overstayers,' I was told by a senior Home Office adviser to Theresa May, who asked not to be named. Overstayers were people who had arrived in the UK legally and continued to live in the country after their visas had expired. 'Given the limitation of resources and legal problems and documentation problems, you wouldn't ever be able to enforce immigration laws through enforcement action,' he said; this broader approach, which involved getting doctors, landlords, police and social workers to do Home Office work, was the logical solution.

The hardliners within the Home Office were keen to go further, hoping to make schools report parents without papers to Immigration Enforcement teams. 'Frankly the one way in which you will be most confident of locating people is connected to the future of their kids because that's what everybody cares about,' the senior adviser said. 'We wanted schools to be able to provide information to the authorities.' However, this policy fell by the wayside early on, blocked by the more liberal members of the cabinet who felt it would be unethical.

There was unease among the Liberal Democrats about all the policies they were helping to implement. Sarah Teather, the former Children and Families Minister, particularly disliked the idea of requiring landlords to verify the immigration status of new tenants, describing it as 'an extraordinary change in the relationship between the citizen and the state'. 'To expect a private individual to police our immigration system – what's the difference between that and saying you're not allowed to buy a piece of fruit from Sainsbury's without proving you're not an illegal immigrant?' she asked. 'How is that sensible?'[2]

'It was very clear that some departments thought this was all absolutely bonkers,' Alex Dziedzan, a senior Liberal Democrat aide, said. Particular opposition came from the Department for Education, the Department for Communities and Local Government, the Foreign Office and the Treasury. In backroom meetings, civil servants from those departments did their best to highlight looming problems, but they met resistance from their counterparts at the Home Office. Dziedzan said different departments in government seemed to attract different types of people. 'Civil servants are good at giving reasons why things are unlikely to work. They're quite good at indicating but not actually saying that they think something is horrendous. This inability to speak up when they think something is horrendous is one of the faults of the system. But the Home Office attracts people who have seen perhaps more abuse of the state . . . so they have more willingness to do negative things, they seem more inoculated against compassion.'

A senior official who attended some of the civil service meetings designed to develop MATBAPS policies told me that there was a 'reign of terror' within the Home Office, where Theresa May's two most senior aides, Nick Timothy and Fiona Hill, were felt to 'rule with an iron fist'. 'Swearing was fairly common. It would have been a brave civil servant who said, "Hang on a minute, there could be a problem." Inconvenient facts were not welcome in any way, shape or form.'

Unexpectedly, opposition also came from within the Conservatives, voiced by Eric Pickles, the Communities and Local Government Minister, who warned that asking landlords to carry out immigration checks on prospective tenants could have terrible consequences.

'Prime Minister, can I be blunt with you? I think this is a seriously bad idea. Checking immigration papers is really hard. We could end up in a situation where anyone foreign-looking cannot get into private rented accommodation because landlords just will not want to take the risk of getting it wrong.'[3]

David Laws's memoir, *Coalition*, records how Cameron stormed out of the MATBAPS meeting after this exchange, frustrated that his enthusiasm for ramped-up immigration checks was not more widely shared among colleagues.

'There were many Tories who were uncomfortable about these policies, who could see the implementation risks. But there was also at that time an overriding panic in Number 10 through Cameron, and at the Home Office through May, about uncontrolled immigration. This has to be put in the context of Cameron panicking about the UKIP vote going up. He was looking for bread-and-butter solutions that would please people who might otherwise go off and vote for UKIP,' Laws told me.

One of Cameron's closest cabinet allies said the prime minister was getting increasingly irritated by the half-hearted proposals ministerial departments were sending back for inclusion in the 2014 Immigration Act. The ally, who wished to remain anonymous, said, 'He was very frustrated. He felt the ideas were limp and tame. This was meant to be a platform to show that we were doing something on our immigration targets.' Cameron asked ministers and civil servants to come up with more aggressive new schemes to make life more difficult for illegal immigrants. 'He felt that the government machine was not delivering the ideas. He felt we had to deliver on this target; it was becoming a more and more obvious failure.'

Some within the cabinet wished they had never come up with the target in the first place. It had been seen initially as a non-controversial alternative to an aggressive immigration policy, and was never envisaged as a major commitment. Immigration figures are published quarterly by the Office for National Statistics and the Home Office, and scrutinised by the media. There was no way to hide failure. The government's continued inability to deliver on this commitment was regularly headline news, fuelling Cameron's determination to find a solution.

Those present at the meetings remember that the impetus for the policies was pushed with equal enthusiasm by David Cameron and Theresa May. May was also increasingly exasperated with the failure of her colleagues to support the hostile environment policies. One of her cabinet colleagues told me he was surprised at the vigour with which she pursued it, given her early political position-ing was much towards the liberal end of the party. Working in the Home Office, where you are endlessly confronted with terrorism and criminality, gives politicians a very pessimistic view of Britain, which possibly hardened her approach, he suggested. Equally, for someone who had an eye on the future leadership of the party, an ability to talk tough on this area was a useful selling point. 'She had a dogged determination on immigration. She wanted to get a tough reputation on immigration.'

Some ministers who attended the MATBAPS sessions saw the whole exercise as simply being about efficiency – ensuring that existing immigration legislation was as effectively implemented as possible; it was a practical matter, not an issue of ideology. But oth-ers found the ethos driving the policies extremely worrying. There was a widely shared unease at the 'papers, please' culture, with asso-ciations of the arbitrary everyday document checks more familiar in a police state. Bob Kerslake told the BBC later that the hostile environment policies were seen by some ministers as 'almost rem-iniscent of Nazi Germany'. He was irritated at the government's defence that any problems which emerged were 'all down to bad implementation by civil servants of an essentially sound policy'. He declined to say who, but revealed that some ministers had expressed deep unhappiness about the policies in the meetings he sat in on.

He was uncomfortable about the direction of policy. 'The tens of thousands commitment was undeliverable. It was disproportion-ately driving behaviour in Whitehall,' he said. Part of his concern was based on the Home Office's reputation for poor data-keeping.

Kerslake's civil service insider's insight on this point is particu-larly telling. 'Had the systems been good enough to be precise, absolutely definitive about who was illegally here, that would have been one thing. But, as we know, the systems were far from precise,' he said. His conclusion cuts through to the heart of the issue. 'It was that combination of a comprehensive regime of making life pretty impossible for people who were deemed to be illegal coupled with a system that was far from robust in determining who was illegal that created the problems.'

The Conservative ex-minister Oliver Letwin, who as Cabinet Office Minister had helped to steer through many of the proposals raised in the MATBAPS meetings, later told me it never occurred to anyone that the Home Office itself might not be able to tell who was here illegally. 'We assumed that the one thing that the Home Office would know is whether someone was here lawfully,' he said.

The Liberal Democrats were opposed to a lot of the measures proposed. 'We felt most of this was totally abhorrent,' Dziedzan said. Their approach was to try to get proposals kicked into the long grass, without threatening the survival of the coalition. They managed to dispense with the idea of getting schools to do mandatory checks on the immigration status of pupils. 'I rather wish in hindsight we had been more forceful.'

Meanwhile UKIP continued to turn up the dial on immigration. In 2013 Nigel Farage told his party conference: 'Ten thousand a week. Half a million a year. Five million economic migrants in ten years coming to this country. Unprecedented. Never happened before. The effects are obvious in every part of our national life. The strain these numbers are putting on public services. Schools. The shortage of school places in primaries and secondary schools. The NHS. The sheer weight of numbers that adds to the other problems. Housing. Demand pushes up prices. Wages are driven down by the massive over-supply of unskilled labour.'[4]

His figures and arguments need careful analysis. Farage is talking about migration into the UK, but neglects to mention how many people left the country over the same period and doesn't acknowledge that a proportion of those coming into the country are British people returning after a period away. Net non-British migration for 2013 was 266,000, approximately half the number he cites. Since most arrivals were working and paying taxes, the degree to which they should be blamed for strains to public services is debatable.

A 2013 study suggested that migrants coming to the UK since 2000 had made a net contribution of £25 billion to public finances,[5] but no one from the government attempted to articulate the position that immigration was boosting revenues, or to point out that a reduction of net migration on the scale promised risked seriously damaging the economy.

Polling undertaken by the Conservative peer Lord Ashcroft highlighted the growing strength of UKIP, suggesting that support for the party in the thirty most marginal Conservative seats had risen from 3 per cent in 2010 to 11 per cent in 2013. UKIP was squeezing support for the Conservatives and could split the right of the party, Ashcroft warned, increasing the risk that Labour would win the 2015 election.[6] Anti-immigration rhetoric was looking like an increasingly potent electoral tool. Both Cameron and May were convinced that pushing on with these policies was the best way to stem the flow of Conservative voters switching to UKIP.

In June 2013, the Home Office set up the ominously titled Interventions and Sanctions Directorate, a sub-department within Immigration Enforcement, whose work was never publicised and whose existence was only uncovered by questions asked under the Freedom of Information Act. This unit was created to 'encourage greater compliance with the immigration rules', had 'responsibility for removing incentives for people to stay illegally', and worked to encourage those here illegally to sort out their status or leave. 'This is achieved by ensuring a range of interventions and sanctions are systematically applied to deny access to services and benefits for those who are unlawfully in the UK'. The unit 'works closely with government departments and a range of other partners across the public and private sectors to identify those migrants accessing such services and benefits to which they are not entitled'.[7] The team was also responsible for administering financial penalties for those found to be employing illegal immigrants.

———

The Conservatives' hostile environment policies were not an entirely new phenomenon; they built on similar initiatives brought in by both main parties over decades. Employment checks on the immigration status of staff had been introduced under Labour, although they were relatively rarely used. Between 1993 and 2009 the number of immigration enforcement officers grew from 120 to 7,500; successive acts gave these officers more powers of arrest, search and use of force. Between 1996 and 2006 over 1,600 more immigration detention places were created by Labour ministers. But the focus under Labour was on removing people deemed to be here illegally; the sanctions designed to make life tougher for people with irregular immigration status were much more light-touch, more of an aspiration than a reality. Theresa May's Home Office pursued these policies with a vastly increased intensity.

As ministers prepared the 2014 Immigration Act, which included the hostile environment measures,[8] there was no shortage of warnings about the likely discriminatory impact of the policies. Detailed submissions were made by legal charities, unions, healthcare organisations, homelessness charities, human rights and race relations groups and housing bodies. The detail and range of the advice that was ignored is impressive.

The Joint Council for the Welfare of Immigrants cautioned, 'Forcing ordinary citizens who are not qualified in immigration law to check someone's legality will result in mistakes and inadvertent discrimination. It will serve to create a hostile environment for ALL migrants . . . making a significant part of the ethnic minority population feel unwelcome in their own country.'[9] The organisation predicted that 'these measures will divide society, creating a two-tier Britain, a return to the days of "no dogs, no blacks, no Irish" and of ill people with no access to healthcare walking the streets of Britain.'[10]

Diane Abbott, who was then a backbench Labour MP, warned repeatedly that the measures were discriminatory. 'It's almost impossible to produce a hostile environment for immigrants and not produce a hostile environment for people who look like immigrants,' she wrote later.

The Immigration Law Practitioners Association said the right to rent scheme (whereby landlords were obliged to check the immigration status of prospective tenants) would be 'intrusive, bullying, ineffective and expensive and likely racist and unlawful to boot'. The Residential Landlords Association pointed out that there were potentially 404 different types of European identity documents that landlords needed to be familiar with in order to check the immigration status of a potential tenant, and warned that landlords might find it simpler not to house anyone they judged to be in some way foreign.

People in the immigration sector were doing all they could to try to explain to Home Office ministers that there were many reasons why people could be undocumented. Lack of documents was not always a sign that someone's immigration status was irregular – it could simply be that they were not able to afford the astronomical and soaring application fees to regularise things, or could not pay for legal advice to guide them, or had never needed to apply for a passport, or were in the long process of applying for status, or had been the victim of a Home Office administrative error.

Until recently there was absolutely no reason for a British

citizen to hold a passport unless they were planning to travel out of the country. It is only since the introduction of hostile environment policies that people who cannot produce a British passport (particularly those without white skin) have suddenly found themselves under suspicion of violating immigration rules.

Immigration lawyer Colin Yeo wrote: 'It is not just the scheming, deliberate or flagrant "illegal immigrant" of popular and Ministerial imagination who breaks immigration laws. Very minor errors and omissions can transform a migrant into an "unlawful immigrant" and can cast them into the twilight world of the hostile environment.'[11]

Yeo was clear that the policies were discriminatory. 'If you are white, middle class, middle aged, take holidays abroad, own your home and have long term employment, you are immune to the effects of the hostile environment. You will rarely be checked and if you are then you possess a passport and you feel secure in your status and your societal role. It will be hard for you to understand the demeaning, emotional and racialised nature of these checks,' he wrote. 'A white person with a local accent may well be regarded as low risk and employable without checks. A black person or a person with a foreign name or an accent may be regarded as high risk and therefore unemployable without checks.'

The clearest warning that the immigration changes might affect the group of people who later became known as the Windrush generation came in a report called *Chasing Status*, published in late 2014, which stated with exceptional prescience: 'Besides those who knowingly have no legal right to be in the UK, there is also another virtually invisible – and rarely acknowledged – group, who can't easily prove their legal status (because of lost documents, or poor government record-keeping) or whose status is "irregular" for a variety of legitimate reasons.'[12]

These people, the report's author, Fiona Bawdon, wrote, had

recently begun to find themselves prevented from working or claiming benefits after a lifetime in Britain. 'Having long taken their Britishness for granted, such people can't believe their nationality, much less their lawful presence, is being questioned.' Those worst affected were older people who had been in the UK for four or five decades, having arrived at a time when their status was automatic. Their length of stay had made them confident that their immigration status was in order. 'They would have assumed it was permanent and irreversible,' Bawdon wrote.

This group tended to have very little money for travel so in most cases had never bothered applying for passports, and if they were aware there was a problem they lacked the money for legal assistance in sorting it out. Just under half the people interviewed for Bawdon's report were Jamaican, but others similarly affected were from Sri Lanka, Kenya, Zimbabwe and the US – highlighting with foresight that this was an issue that went well beyond Caribbean nations. 'Our research shows they are being driven into unemployment, homelessness and destitution by laws already in place. Further changes introduced by the 2014 Immigration Act will only exacerbate their plight.'

These people were 'the unintended and unacknowledged victims of increasingly draconian immigration laws'. Bawdon recommended restoring legal aid for those who had lived in the UK since 1973 and introducing a dedicated team in the Home Office with the understanding and expertise to deal with such cases appropriately. The Home Office declined to do either. We know that officials read the research because they emailed a colleague of mine at the *Guardian* with a statement for inclusion in a piece on the report, announcing that there were 'no plans to introduce a specialist unit to deal with such cases – all cases are considered on their own merits'. Had officials followed her advice, much of the pain experienced by people like Paulette and Anthony could have been avoided.

The Home Office itself estimated in 2014 that there were half a million settled migrants living in the UK who did not hold a biometric residence permit to prove their right to reside and access public services. An official impact assessment on the right to rent policy noted that 'some non-UK born older people may have additional difficulties in providing original documentation. Some may have had their immigration records destroyed. Some will have originally come into the country under old legislation but may have difficulty in evidencing this.' This warning also highlighted the risks posed to precisely the group of people who would later be described as the Windrush generation. Again, Home Office ministers ignored the warning.

A senior civil servant told me it was remarkable that a caveat of this nature had even managed to get through the numerous revisions to the impact assessment. These assessments are required by law to consider whether new policies could discriminate against vulnerable people. 'Impact assessments are written so they don't scare the horses; to avoid presenting anything embarrassing – so the fact that this warning got in there at all is significant.'

Within the charity sector there was despondency about the willingness of the government to listen to their urgent advice. Sally Daghlian, who heads the migrant support charity Praxis, reported that it was increasingly felt that genuine concerns were ignored and changes were brought in regardless of the legal and voluntary sector's responses.

The Runnymede Trust warned, 'Every deportation remains a "positive" contribution to this unhittable, and knowingly unhittable, target. To have such a knowingly unimplementable policy, even merely as an aspiration, sends a strong signal to officials: do whatever you can to drive down immigration numbers, even if this is perverse.'

By this point David Cameron had expressed his distaste for these 'equality impact assessments', which he dismissed as unnecessary red tape. There were 'smart people in Whitehall' who thought about equalities when they were devising policies, he had said. 'We don't need all this extra tick-box stuff.'[13]

But the occupants of Whitehall who devised these policies, just like the politicians in parliament, were drawn from a very narrow section of society. The people making the decisions – the ministers and the civil servants – were not likely themselves to have been affected by the hostile environment. If parliament was truly representative of the population, it would have one hundred black and minority ethnic MPs; the number currently stands at fifty. The 2018 Civil Service Fast Stream annual report revealed that not a single person of black Caribbean origin had been given a place on the graduate high flyers' scheme that aims to recruit future leaders of government departments. The success rate for black Caribbean applicants for the scheme between 2010 and 2016 was 0.64 per cent; white British applicants were around six times more likely to get places.

'Most senior officials see things from the point of view of an affluent, white, Oxbridge, Home Counties type,' a senior Whitehall official told the *Huffington Post*, in response to the figures. 'There is no doubt that if there were more people from a black British background in senior jobs then Windrush would not have happened. But if you don't know anybody from that kind of background, you just don't have the kind of perspective that helps you avoid such hideous errors.'

When Cameron argued that there were 'smart people in Whitehall' thinking about equalities, he didn't consider that the smart people might come from too narrow a background to allow them to appreciate the true impact of the policies they were developing.

In retrospect, it is clear that the smart civil servants had failed to anticipate a lot of the possible fallout from the policies, and chose to ignore repeated warnings.[14]

In May 2014 UKIP took 27.5 per cent of the national vote in the

European elections, up from 16.5 per cent in the previous European elections of 2009, ahead of Labour and the Conservatives. Farage claimed ebulliently that it was the 'most extraordinary result that has been seen in British politics for a hundred years'. The Conservatives responded by pressing ahead with greater vigour on the drive to toughen their immigration policies.

George Osborne said the cabinet would have liked to quietly drop its failing tens of thousands target before the 2015 election, but the party was hit by the double defections of two Conservative MPs, Douglas Carswell and Mark Reckless, to UKIP in 2014, 'which steeled a resolve not to take the immigration target out of the manifesto'.

Labour was also impacted by UKIP's soaring popularity and became increasingly anxious about marginal seats in the northeast. They responded in exactly the same way as the Conservatives, persuaded that the only answer was to harden their stance on immigration. The party remained scarred by former leader Gordon Brown's casual dismissal of ex-Labour supporter Gillian Duffy as 'bigoted' when she confronted him about the impact of immigration in her area during the 2010 election campaign. In the lead-up to the 2015 general election, the party bulk-produced cheerful bright red mugs which they offered for sale to members, with a slogan they felt supporters would enjoy looking at as they sipped their tea: 'Controls on Immigration. I'm voting Labour.'

After the 2015 election, when the wipeout of the Liberal Democrats allowed the Conservatives to gain sole control of the government, May and Cameron were able to push forward unencumbered by the more delicate sensitivities of their former partners. The 2016 Immigration Act included some of the tougher hostile environment measures rejected by the Liberal Democrats during the coalition. Both employers who hired illegal migrants and the workers themselves now faced criminal sanctions; the driving licences of those without a proven right to be in the UK could be revoked; not only did it become harder to open bank accounts, but existing accounts could be frozen; a landlord could now face up to five years in prison for knowingly renting to an illegal migrant; the government's 'deport first, appeal later' policy was extended to all migrants (not just those with criminal convictions). Some immigration officials became 'embedded' in the Driver and Vehicle Licensing Agency, in some police custody suites, and also in some local authority housing and children's services departments. Schools were now required to record the nationality and country of birth of pupils, and this data was originally intended to be handed to the Home Office; this data-sharing was ended after parents complained in late 2016,[15] but not before details of eighteen thousand families had been shared.[16]

Concerns about the policies continued to be expressed. A report by the homelessness charity Shelter had noted in July 2015 that 44 per cent of landlords said as a result of the new measures they would be less likely to let their properties to people and families who 'appear to be immigrants'.

The burden of proof had also shifted. Anyone who could not produce a British passport was deemed to have violated immigration rules until they could prove that they hadn't. It was not up to the Home Office to disprove entitlement but up to the individual to show that they qualified.

———

The warnings raised by campaigners and some politicians that the hostile environment policies would catch the wrong people were well founded.

Michael Braithwaite had lived in London since he was nine, when he had arrived from Barbados. Now aged sixty-four, he was an experienced special needs teaching assistant and had worked at the same primary school in North London for fifteen years before he was called to a meeting with the head teacher one day in January 2017. For a few months he had been aware of rumblings from the HR department about papers that needed clarifying, but it was only when he sat down with the head that he realised things were very serious. His boss had printed out an information pack, headed: 'Penalties for employing illegal workers'. 'You can be sent to jail for five years if you're found guilty of employing someone who you knew or had "reasonable cause to believe" didn't have the right to work in the UK,' the document warned, specifying that employers faced fines of up to £20,000 for each illegal worker they hired.

The head teacher was 'terrified', Michael told me when we spoke in March 2017, after being put in contact by the Joint Council for the Welfare of Immigrants (JCWI), whose lawyers were assisting him. 'His eyes were scared, his mannerisms were nervous. He showed me the forms. He kept asking: "What are you going to do, Michael?"'

Michael felt let down by his employer's lack of loyalty. 'I told him I was confused. I've been here fifty years, working in this school for fifteen years and suddenly this?'

An official from the human resources department of the local council called him to explain that she was worried by his lack of papers. 'I'm supposed to send you packing,' she told him. 'From what I'm seeing here, you're not even supposed to be in the country. But looking at your record, you've been working for us for fifteen years. How can I do that? It can't be right.'

She advised him to seek help urgently but Michael was wary about bringing further attention to his situation. 'I was so terrified, I didn't want to go to my MP. I'd read about people being carted off to detention centres.'

In February 2017 he was called in to the school for a formal meeting with his employers. 'I felt like I was on trial.' The school's

HR representative described him as an illegal immigrant, which he found both hurtful and preposterous. He was sent out of the room for a few minutes to allow the head to consider the situation; when he was called back in he was sacked.

Instead of leaving immediately, Michael went to help his colleagues take pupils swimming. He knew that if he didn't help with the weekly trip, it risked being cancelled. 'There were sixty kids who needed to go swimming – I'd been working with those kids for four years.' Once he had helped walk two groups of children down the road to the swimming pool and then accompanied them back to school, he quietly collected a box of belongings from the store room and left.

Michael was devastated. 'That job was such a good job and it was taken away from me in the snap of a finger. There was a hole in my heart. I got up each morning and walked to sit in the park. Sometimes I considered topping myself.' He worried about being taken away for deportation. 'I was always expecting my doorbell to ring at 6 a.m. – that's when they are meant to come. It made me feel like I was an alien.'

The new checks on driving licences were also successfully rooting out hard-working British people, such as ambulance driver Winston Robinson, then fifty-nine, who received a letter from the Interventions and Sanctions Directorate informing him he was at risk of losing his licence because 'according to our records you have no lawful basis to be in the UK' and telling him, 'You should take steps to leave the UK immediately.'

It is hard to think of more vital members of society than ambulance drivers and special needs teaching assistants, but Home Office officials, pushing ahead relentlessly with the implementation of the hostile environment, had no discretion to consider the wisdom of what they were doing.

As questions were being asked about Winston's driving licence (which was clearly essential to his job), his passportless status was flashing up in his employer's files. In October 2016, he was called in to see the HR director at ERS Medical, a private company which provided ambulance services to London hospitals, and told he was going to be sacked because he had no British passport. 'She was very calm about it. She mentioned the possibility of a substantial fine.' Winston told her that there should be no question about his status, since he had arrived fifty years earlier from Jamaica in 1966, at the age of nine.

She agreed that the rules didn't seem to make a lot of sense. 'What you are saying to me makes this all look stupid. But we have to follow the rules. We can't keep you on.'

'I felt like jumping off a bridge. But I didn't argue; there was no point. She was a nice woman, she said good luck. It was futile to argue.'

He was paid benefits for a few months but these were stopped once Jobcentre staff identified him as someone without the correct papers. The combined effect of being unemployed and denied benefits pushed him around £8,000 into debt. The sense of hurt about what had happened to him was as preoccupying as the practical financial fallout from the dismissal.

'The lack of consideration – no one took the time to look at me again and think, maybe I'm not the person you're looking for. They called me an overstayer, but I was nine years old when I came. What power did I have to jump on a plane and come and hide in your country? What nine-year-old does that? The whole thing is ridiculous. I didn't come like a stowaway on a banana boat in the middle of the night. I came here officially, legally.'

Winston had really liked his job as an ambulance driver. 'I was a normal guy with a normal life until the system betrayed me. I was doing a useful job. I served a purpose in society and all of a sudden that was ripped up.'

As a teenager in 1970s London, Winston had had a lot of trouble with teddy boys and Hells Angels. The difficulties he was now having with the Home Office made him feel the same sense of being targeted for the colour of his skin.

———

Just as campaigners had warned, the hostile environment policies had a clearly racially weighted outcome. A High Court judgement in early 2019 ruled that the right to rent policy, which forced landlords to check the papers of prospective tenants, was racially discriminatory. Research into how the policy was working in practice showed landlords weren't so bothered about checking the papers of white people.

Were the rest of the hostile environment policies racist? Alex Dziedzan, the former Liberal Democrat special adviser, said: 'People will argue, "No, we are not concerned about race, we are concerned about people who are here illegally and not entitled to work here." But the long and the short of it is that it is going to affect a racial minority in this country, so is it racist? Yes, I think it is. Racism doesn't have to be using the N word or not hiring a black candidate; it is structural and systematic.'

A former senior adviser to Theresa May told me he still believed that the hostile environment policy was sound and justified. 'Some people were concerned that it would lead to racist decisions by landlords. Our view was that it should be easy to demonstrate that you are legally in the country or not,' he said, still failing to grasp the difficulties many people have in evidencing immigration status. 'At the point when the hostile environment policies were introduced it was not clear that such a group of undocumented people existed.'

But there was a more fundamental failure underlying the decision to introduce these policies – the inability to admit that immigrants are a force for good rather than a drain on the economy.

Former Cabinet Office Minister Oliver Letwin sees the development of these policies as the result of a crucial misjudgement, stretching back to the 1990s. 'We all just made a massive error in the rhetoric from that point onwards. We completely failed to explain the countervailing benefits of migration, so the whole argument was won by default by those who argued that migration was a bad thing. And if the argument is won that migration is a bad thing, then the question arises: well, how do you limit it? If there's a problem then obviously all the sensible people, having agreed that it is a problem, will also agree that they want to reduce it. We made a collective error in the political establishment right from Blair through to the Conservatives. There was a collective, tacit agreement between the two major parties that something had to be done to reduce the level of net migration.

'This sort of mindset – how do we limit the extent of migration? – was built in for both parties. The difficulty with this thesis was that it was not a problem. There may be in the future a problem with excess levels of migration from the point of view of access to public services, infrastructure, but we completely lost the opposite argument that it was sustaining our economy and much of our public services.'

George Osborne agreed there was a fundamental problem with the rhetoric. 'To always present immigration as a problem rather than as something that both is a challenge but also something that is a great benefit – not just economically but in terms of creating a better society – was a mistake.'

A similar argument was made by Labour's shadow Home Secretary, Diane Abbott, who admitted that Labour should accept some of the blame for the development of the hostile environment policies. 'There was an increasingly harsh rhetoric on immigration, which was shared by the entire political class. The gradually hardening rhetoric led to layers of hardening legislation. It just rolled forward inexorably. If you talk about migrants in the way that the political classes want to talk about migrants you dehumanise them, so you don't stop and think: what happens if you're asking for paperwork from people who reasonably enough don't have it?

'It was a very gradual process that accelerated around Theresa May. But it would be unfair to say that a hostile approach to immigration started with her.'

Were the policies racist? 'They reflected an increasingly harsh rhetoric around immigration,' Abbott said. 'The Tories had the hot breath of UKIP around their neck. If you bring in a set of arrangements which are designed to trap illegal migrants, they will start trapping people who are here perfectly legally who just happen to be black.'

Theresa May's former Home Office advisers like to highlight the work she did with the police to restrict the discriminatory use of stop and search powers and her decision to launch a race disparity audit to combat inequalities across all government departments as proof that she would never have backed racist policies. But many who worked with her acknowledge she had a blind spot on immigration. Shortly after becoming prime minister in 2016 she told the Conservative party conference: 'If you believe you're a citizen of the world, you're a citizen of nowhere.' It was ostensibly an attack on global cosmopolitan elites, but it was also a dog-whistle to the party's flag-waving nationalists at a time of rising post-Brexit xenophobia, another hostile demarcation of who does and does not belong in Britain.

The effect of the hostile environment policies was clearly discriminatory. If ministers had felt it was important to worry about the potential for racially discriminatory consequences, they would have listened to the chorus of warnings. The decision to ignore them reveals that they didn't much care.

WHISTLEBLOWERS

In November 2017 an ex-Home Office employee sat at his computer reading about Paulette Wilson on the *Guardian* website, his heart sinking as he scanned through the details of her attempts to gather evidence of her arrival in the UK. In the weeks which followed, he read about Anthony Bryan, Hubert Howard, Renford McIntyre and Sylvester Marshall, and each time he saw another article which mentioned the difficulties people were having in proving that they had arrived here before 1 January 1973, he felt newly horrified. He would call over to his wife, asking her to come and look, reminding her why the stories made him so angry.

'They destroyed the files that would have helped. This would have been a five-minute job. This whole thing could have been stopped,' he said. 'This is the exact profile of someone who would have benefited from the files.'

'What can you do about it?' his wife asked him.

'I can't help them now.'

But the nagging sense that this was one part of the jigsaw that no one was talking about disturbed him and he was unable to put it out of his mind. He decided to go public with what he knew.

———

Martin Jones (as I'll have to call him, since Home Office whistleblowers do not like to be named) took a temporary job with the Home Office's Data Protection Unit in 2009. He was looking for a new challenge, had no real pressure to earn a big salary, but wanted to do something stimulating. He liked the calm stillness in the open-plan room where he worked. In his imagination the scene was a modern incarnation of a Benedictine monastery, with monks working silently on manuscript illuminations – only the team of around sixty workers were peacefully reading through Home Office files, ploughing through hundreds of pages a day, carefully blacking out sensitive bits of personal information such as phone numbers, or names of officials who had made decisions.

Individuals who are struggling with their immigration status can apply to the Home Office to see their complete files held by the department; until 2018 it cost £10 and subsequently the fee was waived, but the actual cost of finding and preparing the documents is substantial. Before the files are released, officials have to remove or black out information on third parties, and this is what Martin did for a number of years, sitting in his office on Wellesley Road in Croydon, South London, his headphones plugged in to block out the noise of ambulances screaming along the street below.

This part of Croydon is a strangely dehumanising place with its cluster of brutalist 1960s buildings which form the Home Office headquarters, named (at the height of excitement over the moon landings) Lunar House and Apollo House. These are towering, twenty-storey grey concrete edifices, raised on concrete legs, with stripes of glass windows – in a black-and-white checked pattern, according to whether workers inside have raised or lowered the white blinds. The buildings are so tall in this part of central Croydon you have to tilt your head upwards to see blue sky; disagreeable gusts of gritty wind get blasted down the air tunnel between the towers. Martin told me he had seen people blown over by the wind.

As you walk from the tube, the Home Office is well signposted, and a stream of global arrivals are visible making their way to Lunar House to try to sort out their papers. No one looks cheerful; visiting the Home Office headquarters is rarely a life-enhancing experience. It feels as though the town planners have even made it hard for the hundreds of immigrants who visit daily to cross the street, erecting barriers in the middle of the road so everyone is forced to walk in search of a gloomy underpass to make their way from one side to the other.

Martin found working for the Home Office not entirely pleasant. Puzzlingly petty rules kept being emailed out to staff: workers were not allowed to wear trainers in the office (even though they were backroom administrators who never met the public) unless they procured a medical note explaining they had an infirmity; charging your mobile phone in the office was not allowed because it constituted stealing electricity from the government. 'Staff were treated appallingly,' he said. The queues for the lifts at lunchtime were so time-consuming that fifteen minutes of a lunch break could be wasted trying to get out of the building, so people made do with eating sandwiches at their desks. Martin was interested in genealogy and put up with the irritations because reading through the files charting people's migration histories turned out to be a reasonably enjoyable way to spend the time. 'I found it interesting and sometimes disturbing; it was absorbing and I got paid at the end of it.'

To begin with he worked on the seventh floor of B block, a thin, matchbox-shaped Home Office building opposite Lunar House, above the Whitgift shopping centre, a fading, gloomily lit sub-terranean shopping mall. Each worker had a large desk because there were so many paper files that they needed to process, in a typical open-plan 1960s office with grey carpet squares glued to the floor, fluorescent strip lighting attached to greying ceiling tiles. Throughout the day, administrative staff would wheel trolleys through the office, bringing new folders that had been ordered up from the Iron Mountain storage depot a mile away. Some of the piles of records were four feet high.

The government had originally thought it would get an annual total of around two or three hundred of these requests to see full Home Office files when they were first introduced in 1998, but by the time Martin started his job there was a backlog of many thousands. 'No one could believe that there would be this many inquiries.' Sometimes foreign students had lost their papers and needed help in proving that they were here legally; at other times it would be a dispute over whether someone had overstayed their visa, or else someone had lost a passport which contained a stamp giving them leave to remain in the UK and needed help proving that the permission had been given. Having the whole file could help individuals, or (if they were lucky enough to be able to afford them) their lawyers, to sort out their cases.

When he first began work in the department, he was aware of colleagues periodically asking for a key to the basement of the next-door building, C block, a mirror-image of the Whitgift B block, which could be accessed by an underground tunnel. If staff found no information on an individual who had been born in the Caribbean or another former colony, they would go to C block's basement to consult an archive of what were called landing cards or registration slips, which recorded a name and date of arrival and the ship's details. Being able to prove an arrival date in the UK is a crucial element of making a citizenship application, because, as we've seen, the 1971 Immigration Act gave people who had already moved to Britain the automatic right to stay indefinitely. 'Sometimes the Passport Office would call up, and people would say: "I'll look in the basement."'

One of the key problems for people in this cohort was that if you were a British citizen the Home Office would not keep a file on you, because this system was only there for keeping records of immigrants. As Windrush-generation people were effectively moved from being seen as citizens to being classified as migrants, they were forced to make applications to regularise their status;

these applications could have been helped by accessing their Home Office files, only most of them discovered they had no Home Office files because the Home Office had never viewed them as migrants who needed files. It was head-spinningly confusing.

For whatever reason, now forgotten with the passing of decades, the Home Office neglected to keep a record of those people from the Commonwealth who were granted leave to remain on arrival. The result was that when applicants wrote in for their files, there was often nothing to send them. One of the few things that people in the department were able to do was to go and see if a registry slip was available in the basement next door.

Some time towards the end of 2009, Martin heard angry voices in the office and walked over to listen to an animated discussion. 'I'm quite nosy,' he told me. His manager was explaining that officials in another department had told him that the landing cards were to be destroyed.

'You can't do that – we still use those files,' one of his colleagues was saying. 'You can't destroy them.'

'They were very angry. Some of them had worked in the department for twenty years. They were astonished that the papers were going to be destroyed,' Martin told me later.

The manager just shrugged. 'I'm not doing it. I've just been told it's happening. I've got no say in it.'

'What happens if there is a case of a dispute?' Martin asked. He said he was told that the vast majority of people named on the registry cards were in their seventies and eighties, that most of their cases would have been resolved, the remainder must be fairly small in number and that the office did 'not have the resources to keep them'. He remembers protesting: 'Even if half the people are dead, they are historical records.' His manager responded that the cards were 'redundant'.

Martin and a group of four or five colleagues harangued the

manager until he agreed to go back and tell senior officials that there was unhappiness in his department over the decision. They told him to suggest that the files should be microfiched or offered to a black cultural organisation, an ancestry website or the Public Records Office – anywhere that would appreciate their historical value. 'We thought these were all viable options.' In the end the manager reluctantly agreed to make those suggestions to the next level of management, but he was unenthusiastic about it because this represented a breach of protocol in the civil service's clearly demarcated hierarchy. 'I think it was uncomfortable for him. He probably would have been shouted at by senior people asking him why he was complicating things. But he said he would do it.'

There was a lot of irritation among Martin's colleagues that day about the decision. They were the only department to have a real sense of the potential significance of the files.

A few days later the department's manager said he had put forward the objections. He told his team that microfiching the files had been deemed too expensive but he had no sense of whether the other proposals had been listened to. In the Home Office chain of command, this was a plea from staff in a very low-ranking department to senior officials at a much higher pay grade; there was little expectation that their concerns would be taken seriously. There were so many mini-empires in the vast Home Office that it was hard for the vassals in the Data Protection Unit to believe that anyone cared what they thought.

'We won't be in the loop,' the manager said. He had been told that the Home Office had to vacate the next-door building because everyone was being relocated to Lunar House opposite. Already many floors in the two Whitgift blocks had been emptied. Every month that the basement files remained there, the Home Office had to continue paying rent. 'The only reason given was that they had to clear the building.'

That was the last he heard about it. At some point in 2010 the files were destroyed and Martin's department was moved to the seventeenth floor of Lunar House. It was just one of a number of strange decisions made within the puzzling organisation where he had wound up spending the last few years of his professional life. The immigration section of the Home Office was so big that staff had little understanding of what their colleagues on the floor below were doing, let alone what teams in Liverpool and Sheffield were working on. The department wasn't known for being well organised. Martin remembers a manager discovering a whole forgotten room full of files, of unknown origin and purpose; it took staff weeks to sort through the papers and despatch them elsewhere. Working for the Home Office was often confusing.

At the time he was distressed by the decision to get rid of the files because he felt it showed a lack of respect for a piece of history. But the significance of the decision only became really clear a few years later when he and colleagues began to notice a rise in the number of people asking for their files, anxious for material that might help to document their arrival in the UK and secure their immigration status. It was only at this point that the department really began to understand the damaging consequences of the destruction of the cards. In the wake of the hostile environment policies which were requiring people to provide passports or other documents proving their right to be in the UK, the department was getting more and more requests for files which did not exist. The previous solution of nipping to the basement to search for the registration slips was no longer available.

'Every week or two, someone would say: "I've got another one here,"' Martin said. 'People were writing to say: "I've been here forty-five years, I've never had a passport, I've never needed a passport. Now I'm being told I'm not British, because there is no record of me." Because it was no longer possible to search in the archive of landing cards, people would be sent a standard letter that would state: "We have searched our records, we can find no trace of you in our files.'"

Sylvester Marshall received this letter. Paulette Wilson's immigration adviser received a letter saying: 'I have been unable to locate any record of Ms Wilson's current immigration status on our records.' Again and again, Windrush victims appealed to the Home Office for help and were told there was no information to suggest they existed.

The department's older staff, in particular, hated having to send out this standard, single-page letter; they minded not being able to help because they knew these requests were important.

Martin remembers getting a request from a solicitor in around 2015 for the files of a retired nurse who had come from Jamaica as a child, with her aunt. 'She had had a whole career in the NHS, working as a nurse, had children and grandchildren, and now she wanted to go back to Jamaica to see her mother's grave. But when she applied for her passport, that's when she hit the wall. People were asking her: "Who are you? What gave you the right to be here in the first place?" The solicitor wrote asking if there was anything we could do. Knowing the background, I knew there was a time when I could have said: "Can I have a key? I'll be back in ten minutes." That wasn't possible any longer.' He made an effort to help, getting permission from a manager to put his other files aside for a while to prioritise this case, and managed to unearth some records on the aunt, which helped – but he felt frustrated at how complicated and suspicious the system had become. He was irritated by the notion of people having to prove their eligibility.

'Proof is something you do in a scientific experiment. Probability is something you do with human beings. When you have someone who has been married here for over thirty-five years, has three children here, how can she not be telling the truth? I feel angry that people are being treated in a way which is just so abhorrent. People are afraid to apply for citizenship because they don't actually believe they know where they stand in a country they thought was their own.'

It enraged Martin to read about people who had arrived during the Windrush era now being told that there was no trace of them in Home Office records. 'These cards represented the arrivals of people who went on to dedicate their lives to this country. It was like in one stroke they were erased from history.'

He kept thinking that perhaps someone else would raise the issue of the destroyed documents, but when no one mentioned it, he emailed David Lammy MP (who was speaking out about these cases) to voice his concern. David Lammy's assistant, Jack McKenna, put Martin in touch with me. We had a long conversation by phone, and later met in Croydon to talk in greater detail about what had happened.

I wasn't totally sure of the significance of the revelation and was concerned that Martin had never seen the files himself; he had only spoken to colleagues who had gone down to the basement to check the archives, and so he was unable to describe the records. I wasn't sure how many cards had been there, and whether there were records for people who had arrived by plane as well as by ship. I hoped there might be someone else who had worked in the department at the time who would be willing to talk to me, but Martin was only in touch with people who were still employed there, and he said that they were not willing to talk, because civil service protocols prohibit unauthorised conversations with the media and they would risk losing their jobs and pensions.

In the meantime I put the facts as Martin had explained them to me to the Home Office, and received a very detailed response confirming everything he had said.

'In 2010, the decision was taken by the UK Border Agency to securely dispose of some documents known as registration slips,' the emailed response stated.

These slips provided details of an individual's date of entry but did not provide any reliable evidence relating to ongoing residence in the UK or their immigration status. This decision was taken in line with the Fourth and Fifth Data Protection Principles i.e. to ensure personal data held is accurate and up to date and should not be kept for longer than necessary. Keeping these records would have represented a potential breach of these principles. In deciding immigration cases, the Home Office considers alternative evidence, such as tax records, utility bills and tenancy agreements, as evidence of ongoing residency in the UK in these exceptional circumstances. The disposal of registration slips would therefore have no bearing on immigration cases whereby Commonwealth citizens are proving residency in the UK.

There were many elements of this unusually detailed response that were quite odd. In reality, Home Office staff members had been extremely reluctant to consider alternative records such as National Insurance contributions, utility bills and tax records unless they were presented with a meticulous dossier of papers proving residency every year, going back decades. It simply wasn't true that the destruction of the files had no bearing on immigration cases.

Martin was unimpressed by the response. He did not believe that the decision to destroy documents had been in any way motivated by data protection principles – officials had seemed only concerned about the amount of space the files took up and the urgent need to evacuate a building which had been sold off to developers. C block at the Whitgift centre, sandwiched next to a concrete National Car Park and Sainsbury's, is still waiting for redevelopment, and ambitious plans to transform the shabby shopping centre into a glossier retail mall have not yet been realised. Tangled vertical Venetian blinds hang sadly in the windows of the empty building.

David Lammy expressed a widely felt anger when he heard about the destruction of the files. 'This revelation from a whistleblower reveals that the problems being faced by the Windrush generation are not down to one-off bureaucratic errors but as a direct result of systemic incompetence, callousness and cruelty within our immigration system,' he wrote in an email to me. 'It is an absolute disgrace that the Home Office has destroyed these documents and then forced Windrush generation migrants to try and prove their status, threatening them with deportation and stripping them of their rights.'

———

At the same time as the introduction of the hostile environment there were other changes underway inside the Home Office. The budget cuts imposed by the coalition government's commitment to austerity meant that there were fewer opportunities for individuals to talk to case workers.

The number of Home Office public inquiry offices where there were case workers on hand was cut to just two, in London and Sheffield. Even here there was no longer any way that people turning up for a weekly or monthly reporting session could actually speak to a case worker; they were physically located in the building, but no longer routinely booked face-to-face appointments. Most of the applications which would previously have involved a meeting with a case worker became paper-based processes that cut out interviews entirely. Previously, in any unusual right to remain case, an applicant would probably have seen an executive officer – an experienced member of staff. This no longer happened.

Lucy Moreton, General Secretary of the Immigration Service Union, which represents Home Office staff, told me that as a result the whole decision-making process changed. 'The hostile environment was a bad idea, because it changed the emphasis from innocent until proven guilty, to guilty until you can jolly well prove otherwise, but the cause of [the Windrush difficulties] was not the hostile environment alone – the root cause was the staffing cuts and the loss of expertise.'

As well as cutting staff numbers by about a quarter between 2012 and 2015, there was a decision to employ more junior people to deal with these cases, she said. 'They moved the first instance decision maker down a grade, from an experienced executive officer who understood the immigration rules, who saw someone face to face, who spoke to them, to an administrative officer – largely agency staff at the time. They were given a bundle of application papers and a checklist, one of which includes asking for three proofs of residence for every year,' Moreton said. Agency staff tended to be less experienced and less well qualified, and to stay in the job for shorter periods.

Staff were almost never able to use discretion, which began to dehumanise the system, she said. 'That human interaction was removed and that had been a key part of making the decision more robust. These two things together combined to produce an environment where, if you didn't have the right bits of paper, nobody intervened and you were simply rejected.' Once applicants were rejected, their papers were made into an intelligence package and despatched to the Immigration Enforcement division, who would then go out to make arrests. Home Office staff surveys show that morale dropped massively from 2012 onwards, when the cuts to jobs began, and remains incredibly low, Moreton said.

The removal of the human contact meant it was no longer possible to have a five-minute conversation with an applicant and work out whether you felt their account was broadly plausible. Previously, Moreton said, the stories of undocumented people could be easily corroborated by asking a few questions about their childhood in

Britain. She would ask people, for example, if they remembered the Humphreys. Humphreys were invisible characters who featured in TV campaigns by the Milk Marketing Board in the early 1970s, with numerous advertisements in which a red-and-white drinking straw would silently emerge from the side of the screen to drain the glass of milk that one of a number of celebrities (*Carry On* star Sid James, or Rod Hull and his emu) was planning to drink. If the straw rang no bells, Moreton might ask about the 1976 drought and the wildfires that accompanied it, or the Queen's silver jubilee in 1977. 'A few questions and a little bit of a conversation will sort it out. People remember things from school, things on television, things that were very public,' she said. But the staffing cuts meant this was no longer possible. She sympathised with the difficulties people experienced. 'I can't prove that I was in the UK in 1973; nobody can because we didn't keep papers in that way back then.'

Moreton said she didn't know the details of the destruction of the registry slips at the Whitgift centre offices, but there had been similar decisions to get rid of old landing cards in the past. 'I think the question was: were we going to pay a fortune to digitise them or were we not? The record was incomplete anyway; a lot had been lost, some had been destroyed in a flood. The decision to destroy them rather than digitise them was a financial one.'

One Windrush victim trying to regularise his status, Franklin Azolukwam, was even told by the Home Office that they believed his papers had been lost in this flood in Croydon. Another set of files was lost in an accident in the Whitgift centre in the early 2000s. 'There was an environmental catastrophe. They were stored in a bunker which became filled with toxic gas and nobody was able to go in there. The entire contents were destroyed; we lost an awful lot then – passports, Home Office files, all sorts of stuff was there,' Moreton said. But she was uncertain how relevant the destruction of files was to the people whose cases I was researching. 'It's not that we had given them documents which we had then destroyed, it's that they had never had them because they had never needed them.'

The loss of the landing cards was one element of a bureaucratic nightmare. Many experienced Home Office workers realised that all the changes were proving disastrous. 'The removal of face-to-face meetings, and just the loss of operational experience . . . a lot of things came together to make a perfect storm,' Moreton said.

———

Martin Jones was not the only person with experience of working for the Home Office who was feeling uneasy about the unfolding scandal. I was called by several other staffers in early 2018 who were also angry. A Home Office employee who had worked in the Immigration and Citizenship Departments in Liverpool for decades called to vent his fury at the way the cases of long-term residents were being handled. He felt loyal to the institution where he had spent so much of his working life but was concerned that things had changed.

'The introduction of the hostile environment policy meant the mentality was: "I'm going to say no, unless you can prove me wrong," whereas before, we'd been a lot more lenient towards the Commonwealth immigrants. We had no problem about going after everyone else, but the Commonwealth immigrants had always been a different kettle of fish,' the official (who asked not to be named) said. 'That changed about five or six years ago with the hostile environment. Some of the immigration people welcomed it. There was a "Gotcha" attitude – some people enjoyed it; I didn't like that.'

The Liverpool ex-Home Office worker said there was a younger cohort of immigration employees who were more aggressive in their attitude to undocumented Windrush generation residents struggling to establish their right to remain in the UK. 'People who were coming into the department were new and didn't have the background knowledge about immigration in the 1960s that I had,' he said. 'I was saying to them: "Look, they're more British than you! How can you, a twenty-seven-year-old fellow, refuse a fifty-four-year-old fellow, and say he's not entitled to remain in a country he's lived in for fifty-one years?" It is madness.

'There were some people who enjoyed saying: "I've caught you, you are illegal." But they weren't illegal at all. The Jamaicans and Trinidadians – these are Commonwealth people, who were British subjects or citizens of the UK and colonies, before their countries became independent.'

He was 'shocked and ashamed' to read about cases of Windrush generation residents, who had been here for over half a century, being detained. 'I'm astounded by it all,' he said.

'How are you expecting them to have four documents for every year that they've been here? It's pathetic. Particularly because we have been trusting them all these years – they were the same as us, only a different colour. They've been done a huge disservice.'

Previously staff had been allowed to apply reasonable discretion towards applicants in this group. 'Some had come on their parents' passport. Some of them came on their own passports – most of them didn't still have them, of course they didn't, they've been here for forty years,' he said. 'So the policy in the Citizenship Department was: if they say they have been here for that long, OK, provided they pass the character checks and they're not mass murderers, then in they come, give them British citizenship.' The policy had been 'to accept that people were telling the truth because there was no reason to doubt them', he said. If people did have their passports then staff loved looking at the old documents, passing them around the office for everyone to appreciate these curious period pieces, with outdated hairstyles and old-fashioned handwriting.

There was a cultural difference between people who worked in immigration, where there was a more aggressive enforcement approach, and people who were employed by the Nationality and Citizenship Department to help people with their naturalisation. 'The reality was that a lot of the staff that were dealing with these cases – they had no experience, no background in this area, the way we did. The hostile environment wasn't really intended for the Windrush people . . . I think people were quite quick to pull the trigger – because there were targets. The Immigration people were a different breed to us in the Nationality and Citizenship Department. Our motto was: "How can we help?" In Immigration, theirs was: "Prove it,"' he said. 'I would always say: "Just remember these are people's lives, these are not pieces of paper you're dealing with." I always got the impression that they had a rather jaundiced view on life – the more recent intake . . .'

Another retired immigration employee who had spent decades working in Lunar House was also concerned by worsening Home Office attitudes towards people seeking to regularise their status. 'In my day, working in immigration, we very much had the individual's situation in our minds. We did not work from crib sheets or take a this-is-what-the-rules-say approach – you looked at each person's case sympathetically and with discretion. I don't think that happens nowadays,' she said. She agreed that there was increasingly a desire to catch people out rather than to help them.

'I am also concerned that European Union citizens could find themselves in exactly this situation after Brexit because there will be no end of people who have been here years and won't have any documentation either.'

———

I spent some time standing on the windy Croydon pavement looking for the basement of the Whitgift centre's C block, peering down a concrete ramp towards a small door in a wall with no windows, just air vents; I don't know that this was the right entrance, but the rest of the abandoned building was inaccessible. I had a lot of unanswered questions about precisely what the registry slips looked like, how they were sorted, how large the archive was. The Home Office press office refused a request for a briefing on what had happened, with customary good humour: 'Unfortunately we will have to decline your request, but thanks for getting in touch.'

But increasingly it was clear that the document destruction was just one complicating factor in a Home Office landscape where staffing cuts had made decision-making less nuanced and where pressure from ministers to reduce net migration figures meant that employees were increasingly inclined to disbelieve applicants.

In a damning assessment of the Home Office's record during this period, the Joint Council for the Welfare of Immigrants identified 'extremely poor decision making by Home Office staff who are underpaid, undertrained and under cultural and formal pressure to refuse applications (currently over 50% of appeals against Home Office decisions are successful)'. Immigration lawyer Colin Yeo said the Home Office was 'afflicted by an aggressively defensive culture that has been likened to the famous Millwall chant of "No one likes us, we don't care."' This defensiveness meant civil servants and ministers were impervious to legitimate criticism. In these circumstances, individuals fighting to prove that they were right and the Home Office was wrong barely stood a chance.

FRIGHTENING PEOPLE TO LEAVE

Another potent and low-cost tool in the Home Office's arsenal was fear. The government developed a package of measures that they hoped would scare anyone with uncertain immigration status into leaving the UK.

To help with the task, they signed a deal worth up to £40 million with the huge private outsourcing company Capita, contracting the firm to track down around 174,000 people who were on a Home Office database of suspected illegal immigrants. Capita was to bombard individuals with an alarming combination of phone calls, letters and, most controversially, text messages, encouraging them to leave the country. The contract was drawn up according to a payment by results model. 'Capita will be paid for the number of people they make contact with [who then] leave,' the head of the UK Border Agency, Rob Whiteman, said. 'If nobody leaves, nobody will get paid.' The company had agreed an extra bonus payment with the government, so that it would receive a further 12.5 per cent if the total number of removals exceeded a set target by 10 per cent; the design of the contract made it financially rewarding for the organisation to push people out of the country.

Gladstone Ewart Augustus Wilson received an unexpected text message in 2014 informing him that the government suspected him of being in the UK illegally. The text was abrupt: 'Message from the Home Office. Our records show that you may not have leave to remain in the UK. Please contact us to discuss your case.' He was puzzled by the text; he had been living in the UK for forty-six years, since arriving from Jamaica at the age of twelve. 'It didn't make sense,' he told me when we met.

Some time later he received another, equally brief but much more alarming text message: 'Message from the UK Border Agency. You are required to leave the UK as you no longer have right to remain.'

He didn't know that these texts had already been sent by Capita to over sixty thousand people. Somehow Gladstone had been added to the list of people the government believed to be here illegally – known as its 'migration refusal pool'. He was targeted with a flurry of messages designed to eject him from the UK – despite the fact that his family had brought him to the country entirely legally as a child, and despite the fact that he had every right to continue to live here. 'I got very panicky. It made me feel like a criminal.'

Hundreds of messages ended up being sent to people who were in the UK legitimately. One of them was sent to Suresh Grover, a prominent race equalities campaigner who had been in the country legally since 1966; he was horrified, but when he called Capita to complain he struggled to get the call centre operative to understand that a mistake had been made. Another was sent to British citizen Bobby Chan, an accredited immigration adviser at a central London law centre.

The complete absence of any forensic precision in the targeting of the messages was worrying, but there was also something about the relaxed, informal style of text messaging that felt tonally inappropriate, at odds with the seriousness expected of an official government notification requiring you to leave the country.

Labour's immigration spokesperson, David Hanson, said the messages would 'rightly cause distress and offence to British citizens, many of whom have done much to contribute to our society. It is simply wrong for this sort of message to be sent by text and to be so poorly targeted.' He criticised the government for 'using taxpayers' hard-earned money to offend and alienate its own citizens'. Alison Harvey, General Secretary of the Immigration Law Practitioners' Association, said: 'In theory, this is a group of people

1. Passengers disembarking from SS *Empire Windrush* at Tilbury docks on 22 June 1948. The arrival of around 500 passengers from the Caribbean on this ship has come to symbolise the start of the post-war wave of migration.

2. Alford Gardner served in the RAF as a ground engineer in England during the Second World War. He borrowed money from his father to buy a ticket on *Windrush* so he could return to Britain permanently in 1948.

3. Alford, now ninety-three, was dismayed to witness the unfolding of the Windrush scandal. 'It is a disgrace. To think of the hard work we put in to get things as they are in England today . . . I never thought such things would happen. It's definitely racism.'

4. (LEFT) Hubert Howard arrived in Britain from Jamaica on his mother's British passport, aged three in 1960, two years before Jamaica became independent. He has no memory of Jamaica.

5. (RIGHT) A stamp in the passport shows they were given indefinite leave to remain on arrival.

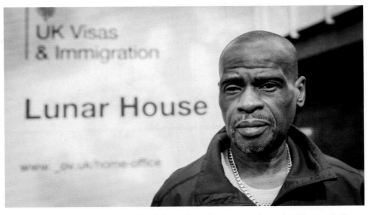

6. Hubert, sixty-one, was sacked from his job in 2012 when the Home Office classified him as an illegal immigrant. He was unable to travel to visit his mother when she was dying. 'It has completely ruined my life.'
He is still fighting to get British citizenship.

7. Paulette Wilson, sixty-two, with her daughter Natalie Barnes.
Paulette came to Britain in 1968, when she was ten or eleven. She worked as
a cook for decades, spending some time as a canteen worker in the House of
Commons, serving MPs. Half a century later she was told she was an illegal
immigrant, arrested and sent to an immigration detention centre.
She only narrowly escaped deportation.

8. Anthony Bryan, sixty-one, arrived from Jamaica in 1965, aged eight.
He went to school in London, worked and paid taxes here for decades, before
being told in 2015 he had no right to be in the UK and would be sent back to
a country he had not visited in over fifty years. He attempted repeatedly to
explain to Home Office staff that a mistake had been made, but no one
would listen. He spent five weeks in detention.

9. Renford McIntyre, sixty-four, lost his job as a driver for the NHS when the Home Office wrongly branded him an immigration offender. He was told he was not allowed to work and not eligible for benefits. He became homeless and had to sleep in an office in an industrial unit. He had lived in Britain for almost fifty years, having arrived in 1968. He remains heavily in debt and has received no apology from the government.

10. In November 2017, car mechanic Sylvester Marshall, sixty-three, was told that unless he could produce a British passport he would be charged £54,000 for the radiotherapy treatment he was due to start for prostate cancer. He was unable to pay, so did not receive the treatment he needed. He had arrived in the UK legally, as a teenager in 1973.

11. Vernon Vanriel, sixty-four, was stranded homeless in Jamaica for thirteen years, unable to return to his family in London. For a while he lived in an abandoned roadside grocery shack. A former professional boxer, he had lived in Britain for forty-three years since the age of six.

12. Joycelyn John, fifty-nine, arrived from Grenada in 1963. She worked as a chamber maid at the Ritz and as a receptionist for the Metropolitan Police, but fifty years after coming to Britain she was told she was an illegal immigrant. Frightened of being arrested and deported, she was pressurised into returning 'voluntarily' to Grenada, the country she had left when she was three.

13. Prime minister Theresa May gives a half-apology, having belatedly scheduled a meeting with Caribbean leaders on the second day of the Commonwealth Heads of Government Summit, 17 April 2018. She said she was 'sorry for any anxiety that has been caused'.

business → *G2*

Tuesday
17 April 2018
Issue № 53,385
theguardian.com
£2.00

The Guardian

May defends joining Syria strikes before parliament had its say

Pippa Crerar
Jessica Elgot

Rudd tells MPs: we were wrong over Windrush citizens

Theresa May has said that waiting for the UN to authorise military action in future would effectively give Russia a veto on British foreign policy as she defended her decision to join international air strikes against the Syrian regime.

The prime minister accused Moscow of preventing inspectors from reaching the site of the chemical weapons attack on Douma and suggested that Bashar al-Assad's forces, backed by the Russians, were attempting to destroy evidence of the attack.

She faced down her critics in a heated debate in the Commons in

14. *Guardian* editors put the Windrush issue on the front page every day for two weeks from 16 April 2018, ensuring that the voices of those affected were finally heard.

Home Office

2 Marsham Street, London SW1P 4DF
www.homeoffice.gov.uk

Dear Prime Minister,   April 29, 2018

It is with great regret that I am resigning as Home Secretary. I feel it is necessary to do so because I inadvertently misled the Home Affairs Select Committee over targets for removal of illegal immigrants during their questions on Windrush.

Since appearing before the Select Committee, I have reviewed the advice I was given on this issue and become aware of information provided to my office which makes mention of targets. I should have been aware of this, and I take full responsibility for the fact that I was not.

The Windrush scandal has rightly shone a light on an important issue for our country. As so often, the instincts of the British people are right. They want people who have a right to live here to be treated fairly and humanely, which has sometimes not been the case. But they also want the Government to remove those who don't have the right to be here. I had hoped in coming months to devise a policy that would allow the Government to meet both these vital objectives – including bringing forward urgent legislation to ensure the rights of the Windrush generation are protected. The task force is working well, the residence cards are being issued well within the two weeks promised, and the design of the compensation scheme is making good progress.

The Home Office is one of the great offices of state and its job is to keep people safe. It comes with the responsibility to fight terrorism, support and challenge the police and protect people against abuse, as well as manage migration.

It has been a great privilege to serve as your Home Secretary. I have seen first-hand the second to none commitment and bravery of our police, fire and intelligence services, they truly are the best in the world and we should rightly be extremely proud of them.

I have been particularly pleased that we were able to set up the first Global Internet Forum for Counter Terrorism which has led the way with encouraging social media sites to go further and faster in taking down radicalising and terrorist material, which plays such a dangerous part in increasing extremism.

15. Two weeks after the scandal erupts, the Home Secretary
Amber Rudd decides to resign.

16. Sarah O'Connor, Anthony Bryan, Paulette Wilson, Sylvester Marshall and Elwaldo Romeo photographed outside the House of Commons on 1 May 2018, delighted that their stories have pushed the new Home Secretary to promise compensation and reform of the Home Office.

17. Sarah O'Connor, fifty-seven, and her daughter Stephanie O'Connor at Sarah's British citizenship ceremony in August 2018. Sarah had been in the UK since arriving from Jamaica aged six in 1967. She was told she was an illegal immigrant in 2016 and was consequently unable to work. She died a month after this photograph was taken.

who records show have no right to be in the UK and should leave. In practice, I have seen British citizens getting these messages, I have seen people who have invested £1 million in the UK getting these messages, I have seen nurses getting these messages.'

But Downing Street put out a statement to stress that David Cameron personally supported the text campaign. The text messages were part of the strategy of getting people to self-deport – cheaply, quietly and without the messy, expensive and often legally problematic involvement of teams of immigration officers. 'The point of the texting, which the prime minister does agree with, is to get in touch with people who may be here illegally and to say to them . . . that they need to be considering going home voluntarily,' the Downing Street spokesperson said.

In turn, a Capita spokeswoman responded defensively to the suggestion of inaccuracies, when reports began to emerge in 2013, arguing that the company could not in fairness be blamed for any mistakes, because it had been given out-of-date Home Office records to work with.

Fans of the government's enthusiasm for outsourcing core tasks to private companies argue that the private sector is able to bring a lean efficiency to work that the public sector has struggled with. Having spent years writing for the *Guardian* about outsourcing failures (in disability testing, prison maintenance and probation services), I felt the Capita debacle was a very familiar story of the pitfalls of subcontracting key public services to huge independent companies that lack the necessary expertise and are motivated primarily by turning a profit. Capita's minimal success in rounding up illegal immigrants suggests that the private sector's involvement was ultimately neither efficient nor cost-effective.

A year after Capita began its work the 'migration refusal pool' (which the company had been contracted to reduce) totalled 173,562, just a few hundred less than when the programme began, when it had stood at 174,057. Of the 120,000 people whose contact details were sent to Capita, fewer than 1 per cent had left the country as a result of their intervention.[1]

In 2013 and 2014, the Refugee and Migrant Centre in Wolverhampton started to be approached by dozens of older West Indians (Gladstone Wilson among them) who were getting texts, phone calls and letters from Capita, informing them that they should leave the country. Case workers made a point of calling Capita and the Home Office to tell them that mistakes were being made repeatedly with the targeting of these messages. Arten Llazari, the charity's CEO, who has been working to support people with immigration difficulties for over twenty years, was particularly enraged by the Capita texting campaign and the 'scattergun' nature of the work.

'The Capita 2012 contract effectively outsourced part of the creation of the hostile environment to the private sector. In the process many vulnerable citizens mostly of Caribbean descent were harassed and repeatedly threatened with deportation,' he told me. 'Thousands of Windrush people were wrongly included in the database Capita was given by the Home Office. The Home Office knew from at least 2013 that legal residents were being harassed.'

The RMC's warnings to the government were echoed by charities across the country. Immigration adviser Sue Lukes said councils in London were seeing a number of cases a year, and would have reported the problem to the Home Office. Internal Home Office guidance in 2014 indicated that there was an awareness both of the problem and of the potential for it to cause embarrassment to the department. Staff were told: 'It is important you treat these cases in a careful and sensitive manner. You must give applicants every opportunity to send in evidence. This is because there is a risk of adverse publicity if these cases are mishandled.'

Gladstone isn't sure what caused his name to end up on the database, but he wonders if it was the result of applying for a

British passport in 2014 when he wanted to travel to Jamaica to visit his mother when she was ill. The application process proved to be more complicated than he had expected, and his mother died before he was able to visit her. Later, he hoped at least to be able to travel for her funeral, but the information he sent in for the passport application appears to have been forwarded to the Immigration Enforcement department, resulting in his name being put on Capita's illegal migrants list. He began to get Capita texts and shortly after that he was stopped from working as a security guard because his employers had received notification that he was not eligible for employment; his security guard accreditation, which he had taken several tests to acquire, was revoked. He had to start making regular visits to a Home Office reporting centre and found the whole process extremely upsetting. 'They told me if I didn't report I'd get a £5,000 fine or six months in prison,' he said.

'The main pain came when I couldn't go to my mum's funeral.' He said the process had been 'like going to hell and back'. 'Every night I grieve over this. I can't forget.' He felt frustrated that neither Capita nor the Home Office took the time to look at his National Insurance records, which would have instantly shown that he had been in the UK for the past four decades. 'It would have been simple for them to check.'

Capita also sent warnings to Anthony Bryan, assisting the Home Office in its efforts to get him to leave the country. In December 2015, Anthony received a letter from Capita Business Services, on behalf of the Home Office, that began 'Dear Anthony Roy Bryan' before jumping immediately into threatening capitals: 'THERE ARE ONLY A VERY SMALL MINORITY OF PEOPLE LIVING IN THE UNITED KINGDOM ILLEGALLY.'The letter told him that his right to remain in the UK had expired. 'This means that the Home Office intends to remove you from the United Kingdom.' It concluded with an enticing plea: 'Anthony

Roy Bryan there is one simple action that you can take today that might avoid you being forcibly removed and that is to contact our departures team today.'

Anthony decided to ignore the suggestion.

Clearly the Capita contract was unsuccessful if the aim was to identify illegal immigrants and encourage them to leave, since so few departures were triggered by their work. But the Home Office may nevertheless have seen the constant harassment of those with an uncertain immigration status as a constructive step towards the goal of creating a hostile environment.

———

A package of other measures was introduced, designed to scare people into leaving. In the summer of 2013, officials launched the peculiarly named Operation Vaken, which saw vans driving around six London boroughs with high levels of immigration, carrying billboards that warned: 'Go Home or Face Arrest'. They were decorated with pictures of handcuffs and a note of the number of recent immigration arrests locally ('106 arrests in your area'). A line at the bottom of the poster adopted a softer tone: 'We can help you to return home voluntarily without fear of arrest or detention.'

The hope was that the Home Office could get people to self-deport by constantly making them nervous about their immigration status, frightening them into submission.

A YouGov poll showed that 47 per cent of the public approved of the 'Go Home' vans. Around the same time, Home Office vehicles began to be marked clearly with the words 'Immigration Enforcement', to alert people to the hovering presence of border guards, monitoring their movements.

The associations of the 'Go Home' slogan – echoing of decades of racist abuse – caused widespread unease. The Labour MP Diane

Abbott, whose constituency in North London was one of the target areas, said: 'It is not so much dog-whistle politics as an entire brass band. It is akin to scrawling "Paki go home" on the side of buildings.'[2] Simon Woolley, a leading campaigner for race equality, who had been advising Theresa May in the Home Office on police stop and search policy, was horrified. 'The pain of being told "Go back home on the banana boat" has never gone away, so to see a government department using that language was unbelievable. It fed into a narrative that says black people will never belong in this country.'

It was never clear who had decided on the menacing and weirdly Germanic-sounding title of the operation, and perhaps it was nothing more than an odd name. The Home Office dismissed the suggestion that there was anything remarkable in it, commenting only that operations are named in alphabetical order, and that *vaken* means 'awake' in Swedish.

The Home Office said the 'Go Home' vans pilot was about giving illegal immigrants 'the opportunity to leave the country voluntarily and with dignity, rather than be arrested, detained and removed. Voluntary returns are the most cost-effective way of removing illegal immigrants and save the taxpayer money.' The scheme ran for just a month during the summer parliamentary recess, and its success was limited. A Home Office report found later that only eleven people had left the country as a direct result of the advertisements. The official evaluation also revealed that 1,561 text messages were sent to the hotline which offered to help illegal migrants return to their home countries, but 1,034 of these were hoaxes, which took seventeen hours of staff time to handle.[3]

Former adviser Nick Timothy later tried to argue that the vans had been opposed by Theresa May and then disinterred and approved when she was away on a walking holiday in Switzerland. 'Theresa May was criticised for the notorious "go home or face arrest" vans that were deployed in 2013. In fact, she blocked the proposal, but it was revived and approved in a communications plan while she was on holiday,' he wrote. 'She killed the scheme off later that year, but by then the damage had been done.' But others who worked on the project insisted that May had been informed of the intention to pilot the policy and had viewed and commented on the wording on vans, requesting that the language be toughened up so that voters were not left with the impression that taxpayers' money was being used to pay for illegal immigrants to be returned home.[4]

Later when the vans were widely criticised, May distanced herself from them. 'I think they were too blunt an instrument,' she said.

But the branded Immigration Enforcement vans stayed, with their yellow fluorescent stripes and their black-and-white checks, a sinister presence, circling around areas of high migration. Lucy Moreton, General Secretary of the Immigration Service Union, said the decision to paint the vehicles was made at a time when it was becoming clear that the government was failing on its commitment to bring down net migration. 'There was a recognition that we couldn't do anything about immigration, so if we couldn't do anything about it, all we could do was to convince the voting public that we are doing something. So we painted all the vans,' she said. Workers hated the new vehicles because they were frequently vandalised, their windows smashed and tyres slashed by anti-deportation campaigners. 'The cost to repair these stupid vehicles!' she said. 'People are constantly having to abandon them and go and pick them up later because they are not drivable.' But they were kept in service.

———

Some people were so petrified by Home Office threats to detain and remove them that they did eventually opt to leave under a voluntary scheme (although it feels wrong to describe their departure as voluntary in any meaningful sense of the word).

Joycelyn John's experience is one of the most disturbing cases to emerge from the scandal. She arrived in London in 1963 at the age of four with her mother, travelling on a Grenadian passport as a British subject. She went to primary and secondary school in Hammersmith, then began working in hotels in London, for a while at the Ritz, and later at the Hilton. Around 2009 she lost her Grenadian passport, which contained the crucial stamp giving her indefinite leave to remain. She had trouble getting a new passport because her mother (who was unmarried when Joycelyn was born) got married when Joycelyn was eight, and changed her daughter's surname from Mitchell to John. She never registered the change, however, so there was a discrepancy between Joycelyn's birth certificate and the name she used all her adult life.

She spent several years attempting to sort out her papers, without success, and by 2014 she had been classified as someone who was living in Britain illegally. She lost her job and was unable to find new work because she had no papers. She could no longer afford her rent; for a while she was living in a homeless hostel, but lost her bed there because the government does not fund hostel places for people classified as illegal immigrants. She spent two years staying with relatives, sleeping on sofas or on the floor.

During that time, she managed to gather seventy-five pages of evidence proving she had spent a lifetime in the UK – bank statements, dentist's records, medical files, National Insurance and tax records, letters from her primary school, from friends and family – but, inexplicably, this was not enough to satisfy immigration staff.

Every letter Joycelyn received from the Home Office warned her that she was liable to be detained and deported to Grenada, a country she had left more than fifty years earlier. She began to feel nervous about opening the door in case immigration officers were outside, waiting to put handcuffs on her and drive her away. 'I was very frightened,' she told me. An adviser at a migrant support charity in Hackney had suggested that the easiest way to extract herself from the difficulties would be to apply for a ten-year visa, allowing her to stay in her own country. She found it a degrading requirement, since she considered Britain her home, but was ready to comply until she realised the process would cost her more than £800. With no job and no savings, she was unable to pay.

A Home Office leaflet encouraging people to opt for a voluntary departure, illustrated with cheerful, brightly coloured aeroplanes, and published around the same time as the 'Go Home' vans were launched, said: 'We know that many people living in the UK illegally want to go home, but feel scared of approaching the Home Office directly. They may fear being arrested and detained. For those returning voluntarily, there are these key benefits: they avoid being arrested and having to live in detention until a travel document can be obtained; they can leave the UK in a more dignified manner than if their removal is enforced.'

This appeal to the desire for a dignified departure was a shrewd tactic on the part of the Home Office. The idea of being forcibly taken away by guards terrified Joycelyn. 'There's such stigma . . . I didn't want to be taken off the plane in handcuffs.' She was getting deeper and deeper into debt, borrowing money from a younger brother, until eventually she concluded it was no longer fair to continue relying on him. When the hostile environment is working well, it exhausts people into submission. It piles up humiliations and stress and fear until people give up resisting.

In November 2016, she finally decided that a so-called voluntary departure would be easier than trying to survive inside the ever-tightening embrace of Home Office hostility. Officials booked her on a flight on Christmas Day; when she asked if she could spend a last Christmas with her brother and five sisters, staff rebooked her on to a flight on Boxing Day.

She was so desperate, she felt this was the best option. 'I felt ground down. I lost the will to go on fighting,' she told me. By that point, she estimated she must have attempted around a dozen times to explain to Home Office staff – over the phone, in person, in writing – that they had made a mistake, but no one was prepared to listen to her.

'I don't think they looked at the letters I wrote. I think they had a quota to fill, they needed to deport people. Nobody was willing to help.'

She found it hard to understand why the Home Office was prepared to pay for her flight to Grenada, but not to waive the application fee to regularise her status. It made her wonder if staff were working towards a removal target. 'The flight would have been much more expensive than waiving the fee.'

A final Home Office letter told her: 'You are a person who is liable to be detained . . . You must report with your baggage to Gatwick South Virgin Atlantic Airways check-in desk on 27 December.' The letter resorted to the favoured Home Office technique of scaring people with capitals, reminding her that in her last few weeks in Britain: 'YOU MAY NOT ENTER EMPLOY-MENT, PAID OR UNPAID, OR ENGAGE IN ANY BUSI-NESS OR PROFESSION.' It also informed her that her baggage allowance, as she packed up after a lifetime in the UK, was 20 kilos, 'and you will be expected to pay for any excess'.

How did she pack for her journey back to a country she had left as a four-year-old, more than half a century earlier?

'I was on autopilot; I was feeling depressed, lonely and suicidal. I wasn't able to think straight; at times I was hysterical. I packed the morning I left, very last-minute; I'd been expecting a reprieve. I didn't take a lot – just jeans and a few T-shirts, a toothbrush, some Colgate, a towel – it didn't even fill the whole suitcase.' She had £60 to start a new life on the other side of the world, given to her by an ex-boyfriend. She had decided not to tell her sisters she was going that

Christmas, and only confided in her brother. 'I just didn't want any fuss.' She didn't expect she would ever be allowed to return to Britain.

She is clear that her decision to leave was motivated by fear. 'I was terrified.'

Jacqueline McKenzie, an immigration lawyer, believes the Home Office took advantage of Joycelyn's unprotesting personality. 'They probably saw her as someone who was being compliant. She never missed a reporting session.'

Life was very hard in Grenada. Officials seemed to think Joycelyn would have no problem settling down in an entirely unfamiliar environment, but she found everything strange and uncomfortable. She had to scrub her clothes by hand and struggled to cook with the local ingredients. 'It's just a completely different lifestyle. The culture is very different. It's hard to adjust.'

There was no help from the Home Office to get resettled in Grenada; she was given no money to start a new life and found getting work very difficult. 'You're very vulnerable if you're a foreigner. There's no support structure. No one wants to employ you. Once they hear an English accent, forget it. They're suspicious; they think you must be a criminal if you've been deported.'

Joycelyn recounted what had happened to her in a very matter-of-fact way. She only expressed her opinion about the Home Office's consistent refusal to listen to her when I asked her how she felt. Her analysis was succinct. 'The way I was treated was disgusting.'

In her position, I'm not sure I would have been able to restrict myself to such a pithy assessment. I still find it hard to accept that government officials blithely ignored Joycelyn's repeated attempts to explain that she had been wrongly labelled as an illegal immigrant, bombarding her with a series of threatening letters telling her she had no right to live in the UK, eventually making her feel she had no option but to leave her life, her family and the place that had been her home for fifty-three years and relocate to an unfamiliar country 4,300 miles away. The outcome – a fifty-seven-year-old Londoner, jettisoned on an island off the coast of Venezuela, friendless and without money, trying to make a new life for herself – is as absurd as it is tragic.

———

Trevor Johnson was called by Capita in the summer of 2015 and told that Immigration Enforcement staff would be visiting his home that night to take him to a detention centre ahead of deportation to Jamaica, since he had been classified as someone with no leave to be in the UK. He remembers the call clearly, because he felt the young Scottish woman who spoke to him was extremely rude. He told her firmly: 'I'm not going anywhere. I'm sorry, love. I've got a right to be here.' But he was very unsettled and when his daughters, sixteen-year-old Tia and thirteen-year-old Lauren, came home from school, he sat them down and told them he would probably be taken away and deported that night.

'The Home Office is trying to remove me,' he told them.

'Will we have to go with you?' the younger girl asked.

'No, you won't have to come,' Trevor told her. They were anxious about where they would go if he was taken away. Their mother had died ten years earlier and Trevor was bringing them up as a single parent. He tried to be reassuring. 'If anything happens, go to my sisters.'

He stayed up all that night, sitting on the sofa of his flat in South London, waiting as the warm summer evening stretched into darkness, listening for a knock at the door. Every so often he would get up and look out of the front window, peering through the trees on to the street below to see if there was an Immigration Enforcement van parked outside; then he would walk through to the kitchen to look out at the courtyard at the back of the block of flats, to check whether a van had come around the side entrance. 'I would get paranoid, looking out the window, thinking either they could come in from the front or the back. Every time I saw a police car I thought, bloody hell.' The knock never came, and Trevor remains unclear about why he had a call informing him deportation was imminent.

The following day he was able to get help from a local charity, the Lambeth Law Centre, to stave off further deportation attempts, but the Home Office decision to classify Trevor as an illegal immigrant had already nudged his family towards destitution. Trevor was keeping letters from bailiffs and debt collectors in a collection of plastic bags in the corridor. The previous winter he had been forced to beg on the streets of Brixton for money to heat the flat.

The issue of his uncertain immigration status had first emerged in 2001 when he had hoped to visit his father, who had become ill shortly after retiring to Jamaica. Trevor had lost the passport he arrived on, and was told by the Home Office that they had no record of him. He went to Lunar House to see if staff there could help him. 'They couldn't find me.'

At that stage, he was puzzled and irritated by the bureaucratic hiccough but not especially worried. 'I knew I was here legally. I was in no sweat about it.' But twelve years later, after the implementation of the hostile environment policies, this uncertainty over his immigration status worked its way into the official system. He went to the doctor for a routine visit to renew the certificates which confirmed that he was too ill to work (he was troubled by chronic arthritis and a liver problem). The doctor told him that the clinic had had a phone call from the Department for Work and Pensions telling him not to issue the documentation. 'Boom. My benefits were stopped.' He had been attending an adult literacy course (having struggled with reading since his move from Jamaica at the age of ten in 1971 disrupted his schooling). 'The next thing, I went to college and they said you can't come any more.'

For a while the child tax credit payments continued, which was vital because his two daughters were still at home. Then suddenly they stopped and life became very difficult. A friend suggested that he should go to the Jobcentre and ask for a voucher to take to the food bank. Trevor was relieved to see a familiar face at the counter when he arrived. 'It was a guy at the Jobcentre I used to get on well with. I told him, "I'm struggling, I've got two kids, I've heard you issue vouchers for the food bank." He said: "I'll go and check for you." Then he came back and said: "I'm so sorry. You're Jamaican."'

'I didn't argue,' he said. By that point he had lived in the UK for over forty years. 'They knew my situation; I was struggling to feed the two kids. They should have tried to help. I've been here all these years, and they're still calling me a Jamaican. I couldn't believe it.'

With his housing benefit stopped, rent arrears began to accrue. The landlord began possession proceedings and the family faced eviction. His sisters would help out when they could. 'When I had money I would jump on the tube and bring him £100. It wasn't a lot to feed two young people. We all knew what he was going through. We were all really, really upset,' his younger sister, Cardlin, said. 'We helped out when we could. It wasn't enough.'

It was hard, explaining to his daughters what was going on. He told them: 'Daddy might be getting chucked out of the country.' Officials kept phoning up, and the children would listen in silence, trying to work out what was going on. They knew money was tight. They weren't getting any pocket money and the food they were eating at home had changed. Normally Trevor enjoyed cooking well for his daughters, making dishes with meat and spices. Suddenly they were eating food donated via a local day centre (which didn't require an eligibility voucher), tins, pasta, non-perishable goods. Trevor was no longer able to buy his daughters any clothes.

'They didn't know the full extent. They were unhappy but somehow they didn't want to show it,' Trevor said. 'I went plenty of days without eating.'

In the winter there was no money to heat the flat, so Trevor went out to beg for coins to put in the gas and electric meter. He walked to the neighbouring but less familiar area of Camberwell because he didn't want anyone to recognise him. 'Some people were alright. Some people looked at me like they were scared. I'd get a couple of quid here, couple of quid there.' He made himself stay until he had £10. 'I knew my kids wouldn't be warm.'

He begged on the streets three or four times but he was upset by the way people stared at him as he stood with his hand stretched out. He remembered how his father had warned him about the prevailing climate of racism shortly after he arrived in Britain. 'He told me: "If a black man is walking along the street and a lady falls over, they will think you pushed her over. They will come and say you did it. So when you see an old lady coming down that side of the road, you ought to cross to the other side,"' he said. That advice had stayed with him; he hated sensing that people felt threatened by him as he begged on the street corner. 'I decided I couldn't do it any more after that. I don't want people to be scared of me,' he said. 'I'm a proud man. I didn't like doing it. When you need to do something to survive, you make yourself. I wouldn't do it again. It was very, very degrading.'

Trevor understood that the combined impact of the letters and phone calls and the suspension of financial support was designed to push him to leave; life became so difficult that, had it not been for his children, he might have considered a voluntary departure. As it was, he had no option but to struggle on.

They had two Christmases without money. Eighteen months without being allowed to work or receive benefits pushed him heavily into debt for the first time in his life. A local charity gave him a second-hand fridge. 'Four sisters who live on this estate, they gave me food for Christmas. They knew what was going on. There was a tree, but nothing under it. They bought my daughters

Christmas presents. They bought food for us. They understood I had no money for anything.'

Just as upsetting as the acute financial problems was the shattering of his sense of identity. Trevor no longer felt he knew who he was. 'I felt I was English. When this happened I didn't feel English any more.'

———

As part of its campaign to create a climate of fear, the government began encouraging members of the public to inform on people they suspected of being in the UK illegally. David Cameron announced the launch of a National Allegations Database, designed to make it easier for people to make tip-offs to the Home Office. With its sinister name, the service offered chilling echoes of a Soviet denunciation culture, but Cameron was cheerfully upbeat about its function, declaring in 2012 that he wanted 'everyone in the country' to help with the job of tracking illegal immigrants down and 'getting them out of the country'. He appealed for members of the public to help 'reclaim our borders', as if it was a positively patriotic act to report suspicions about undocumented migrants to authorities. In the course of just three months in 2012, the Home Office received 20,812 allegations about the possible presence of illegal immigrants – one every six minutes. The quality of information was questionable, however, and the vast majority of tip-offs did not result in any action being taken.

The campaign to get neighbours to report on neighbours, presumably based on ill-informed judgements about people who looked or sounded 'foreign', heightened the sense of unease felt by anyone who was aware that their immigration status was unclear.

On Valentine's Day 2013, the official Home Office Twitter account declared: 'Roses are red, violets are blue. If your marriage is a sham, we'll be on to you. #happyvalentinesday.' The tweet's gleeful spite and flippant tone offers an insight into the curiously unpleasant culture running through Theresa May's department.

As well as encouraging tip-offs from the public, the government exerted increased pressure on all departments to notify the Home Office about immigration offenders. Reports of possible overstayers from the Department for Work and Pensions to the Home Office jumped from 171 in 2014 to 1,377 in 2015; tip-offs from the police to the Home Office rose from 634 to 3,372 over the same period.

People whose papers were not in order were becoming too nervous to go to the doctor, now that healthcare data could be used for tracking immigration offenders. By 2017 medical staff were being asked to make 'reasonable inquiries' about patients' immigration status. It was evident that it was even becoming dangerous to seek help from the police. A woman who went to a London police station in 2017 to report that she had been raped was subsequently arrested, taken into custody and interrogated about her immigration status.[5] People without papers were being pushed out of normal society, beyond the protection of the state, forced into destitution and homelessness, excluded from employment and denied the support of the NHS and the police.

If the point of the hostile environment was to strip away all safety nets for people who were undocumented, the government had done so effectively. When Theresa May launched the hostile environment, she said: 'What we don't want is a situation where people think that they can come here and overstay because they're able to access everything they need.' She may have viewed it as a mark of success that the measures she and David Cameron introduced were beginning to make life intolerable for thousands of people without papers. The hitch, which officials had still not grasped, was that the majority of undocumented people in Britain were living here entirely legally.

HUNTING FOR PROOF

How many of us are able to lay our hands on our first passport? How many of us can supplement this with three or four pieces of official documentary evidence showing where we were living every year for the past four or five decades?

The hunt for documentary proof of a Britishness they never expected to be questioned brought many people close to breaking point. Strictly speaking, the whole exercise was unnecessary. People were being asked to prove that they qualified for a status that they already possessed. But everyone was confused and most were very vulnerable, having already lost their job or benefits or been denied medical treatment. If the state required proof that they had arrived in the UK before 1 January 1973 and that they had lived here continuously (with no more than a two-year break out of the country), then they had no option but to try to provide it.

The state requires applicants to be organised and to have stable, predictable existences. However, most people's lives are more complex and may be filled with unexpected anomalies that are hard to explain on a tick-box form. The state does not expect your house to burn down and destroy all your records, nor does it anticipate that your ex-partner might unceremoniously dispose of all your possessions, including the passport with your crucial leave-to-remain stamp. The state won't accept that the name on your birth certificate might not be the name you have called yourself all your life (because your mother wanted to forget about your unsupportive father who walked out weeks after your birth, and so she decided to change your surname without thinking there was any need to fill in a form to clarify this). Nor will it tolerate a bureaucratic error made by a careless registrar in another country six decades earlier, who put your father's name in the wrong box, rendering you fatherless. The state wants lives to be simple and well ordered.

The Home Office never seemed to have the capacity to understand that in order even to contemplate accessing records from half a century ago, you have to be a particular kind of person. If you're a homeowner, with a mortgage, someone who takes regular foreign holidays, if you're in stable employment, and your parents are still alive and have hung on to your early school reports – this would be a monumental headache, but it would just about be manageable. When you've been tipped into unemployment by the problem you are seeking to resolve, and you have limited resources or no money at all for bus fares, phone calls, photocopying, legal advice, it becomes much harder. For anyone who had experienced homelessness or serious illness, or family breakdown, it was usually hopeless.

One crucial line in the 1971 Immigration Act made it clear that it was up to the individual to prove they were British, rather than the Home Office's responsibility to prove they were not. 'When any question arises under this Act whether or not a person is a British citizen,' the Act reads, 'it shall lie on the person asserting it to prove that he is.'[1]

The detective work required to find the evidence was extensive and often whole extended families were swept in to help with the search. Everyone going through this process thought the simplest way to resolve the problem would be to get access to the Home Office immigration files recording their entry into the country. It was a source of considerable frustration that this information proved impossible to get hold of.

For all the documentless Windrush people, the search was an agonising process that stretched over months and often years, as they hunted through archives for bits of paper that would conclusively persuade the Home Office bureaucrats that they were telling the truth. All along the way they were disbelieved. The notion of being innocent until proven guilty does not apply in Home Office immigration cases. The Home Office rejections effectively meant: 'You're lying. You're guilty. You're illegal.'

———

Almost everyone caught up in the same search for evidence went through a similar journey from optimism to despair when it became obvious that the hunt for proof was fraught with unexpected complications.

When I met fifty-seven-year-old Sarah O'Connor at her home in Dagenham, East London, in early March 2017, she was feeling very bleak about her prospects of getting the necessary evidence, particularly at a time when the Home Office's restrictions meant she was descending rapidly into serious debt. She had been in Britain since she was six.

Sarah was so worried about being visited by either immigration officials or bailiffs that she was very nervous about opening the front door. The bailiffs had informed her that they would be coming to see which of her possessions they could sell off at auction as part payment for the debts she had run up since losing her job. She didn't think they were likely to find much of any value. 'There's a second-hand computer and a television my daughter gave me. That's it,' she said and laughed. She had already had to sell her car because she couldn't afford to get the MOT done. 'I don't know how I'm meant to survive.'

But she had a surprising ability to see the dark humour in the impossible situation she was facing, and made me laugh by highlighting the multiple absurdities and inconsistencies in the state's treatment of her. After she lost the job that she had been doing for sixteen years in a high street computer shop, she went to the Job-centre to claim unemployment benefits and was upset to be told that she wasn't eligible because she had no proof that she was British.

She had attended primary and secondary school here, held a driving licence, voted in general elections since she was eighteen, had been married for seventeen years to someone British and had four children here (all of whom have British passports), so she couldn't see what conceivable reason they had for doubting her eligibility.

'I've paid all my National Insurance so if anything like this happens I can get help – you've had no problem taking my tax and National Insurance,' she told them. 'You take my money but you won't help me out when things are bad. So do I get all the money back that I've paid all these years?' The Jobcentre official was silenced by her tirade. She laughed at the memory of how fierce she had managed to be.

'How am I meant to survive?' she asked him.

In the weeks that followed she spent hours on the computer researching how she could formally naturalise to officially become British. Aside from the shortage of paperwork that she needed to prove that she had been here for the correct period of time, she was also dismayed by the £1,200 fee required. 'I haven't got £1,200,' she said, horrified but still laughing. 'And it says I've got to take a test to prove I'm British. I'm sorry but the only language I speak is English.'

On the surface she was determined to see the ludicrous, funny side to her predicament, but she admitted she was having trouble sleeping and was beginning to feel unwell as a result of the stress. Her doctor had put her on antidepressants. 'It's wearing me down.' She tried contacting the National Archives for any record of her immigration details, only to receive an email from a member of staff there, informing her: 'Unfortunately I could find no entry for your name.'

She no longer had the paperwork from jobs she did in the 1970s, 80s and 90s, working as a greengrocer and for Ford in Dagenham as a cleaner. 'I don't have the pay slips; I keep receipts and paper slips for six years – then I throw them away. If I didn't the house would overflow with paperwork,' she said. 'It's so ridiculous. I see myself as British.'

She repeatedly rang the Home Office and asked them to find evidence of her arrival in the UK in 1967, or to release their files on her. Eventually an official sent a letter stating: 'I have searched our systems and can find no Home Office record for Ms O'Connor.'

I was getting increasingly frustrated during the regular conversations I had with the Home Office press office, who seemed oblivious to the mounting evidence that something was going badly wrong. I contacted them to ask about Sarah's case, and received an email saying that staff could find no sign that she had made an application for naturalisation. I emailed back to explain (again) that although she had contacted the Home Office to try to resolve her problems, she hadn't made the application to stay because she couldn't afford the fees. Although she had been offered new jobs, she had been prevented from taking them up because she had no passport; meanwhile she had been refused benefits. 'Her daughter is giving her money for food,' I wrote. I couldn't understand why no one was grasping the severity of the crisis that Sarah and others were experiencing.

I liked Sarah, and spoke to her frequently over the following weeks. She would call up and begin: 'It's only me, Sarah,' before describing some new complication with her ongoing efforts to sort out her situation, in a subversively funny way that would make me laugh and feel unhappy at the same time. Once she called to tell me that she had been practising taking the Life in the UK test online, and kept failing – despite having spent fifty years here. Mostly she wanted to talk about how the search for proof of her past was making her feel.

'Am I right in calling myself British or this country my country?' she asked.

———

Again and again those who were spending every moment they had searching for proof of their British past came up against unhelpful, obstructive Home Office doublespeak.

Staff sent letters informing people that new checks needed to be made on them, adding: 'Please note it is no longer possible to make an enquiry in person. Please telephone the number on this letter in the first instance if you need to contact us.' There was no telephone number on the letter.

Others got letters telling them they were liable to be detained and removed. When they tried to telephone the number which had been printed on the document they found it was never answered. Many were upset to see that the letters sent by UK Visas and Immigration came on paper with the slogan 'BUILDING A SAFE, JUST AND TOLERANT SOCIETY' printed at the bottom of every page. The slogan felt starkly at odds with the alarming, unjust and intolerant treatment they were receiving.

If you weren't instructed to call non-existent or non-functioning numbers, you might be invited to discuss your problems with your Home Office case worker, despite the fact that no one could tell you who that person was, or how you might contact them. The Home Office also told people to contact the Citizens Advice Bureau, but the charity was not familiar with this issue, and was ill equipped to offer immigration advice.

At first I had been puzzled and confused by what was happening. Now I just felt angry.

———

I was contacting the Home Office press office every few days with a new case. Sometimes I sensed an edge of annoyance; at one point I was so unsettled by the hostility seeping through the earpiece that I complained that I felt like I was being told off by the team whenever I rang up. There was a pause, and then the official said: 'Well. That's certainly not our intention.'

Repeatedly when I contacted the Home Office to highlight cases of people who had lost their jobs or homes, or who were unable to get passports to visit dying parents, officials seemed to indicate that the fault lay with the individual for failing to provide enough evidence of their right to be here. There was a reluctance to question whether the department's own policies might be causing the difficulties.

I was struck by how quickly cases were getting resolved after I sent the individual's details through to the Home Office. Sometimes a person I had interviewed would get a package with a long-awaited biometric card (conferring a temporary right to remain) couriered to their home within twenty-four hours of the issue being raised. Officials clearly wanted to tidy up cases and make them go away at the first hint of bad publicity.

It was great to feel that highlighting individuals' plights had a positive impact, but clearly this was a terrible way to go about resolving a systemic problem. It just wasn't possible to write about all the cases that were emerging. Comprehensive government action was required, but there was no indication that ministers were worried by what was happening.

The Home Office came up with the same official response to every case I raised. The formulation was so enraging that it set my teeth on edge every time I saw it emailed through as part of a standardised reply to my queries. 'We value the contribution made by Commonwealth citizens who have made a life in the UK,' the Home Office declared in a statement about the refusal to give Sylvester Marshall free NHS radiotherapy as prescribed for his prostate cancer. 'We value the contribution made by Commonwealth citizens who have made a life in the UK,' an official statement began, in answer to my questions about why Michael Braithwaite had been sacked from his job as a special needs teaching assistant. Why was Sarah O'Connor facing bankruptcy, unable to work or claim benefits because no one believed she had a right to be here, despite fifty years in Britain? 'We value the contribution made by Commonwealth citizens who have made a life in the UK.'

It was absurd. The government clearly did not value their contribution in the least, otherwise they would have hurried to fix the problem years earlier. But this was the narrative that officials desperately wanted to project: there had been a regrettable administrative error, a blip. The line was intended to reassure and comfort people who were beginning to look at the Home Office's actions with deep unease. The subtext was: Don't worry! We are good people at heart. Britain's institutions should on no account be seen as fundamentally racist or cruel – because Britain is a fair and good place that values the contribution of its Commonwealth citizens.

Sometimes the Home Office would also comment: 'We understand that these individuals may not have the relevant documentation to support their application, and so we work closely with applicants to consider alternative documentation to prove their ongoing residence.' This simply wasn't true. Everyone I had met was desperate for the Home Office to work closely with them to help them with their case; no one had been offered such support.

Usually the Home Office statements added that the individual concerned should 'take legal advice and submit the appropriate application with correct documentation so we can progress the case'. I felt they were effectively blaming those affected for having not filled a form in correctly. There still seemed to be very little understanding of why people might not have submitted appropriate papers – i.e. that it might be impossible for them to gather the required evidence, get legal advice and pay the application fee. I spent some time explaining to Home Office press officers that it was just not realistic to tell people to seek legal advice if they had been sacked from their job and denied benefits because they had been classified as illegal immigrants – because legal aid for immigration cases had been abolished, and they would have no money to seek advice privately. Equally it was not possible for someone pushed into near destitution by the department's policies to submit the appropriate documentation because the fee for submitting a naturalisation application stood at well over £1,000.

Very occasionally these explanations seemed to sink in – a press officer would agree that this did seem to be a difficult situation, and would promise to see if the fee could be waived – but I had no way of knowing if these concerns were being relayed to anyone more senior.

In a strange effort at damage limitation, the Home Office's Media blog (published daily online for the benefit of journalists, politicians and members of the department) reported that Sylvester Marshall's case had been taken up by Jeremy Corbyn in parliament, and added that Sylvester was 'delighted his case had been resolved'. I had to ring the Home Office, again, to point out that his case had not been resolved, and so it was just a lie to state that Sylvester was delighted about anything, and to ask them to correct their publication (which they agreed to do).

There was another, more important reason to be annoyed by the Home Office formulation: 'We value the contribution made by former Commonwealth citizens who have made a life in the UK.' The clear implication was that these people were good migrants, worthy of sympathy and support. It was true that most of the people I had interviewed had been hard-working taxpayers who had contributed greatly – but what if they had been less instantly appealing? What about people with more troubled lives who had been unable to contribute? The government seemed to be saying that they would like to help these eminently deserving people, but as for the rest – the unemployed, or the undeserving hordes of failed asylum seekers, irregular migrants, overstayers – they should face the heat of the hostile environment. Implicit in the catchphrase, which was repeated and repeated as the scandal grew, was an unspoken desire to divide immigrants into worthy and unworthy, good and bad, deserving and undeserving, which narrowed the scope of what was going wrong, and diminished the need for a comprehensive reversal of policy.

If these good migrants were the exception, it allowed the government to continue to treat everyone else – the 'bad' immigrants – as poorly as it pleased. Officials could go on talking as harshly as they liked about the bogus refugees, the scrounger migrants and criminal asylum seekers who should be granted no sympathy, persisting with the rhetoric of a tough environment for illegal immigrants. This approach meant no questions were asked about the general fairness of the policies, and it meant no one was looking closely at the wider group of people wrongly caught up by hostile environment policies, large numbers of whom were equally deserving of public sympathy. It suggested that these people were exceptional, and distracted attention from the bigger picture of many other groups wrongly classified as illegal immigrants by poor Home Office decisions and bureaucratic delays.

Politicians, when they began to take an interest, repeatedly characterised the Windrush group as intensely loyal to the UK. 'There are few more patriotic groups of British citizens than the generation from the West Indies that we are talking about,' Diane Abbott said. She recalled childhood visits to the homes of her parents' friends who had arrived from the Caribbean in the 1960s. 'It was never unusual to find a big picture of the queen in their living room. These were people that loved their royal family, who were proud of being British. They were a generation with a real commitment to hard work . . . To be so loyal, to be so patriotic, to have such a work ethic and to be treated in the way they have been treated is a shame and a disgrace. It felt like the loyalty that they showed to this country was not being reciprocated.'

All of which was absolutely true, but it felt unhelpful to hive off these valued, patriotic contributors from the rest of the bigger mass of people who were suffering at the hands of the Home Office. What about the people who weren't patriotic? What about asylum seekers who weren't hanging pictures of the queen on their walls? Immigration adviser Sue Lukes cautioned against always focusing on the 'good and unimpeachable' because it made it 'hard to get support for the ordinary and sometimes difficult'.

———

As people continued searching for proof of their Britishness, it gradually became clear that the Home Office had shifted the goalposts. Britain's immigration legislation had profoundly changed since they arrived, without them noticing, pushing them across the invisible but crucial line that stands between legality and illegality.

If the introduction of the hostile environment policies from 2012 onwards had made life much tougher for Windrush victims, the roots of the problem go back decades earlier. To fully understand what had happened, they needed to have knowledge of complex immigration laws passed in 1948, 1962, 1968, 1971 and 1982, all of which had a bearing on their situation. Most politicians had only the haziest understanding of these changes, and only the most specialised immigration lawyer could explain their significance. It was entirely unrealistic to expect those affected by the changes in law to be knowledgeable about the shifting legal horizon, even though the combined effect of the various revisions would turn out to have a critical bearing on their own immigration status. Successive governments failed to explain the implications of the tightening regime.[2]

The legislation is so impenetrable and confusing that it's no surprise those affected didn't grasp the significance of the changes. Nor is it at all strange that, with the absence of free legal advice once the hostile environment kicked in, so many found themselves unable to extract themselves from a nightmarish position – one which was not caused by any mistake they had made, but simply by the retrospective changing of laws governing their immigration status, the rules constantly shifting around them so that people who had arrived here entirely legally found themselves branded as illegals.

The introduction of biometric cards for some foreign nationals in 2008 had made things still more complicated for people without proof of their immigration status, forcing those in a Windrush-type situation to redocument themselves – making them apply and pay for papers that proved a status which they already had.

All the while the costs of getting papers from the Home Office were rising. The Asylum and Immigration Act of 2004 allowed the department to start charging more than the administrative cost for immigration and nationality applications. The cost of sorting out your status was rapidly becoming unaffordable.

When the hostile environment policies were implemented and the immigration regime tightened, ministers simply forgot that their predecessors had allowed hundreds of thousands of people into Britain without ever registering them. Officials were incredibly negligent to be so hazy about the implications of the country's evolving immigration legislation.

————

All of these stories of lives wrecked by a government policy left *Guardian* readers horrified, but there was still nothing to suggest that Home Office ministers were concerned by the unfolding issue or were inclined to do anything other than instruct officials to fix each case when it appeared in the newspaper.

The Home Secretary, Amber Rudd, said later that her officials had reassured her that this was a problem that affected just a small number of people, and that she didn't need to worry about it. 'When I asked my experts about it, I got a very "We're fine; we're on it" type of reply,' she told me. In March Home Office staff told her that there was 'a group of people from the Caribbean that would need better assistance', but said nothing to suggest that the issue needed to be dealt with urgently.

There was still no real understanding within the Home Office of the magnitude of what was going wrong. Officials continued to try to sweep the issue under the carpet, until a *Guardian* front-page story finally transformed the scandal into an international crisis.

A POLITICAL EXPLOSION

Suddenly on 16 April 2018 the government decided that the way it had been treating undocumented Commonwealth people was 'terrible'. I had been contacting the Home Office for six months about this issue, and until now there had never been the slightest hint of such a feeling within the department. It seemed to me that the officials I was talking to mainly found my regular phone calls irritating. No one ever suggested that anyone at a senior level might be interested, and requests for comments from the ministers in charge were rejected. Yet Home Secretary Amber Rudd was unexpectedly overcome with concern for a group of people that she had hitherto never spoken about.

'Frankly, how they have been treated has been wrong – has been appalling – and I am sorry,' she told parliament. 'I would not want anyone who has made their life in the UK to feel unwelcome or to be in any doubt of their right to remain here.' Significantly, she criticised the ethos of the department she had headed for almost two years. 'I am concerned that the Home Office has become too concerned with policy and strategy and sometimes loses sight of the individual.'

This was a very surprising development.

What had happened to prompt such an abrupt shift? A number of things – but a sudden awakened sensitivity to the brutality of the government's own behaviour towards all these people was not one of them. I felt a burning rage at the shamelessness of it all.

The key trigger for this undignified U-turn was a really foolish miscalculation made by the prime minister's office, which caused the government profound embarrassment when we highlighted it on the front page of the *Guardian* on Monday 16 April. The government's handling of events is worth studying in detail as a textbook example of how not to respond to a crisis.

That week the leaders of fifty-two countries were arriving in London for the Commonwealth heads of government meeting. The Mall was decorated with the flags of all of the Commonwealth nations and caterers at Buckingham Palace were preparing for tea parties and state dinners. In normal times, this summit would have been regarded as a routine, inconsequential diplomatic event, heavy with ceremony and light on substance. But with Brexit looming, and as ties with European partners unravelled, the government was unusually determined that relationships with Commonwealth partners should be boosted, so the whole event took on a new significance. The occasion was seen as an important opportunity to shower with love the nations on whom Britain expected to be increasingly reliant once it left the European Union.

The week before the event, the Caribbean High Commissioners gathered to express in public their concern about the number of people whose lives were being ruined by the Home Office. They called on the British government to adopt a more compassionate approach to individuals who had arrived in the UK as children and never formally naturalised. 'I am dismayed that people who gave their all to Britain could be discarded so matter-of-factly,' Guy Hewitt, Barbados High Commissioner, said. 'Seventy years after Windrush, we are again facing a new wave of hostility. This is about people saying, as they said seventy years ago, "Go back home." It is not good enough for people who gave their lives to this country to be treated like this.'

The High Commissioners had assembled other influential voices to express fury at what was happening. The Reverend Dr Wilfred Wood, the Church of England's first black bishop, described the treatment as a 'betrayal of Commonwealth immigrants in Britain' and said that for them to 'find themselves hunted, uprooted and deported like common criminals, comes close to being a crime against humanity'. Andrea Levy, whose father came to Britain on the *Empire Windrush*, said: 'For Britain to treat its former colonial subjects in such a way is a violation of its historical responsibility. Beyond the individuals concerned, it sends a chill through entire communities. It suggests no one, not even your granny, is safe.'

The Home Office responded to the High Commissioners' press conference with a familiar statement: 'We value the contribution made by former Commonwealth citizens who have made a life in the UK.'

Devastatingly, Hewitt revealed that a formal request had been made by the twelve Caribbean nations to meet the prime minister to discuss what was happening, but their request was rejected. 'This will not be possible,' he was told by the prime minister's office at Number 10. The rebuff left the leaders of the Caribbean nations feeling snubbed and convinced that the British government had either failed to appreciate the scale and seriousness of what was happening to large numbers of Commonwealth-born people, or, worse, was aware but did not view it as a priority. It was difficult to see this dismissal as anything other than a clear sign that these countries were not considered worthy of the prime minister's attention.

Caribbean diplomats saw it as a very brutal reflection of the fact that the British government didn't care enough about these elderly, often marginalised people to bother scheduling time to discuss their problems. It smacked of racism.

I contacted the Downing Street press office on Sunday 15 April to see if they could explain the refusal. An official called back while I was cooking lunch, conceding that a request had been received from the Caribbean High Commissioners and confirming that a meeting had not been set up; there would be other opportunities for heads of delegations to meet the prime minister and discuss this 'important issue'.

She also said that the Minister for the Caribbean had met High Commissioners in March and told them that the Home Office would treat the issue as a 'priority' and would be having another discussion about it in June (in three months' time, which did not make it sound like anyone was treating it as a very high priority).

Turning down the meeting was a huge mistake by Downing Street, and one which is still hard to understand. The article highlighting this diplomatic snub went on the *Guardian*'s front page, and the political response was instant. Suddenly ministers who had previously been totally silent were falling over themselves to express profound sorrow about the sufferings of the undocumented Commonwealth people. The brazen speed of the official turnaround was distasteful to watch.

The Minister for Immigration, Caroline Nokes, who hadn't previously spoken about this issue, was on lunchtime television within hours. 'I want to send a message to the West Indian community. We invited you here. We wanted you to come to the UK and rebuild after the Second World War. We absolutely have a duty to make sure that those who haven't had their status regularised, and there may well be many of them, have the opportunity now,' she said. 'I am very conscious that we have made some mistakes, which we cannot continue to make, and I am determined that we won't because these people have contributed an enormous amount.'

Did she need to apologise, a BBC interviewer asked her. 'Oh, I think I've been very clear about how sorry I am about the whole situation,' she said, breezily, and not sounding, to my ears, amazingly sorry.

Very quickly afterwards, Home Secretary Amber Rudd was in parliament expressing her own regret at what had happened. The Home Office would establish a dedicated new team to help people to gather evidence of their right to be here, she announced; fees would be waived so that no one needed to pay for the new documentation they were expected to have.

A number of other significant things had combined to put pressure on the government and force this abrupt shift. The campaigner Patrick Vernon, whose parents emigrated from Jamaica in the 1950s, had made a critical connection between the scandal and the upcoming seventieth anniversary of the arrival of the *Empire Windrush* at Tilbury Docks. He had launched a parliamentary petition, which would trigger a parliamentary debate once a hundred thousand people signed online, calling for an immigration amnesty for those who had arrived as British subjects between 1948 and 1971. Vernon's petition created a potent brand for this group whom for months I had been struggling to describe as 'Caribbean-born, retirement-age, long-term British residents'. This clunky categorisation was extremely hard to put in a headline. Vernon succinctly classed them the 'Windrush generation', which immediately evoked the emotional response that people feel towards the pioneers of migration who arrived on that ship. Although it was a bit of a misnomer (since those affected were strictly speaking the children of the Windrush generation) that branding was incredibly important, making a complicated issue much easier to grasp. Within days, tens of thousands of people had signed the petition, revealing (as we had already realised from the responses of *Guardian* readers) that even if the government was disinclined to take this issue seriously, there was huge public concern about it.

Labour politicians had also stepped up their interventions. Tottenham MP David Lammy delivered a letter to the prime minister that Monday morning, describing the situation as 'immoral and inhumane' and urging the government to find an 'effective, humane, route' to resolve a problem which had caused 'undue stress, anxiety and suffering to many'. The letter carried the signatures of 140 MPs from all parties, gathered over the previous days by Lammy's parliamentary assistant, Jack McKenna. The cross-party signatures provided a clear indication that backbench MPs were more engaged and troubled by the issue than cabinet ministers.

The Caribbean High Commissioners were mobilising behind the scenes, increasingly incensed by what was happening. This was largely down to Guy Hewitt, a non-career diplomat who had been appointed High Commissioner for Barbados after working in business and development. His four-year tenure in London was coming to an end and his patience was wearing thin. He and his colleagues had raised the issue repeatedly at various levels with the Foreign Office, from 2013 onwards. In 2016 the issue of older Caribbean-born residents being wrongly categorised as illegal immigrants was raised formally by Caribbean Foreign Ministers with the then Foreign Secretary, Philip Hammond, during the bi-annual UK–Caribbean forum held that year in Freeport in the Bahamas; nothing happened. 'We kept trying to get the British government to take it seriously; we kept raising it with them in meetings,' Hewitt said. 'They didn't see this as a priority.'

Hewitt was irritated by the cautious approach of the other Caribbean diplomats. 'They tried to tell me how to deal with this kind of situation – writing letters, communicating formally, going through the normal channels, of conflict resolution, exchanging and sharing concerns.' He could see this was not working, and decided to adopt instead the principle of guerrilla diplomacy, jettisoning his profession's polite, measured techniques in favour of direct, combative activism.

'I can still see one of my colleagues . . . his look of absolute horror when I said to him, "I do not believe that we can use the normal channels to resolve this crisis,"' he told me.

He brought together leading race relations campaigner Lord Herman Ouseley, Omar Khan from the Runnymede Trust and

Satbir Singh from the Joint Council for the Welfare of Immigrants, along with David Lammy, and they drew up a timetable of events designed to force the issue on to the political agenda.

But when Downing Street rejected the request for a meeting with Theresa May and all the Caribbean heads of government to discuss the subject during the Commonwealth summit, Hewitt was furious, and went straight to the leading television and radio news shows to express his anger. The refusal reflected 'an implicit prejudice' within the British government, he said. He felt Britain was 'saying to people of my region: "You are no longer welcome on our shores."' He wanted the whole country to understand the enormity of the problem. 'I did not want them to have any sense that this was anything other than a catastrophe,' he said.

Hewitt's undiplomatic willingness to say what he actually thought was very refreshing. He was anxious that the wrongs done to Windrush people should not be forgotten. 'These people came here after the Second World War. They faced incredible abuse and racism but they stuck it out and made Britain the multicultural place it is now. They were conscientious workers, taxpayers, and then this happened. There was such shock and disbelief that a country they gave everything to should question their legitimacy.'

For years, the government had failed to respond to diplomats' warnings, but within minutes of appearing on breakfast television, Hewitt's phone began to 'ring off the hook' with approaches from government officials.

By midday on 16 April the prime minister decided that she needed, after all, to schedule a meeting with her Caribbean colleagues. Hewitt got word that 'the Prime Minister would be very pleased to meet Caribbean Heads or their representatives tomorrow at Downing Street from 11.30 for 30/40 minutes'.

After months of very little coverage, suddenly the BBC and other media outlets had started to report the problem. Perhaps most significantly, the *Daily Mail* had abruptly decided this was an issue that it felt angry about. That Saturday, 14 April, the paper had published a new interview with Sylvester Marshall, summarised (reprinting material from the *Guardian*) the problems suffered by Paulette, Hubert and Renford, and declared that it was launching a campaign.

The cumulative impact of the *Guardian*'s steady coverage over the previous six months had finally become impossible to ignore, but nothing alarms a Conservative government like the threat of a *Daily Mail* campaign, so this development will also have inched unresponsive ministers towards belated action.

On Monday 16 April the *Guardian* reprinted the photographs and stories of everyone interviewed to date – detained grandmothers, sacked special needs teachers, cancer patients denied treatment. The collected accounts provided undeniable evidence of profound and widespread human suffering and helped unleash political chaos.

There were three really significant moments during the urgent parliamentary question on Windrush that Monday. The first was Amber Rudd's startling announcement that this was something she was extremely concerned about. Second was her claim to be worried that 'the Home Office has become too concerned with policy and strategy and sometimes loses sight of the individual', refusing to admit that it was the hostile environment policy itself, not the implementation of it, that was causing problems.

Possibly she found herself in an awkward position; she couldn't criticise the policies introduced by her predecessor, who was now her boss, so she blamed the department instead. This approach was extremely badly received by government employees who were working to implement the hostile environment measures. Rudd seemed to be suggesting that this was all the result of over-zealous behaviour by Home Office workers, and an excessively punctilious implementation of policy. This betrayal of her staff would have fatally damaging consequences for her. 'These are her policies, the policies of her government,' one Home Office source told the *Guardian* later in the week. 'And she was trying to blame them on officials.'

But the most memorable moment came not from Rudd, but from Labour's David Lammy, whose angry accusation that the government had allowed itself to become infected with far-right ideology quickly went viral.

'The relationship between this country and the West Indies and the Caribbean is inextricable. The first British ships arrived in the Caribbean in 1623, and despite slavery and colonisation, twenty-five thousand Caribbeans served in the First and Second World Wars alongside British troops. When my parents and others of their generation arrived in this country under the British Nationality Act 1948, they arrived here as British citizens. It is inhumane and cruel for so many of that Windrush generation to have suffered for so long in this condition and for the Secretary of State to be making a statement on the issue only today,' Lammy said. He asked for details (which we still do not have) on the number of people denied pensions and healthcare and sacked from their jobs. He pinpointed Theresa May as the chief architect of the problems experienced by the Windrush generation.

'This is a day of national shame, and it has come about because of a "hostile environment" and a policy that was begun under [the] prime minister. Let us call it as it is: if you lay down with dogs, you get fleas, and that is what has happened with the far-right rhetoric in this country.'

———

Theresa May also did her best to appear contrite, apologising repeatedly that week, but it's worth dissecting the shifting and shifty nature of the statements because mostly they were not actually very apologetic in substance. It was hard to avoid the feeling that these apologies were primarily expressions of sorrow that the government had been caught out doing something so shabby rather than heartfelt pronouncements of genuine remorse.

A true apology would have said: 'I'm so sorry we have caused this terrible situation; we will do everything we can to make amends.' What we heard were half-apologies and apologies that just revealed irritation at being forced to address the subject at all. These were narrow, cautious indications of regret that seemed to be really saying: 'I'm sorry you feel cross about this,' or 'I'm so sorry that we are still talking about this,' or 'I'm sorry but I've already said I'm sorry on numerous occasions.'

What Theresa May was not apologising for was the decision to create the hostile environment. She made no apology for the discriminatory nature of a policy that was leaving people homeless, jobless, destitute and sometimes suicidal. She was just sorry that the wrong people had been blasted with hostility.

In the rapidly organised sit-down meeting with the Caribbean heads of government, Theresa May admitted in a very relaxed-sounding way that the problems were the unexpected result of policies she had introduced. 'This issue has come to light because of measures we introduced recently to make sure that only those with a legal right to be here can access things like the NHS and rented accommodation, and this has resulted in some people, through no fault of their own, now needing to be able to evidence their immigration status,' she said, before going on to wheel out the government's by now very familiar line. 'I want to reiterate how much we value the contribution that is being made by Commonwealth citizens who have made their lives here in the UK to the United Kingdom, particularly as we come together to celebrate the ties between us. The Home Secretary apologised yesterday for any anxiety caused and I want to apologise to you today because we are genuinely sorry for any anxiety that has been caused.'

The apology was tacked on at the tail of her statement, and was a fairly lousy attempt at regret. She was sorry for 'any anxiety' caused. This translates as: 'I am sorry you were worried,' and is not an admission of guilt or responsibility for anything that might have caused that worry. There seemed very little understanding of the scale of the problem or the depth of the pain caused and certainly no admission here of the profoundly cruel impact of the policies she had designed. Listening to her speak, it sounds as if she is apologising for a trifling mix-up that has occurred on her watch. Theresa May doesn't seem to be someone who finds expressing emotions easy; this had been clear in her reaction to the tragedy of the Grenfell Tower fire the previous year, where she had initially avoided confronting survivors. Perhaps she found it hard to get the tone exactly right in this formal encounter, but still the substance was sorely lacking.

Officials reached out to race relations and migrant support organisations in an attempt at damage limitation. While Guy Hewitt's mobile was buzzing constantly with calls from civil servants trying to organise placatory meetings with Commonwealth diplomats, other groups that had been trying for months to get this issue on to the agenda were suddenly invited to Downing Street to discuss how they might help the government to sort out this mess. The heads of the Runnymede Trust, Omar Khan, and the Joint Council for the Welfare of Immigrants, Satbir Singh, were unexpectedly called to meet officials in Number 10. The government wanted to put out a press release saying that it was handling the problem, and hoped to include some words of approval from both organisations. Khan and Singh were surprised at the request, and said they did not feel inclined to assist with such an unashamed face-saving gesture.

May's political career had begun with a pledge to rid her party of its 'nasty' image. When she became prime minister in July 2016 she stood on the steps of 10 Downing Street and spoke about a number of burning social injustices that she wanted to fight against, among them the injustice that 'if you're black, you're treated more harshly by the criminal justice system than if you're white.' This whole episode was badly eating away at whatever residual capacity she had to promote herself in this light.

At prime minister's question time the following day, May was still speaking from the same script. She acknowledged this was a 'very important issue' which had caused a 'great deal of concern and anxiety'. Again she picked on this peculiarly mild notion of anxiety. In dozens of interviews with people affected I don't recall anyone saying that their main reaction to being classified as an illegal immigrant was anxiety. Talking casually about 'concern and anxiety' was a deliberate attempt to downplay a situation that had seen British citizens unnecessarily held in detention centres and chased out of the country. All week victims were on the news explaining how they had felt suicidal, or had been forced to cut back on food; she can't have been unaware of these reports, but she decided the best response was: 'I want to say sorry to anyone who has felt confusion or anxiety as a result of this.' This seemed like an insulting attempt to minimise what had happened.

Jeremy Corbyn tried to attack the prime minister over the destruction of the registry slips in Lunar House, pointing out that she had been Home Secretary when the files were destroyed. May's advisers had anticipated this question and researched the history of how the C block basement came to be cleared, and the prime minister was able to respond triumphantly: 'The decision to destroy the landing cards was taken in 2009 under a Labour government.' She made no attempt to downplay the significance of the files or of the decision to get rid of them, but was delighted to be able to put some of the blame on to Labour.

By Friday 20 April, Theresa May tried apologising for the

whole crisis again, promising compensation and declaring that the Windrush people were British. 'They are part of us. They helped to build Britain and we are all the stronger for their contributions,' she said. But she was still tonally wrong. The government would do whatever necessary 'to resolve the anxieties' which people had suffered – as if all the pain caused by the Home Office was merely a bit of needless fretting by those affected.

Television headlines and newspaper front pages all week had been about Windrush-related fiascos. The *Guardian* published the whistleblowers' account of documents being destroyed, which had caused further distress to those affected. The Commonwealth summit had been billed as an opportunity to showcase Britain as a globally connected nation that would flourish post-Brexit, but it had been comprehensively overshadowed by the government's harsh approach to the Commonwealth-born Windrush generation. The problem entirely undermined their desire to strengthen ties with old allies ahead of the fracturing of relations with European partners.

Keith Mitchell, prime minister of Grenada, said the use of the phrase 'hostile environment' with regard to immigrants 'doesn't feel good'. 'We have been making the point that Britain, being our former colonial masters, have not necessarily treated us in the post-colonial period in the way we expected.'

———

May's tone went down very badly with the families of those affected. I spent an afternoon that week in the windowless basement of McKenzie, Beute and Pope, the South London law firm run by solicitor Jacqueline McKenzie, talking to Sentina Bristol, a retired nurse, whose fifty-seven-year-old son Dexter had died three weeks earlier as he tried to sort out his papers. She was certain that the stress caused by the Home Office's decision to question his status had caused his death. A few months earlier, he had been prevented from taking up a cleaning job and been denied unemployment benefits because officials did not believe he was in the UK legally. Dexter had moved from Grenada to London when he was eight, forty-nine years earlier.

He was distraught at having his right to live here questioned. 'He died with hatred in his heart about the Home Office. He was powerless. He couldn't do anything; I couldn't do anything,' Sentina told me.

Despite her very raw grief she was incisive about what had happened and who was responsible. 'I think Theresa May should resign. My son is British. We didn't come here illegally,' she said. Grenada only gained independence in 1974, so it was still a British colony when they travelled to the UK, which meant they came as British subjects. They didn't think they were emigrating, just making an internal journey. Sentina had always felt profoundly patriotic, recounting how as a child her whole school in Grenada had dressed up in red, white and blue, and marched in the recreation ground, to celebrate a visit by Princess Margaret.

'When I moved to Britain I felt like I was leaving home and coming home. It was all the same. Grenada was under British rule.'

Her anger was powerful. 'This is racism. He was the victim of their policies, and it is a tragedy,' she said. 'There was a lot of racism when I came here, but I was young, I could handle it; I just ignored it. This is worse, this is the government. They are intelligent people, they are people of power. We expect better from them. No one expected this country to turn into what it is now.'

Jacqueline McKenzie, one of the most well-informed lawyers on this problem, who had helped numerous Windrush people sort out their status, said she was heartbroken by Dexter's death. 'This is the worst case I've ever seen. We went to extreme lengths to try to get this sorted out.'

The Home Office offered condolences (adding in passing, 'this is about people who have contributed so much to our society'), but noted that Dexter had not yet made an application to regularise his situation – indicating, as usual, that officials felt the fault lay on his side. But Dexter hadn't submitted an application simply because he had still been struggling to gather all the necessary documents before paying the expensive, non-refundable fee.

———

Sylvester Marshall had still not received his radiotherapy treatment. Theresa May announced on 18 April that Sylvester was 'not part of the Windrush generation' – presumably because he had arrived a few months on the wrong side of the cut-off date of 1 January 1973. This legally accurate but surprisingly tough response was another indication that she felt no real unease about her government's conduct towards people who had lived and worked here for decades. She added that he would, nevertheless, 'be receiving the treatment he needs'.

This came as news to Sylvester, who had been given no information about a change in his situation. He had had a brief phone call a few weeks earlier from the hospital consultant, who had congratulated him on looking well in a video interview on the *Guardian* website but had said little to make him feel reassured. The following Monday, however, there was an unexpected development when the Royal Marsden Hospital sent a private taxi to his Brixton hostel to take him for urgent blood tests.

The sudden appearance of the car surprised everyone at the homelessness charity St Mungo's. 'I've never seen that happen before, ever,' said his case worker (asking not to be named).

The following day a second car was sent by the hospital to collect him for another appointment, and the St Mungo's case worker accompanied him. 'Sometimes if patients can't get to an appointment, they send hospital transport – but that's not what this was. It felt much swankier, more like we were being driven by a chauffeur. I've been doing this work for seven years, and I probably go to hospital once a week with a client on average. Most of the clients have got some reason why it would be hard for them to go by public transport – either a physical or a mental health condition – but it would be unheard of that the hospital would send a car.'

Those involved with Sylvester's case believed that attempts were being made to speed up his treatment before it could be used again as political ammunition at the following Wednesday prime minister's question time stand-off between May and Corbyn. Chuka Umunna, Sylvester's MP, said he understood that the Home Office had been told by Downing Street: 'Sort this, and sort it before next Wednesday.'

Staff at the hospital were waiting. 'As soon as we said the name Sylvester, someone came and personally walked us to the appointment,' the case worker said, adding that this was also highly unusual.

'He was very, very nice,' Sylvester told me, describing this hospital employee. 'He was waiting for me at reception, and he waited while I had the meeting, and then he took me back and organised a cab home. I couldn't believe how nice he was.'

They had an appointment with the hospital's consultant, Mr Khoo, a well-respected prostate cancer specialist, who informed them that Sylvester's radiotherapy would start on 1 May, in a week's time. There was no discussion of the pause in treatment, no mention of Sylvester having been suspected of being an illegal immigrant, and no apology. 'There was no acknowledgement of what had happened. I was so shocked that this was happening that I didn't ask the questions that I wish I had. We went back again in the posh car,' the case worker said.

Sylvester was delighted, relieved that there had been no mention of a £54,000 price tag for the treatment, but surprised by the sudden rush to resolve the situation after six months of extreme worry. 'They are scared of all the publicity in the media; it has really shaken them up,' he said. 'The Home Office has known about my problems for years. I think this is all down to the media noise.'

Jeremy Bloom, Sylvester's lawyer, had little doubt that the decision to treat was somehow accelerated so that the treatment would be underway before Jeremy Corbyn could raise it with Theresa May for a third time in PMQs. 'That's made even more apparent by the fact that the hospital never explained why it changed its position,' he told me. He was angry on Sylvester's behalf at the government's prolonged refusal to assist him and the suddenness with which its position shifted once the issue became politically toxic.

The hospital was unable to comment on how its decision had been reversed so suddenly, except to say that they had been told that Sylvester was going to be granted indefinite leave to remain, making him eligible for free NHS care. It was a Home Office decision, and they were just caught in the middle, they said; the hospital had no choice but to act according to instructions. However, the decision to treat Sylvester – and to send a car to collect him – came before he got his papers, so what happened to trigger the U-turn remains opaque.

———

It was undeniably exciting to see this political turmoil caused by the relentless publication of articles on a subject that no one had previously wanted to think about. Everyone has moments of existential doubt about whether what they do serves any purpose, but those two weeks, in which the government was held to account and forced to act, showcased the power of the *Guardian* and the enormous capacity of journalism to trigger change.

Within the building, there was total dedication to getting the coverage right. A team of reporters was allocated to interviewing the huge number of newly emerging Windrush victims. Politicians were finally being contacted by constituents who had previously been nervous about giving details of their cases to officials; they were also belatedly looking through their constituency casebooks to see if there were Windrush victims among the immigration caseload, and finally they were speaking up about the huge variety of difficulties these people were facing as a result of Home Office policy.

It had been hard initially to persuade people to talk to us about being classified as an illegal immigrant; now we were overwhelmed with people who wanted to talk about their treatment at the hands of the Home Office.

It was clear that the reporting of this issue had worked because it had humanised those affected, and this had been largely the result of an early decision by the newspaper's picture editors to commission beautiful portraits of everyone interviewed. There was a powerful disconnect between the imagined, inaccurate vision of an illegal immigrant (someone who has entered the country hanging from the undercarriage of a lorry) and the peaceful images of those affected, taken at home, with their families.

Editors put the story on the front page day after day. Any hope that the government might have had that the issue would quickly exhaust itself was repeatedly dashed by the publication of new damaging revelations about Home Office failures.

Thousands of emails started flooding in from people who wanted to describe their experiences of the hostile environment. A senior British diplomat described how his baby son had been denied a British passport after being born abroad. 'You cannot be more British than the British High Commissioner,' Arthur Snell, the former High Commissioner to Trinidad and Tobago, noted. 'But that wasn't British enough.' The Home Office treated everyone 'with disdain, to the point of absurdity', he said. It was adhering to a policy that requires the applicant to prove 'in the face of a very, very sceptical and negative institution' that he or she had the right to be British. 'You can expect the Home Office to answer in the negative wherever they can.' He was able to go through the expensive procedure of reapplying, but recognised the system was harder for 'people with fewer resources, fewer networks, fewer connections'.

For a while I was unable to read all my emails because there were so many unhappy stories of cruel bureaucratic mishandling of cases. Caroline Bannock, a senior journalist who runs the *Guardian*'s community team, created a huge database collecting all the stories together and made sure everyone who emailed got an answer with information on where to go for advice and how to contact the new Windrush Taskforce, set up by Amber Rudd to help people resolve their citizenship status.

We tried to speak to as many people affected as possible, but it was clear that the impact of the hostile environment policies stretched well beyond the Windrush group. The range of problems was extraordinary and everyone who wrote to us had to some degree an expectation that if we published something about their situation, the Home Office would change its mind. It felt like an enormous weight of responsibility and we repeatedly discussed at length how we should handle the cases. We weren't able to write about most of these problems immediately, but reading the cases and digesting the details was very educational for everyone in the newsroom, providing a powerful picture of ingrained flaws within the Home Office. We picked out themes of how things were going wrong – documents being lost, fees becoming unaffordable, the burden of proof becoming unacceptably high, misdirected Immigration Enforcement raids – and began to focus on them.

Colleagues worked late and over the weekends to make sure that this issue was properly reported. I felt lucky to work with people who really care about what they are doing and about getting things right, and who are calmly efficient, very professional, making the right calls about how to proceed with the coverage.

I began the week of 16 April delighted that politicians were finally paying attention, but by the end of the week the excitement had worn off. I just felt incredibly sad that there were so many more stories emerging of lives torn apart by bureaucratic cruelty. The scale of the misery was devastating.

One morning I came into work to find twenty-four messages on my answerphone from desperate people battling with the Home Office to get their citizenship, each of them convinced that I could help. 'I'm a Windrush person. I came on my sister's passport. Are they going to come and arrest me?' one asked. Another woman got in touch to say her mother was worried she was going to be deported. 'My mother was sent to the UK when she was fourteen years old. Over the last few days she has stopped talking completely. I am scared and depressed.'

I wanted to cry at my desk when I opened a letter from the mother of a young woman who had arrived in Britain in 1974 from Jamaica at the age of one. In 2015, after being classified as an illegal immigrant, told she would be deported and sent to Yarl's Wood, she had taken an overdose and died. 'Without the time she spent in Yarl's Wood, which we understand was extremely unpleasant and the threat of deportation, my daughter would be alive today,' she wrote. The government had been aiming to bring down immigration at any cost, she continued. 'One of the costs as far as I am concerned was my daughter's life. No parent should have to bury their child in circumstances like that.'

Alongside these upsetting calls and letters, there were many from readers offering financial support to victims, and from lawyers offering pro bono assistance. Someone from Dorset sent a shoebox full of bars of chocolate, writing that he imagined that reporters needed the sugar kick to keep up energy levels.

At a time when journalists' reputation with the public feels at a low, amid accusations of fake news and distrust of the mainstream media, it felt positive to help demonstrate why the existence of independent critical media organisations is so important. Even Amber Rudd paid tribute to the 'media outlets which relentlessly exposed the situation of which these individuals had been on the receiving end. It is their extraordinary work that has led to this sea change in the protection of the Windrush cohort, and the changes that will be made in the future.'

If the scene at the office was a smooth-running model of professionalism, at home it was chaos. I wrote until two in the morning, and got up at five to catch up on reading. I tapped out so many articles over those two weeks that my right arm began to ache painfully from bad typing, making it hard to sleep. My dictaphone overheated from overuse and one of its batteries exploded with a surprising pop next to my computer, so that I had to run to Argos and buy a new one before I could continue working. I had to retreat entirely from family life to make sure I poured out every bit of information I had. Shoes went missing, homework was left undone, meals were uncooked. No one much minded. There was an unexpected heatwave and I was aware of the arrival of a plague of ants and flies and fleas (and possibly nits) and there was no time to deal with it.

I'm married to a Conservative MP (Jo Johnson) who at the time was a minister in Theresa May's government. As a news reporter, I have to be politically independent; I let him get on with his job and he doesn't interfere in mine. Life is busy and complicated and mostly we're focused on the pressing day-to-day issues around children. Clearly there are huge areas of disagreement but we try to step around anything too contentious for the sake of family harmony. But the fact did not go unnoticed. One Sunday morning he had to go on television to defend Amber Rudd, returning home at lunchtime to look after the children so I could talk on the radio about how the government had got things badly wrong. I can see why it looks weird from the outside; that weekend it felt very weird. I only had one brief exchange with his brother Boris, who was then Foreign Secretary, about the issue, at a noisy family birthday party later in the year, when he said: 'You really fucked the Commonwealth summit.'

During a live interview with Jamaican radio, which the *Guardian* had organised to see if anyone who had been deported to Jamaica would get in touch with us, I was asked if it was uncomfortable to do this reporting while being married to a government minister. I explained it wasn't really any more uncomfortable than usual; people have complicated lives.

———

Prime minister's question time on 25 April began with the strange British spectacle of both Theresa May and Jeremy Corbyn (a life-long republican) congratulating the Duke and Duchess of Cambridge on the recent birth of their son, before they switched to the real matter of the day, and Corbyn began to attack May for her role in introducing the hostile environment. He asked her to scrap the hostile environment and end the 'bogus immigration targets which have driven the hostile culture', concluding by asking: 'Is it not time she took responsibility and resigned?'

Her response (a non sequitur, but characteristic of the low-level squabbling that passes for debate in the Commons) was simply: 'Let us look and see what a Labour government would be like because a Labour government would wreck our economy, would damage people's jobs, would tax people and would end up with debt for future generations.'

But the issue was uniting politicians on the left and right. The right-wing Conservative MP Jacob Rees-Mogg repeatedly expressed outrage about the Home Office treatment of Windrush victims. 'It's absolutely dreadful – these people are as British as you and I are and it's really extraordinary that the Home Office is coming out with this ghastly bureaucratic guff saying that they've got to show they're British. Nobody's asking us to prove that we're British when we go and use public services,' he noted. Labour's shadow equalities minister, Dawn Butler, accused the government of racism. 'Theresa May has presided over racist legislation that has discriminated against a whole generation of people from the Commonwealth.'

Amber Rudd had returned to the House of Commons on Monday 23 April to give a more detailed account of what had gone wrong and to explain how things would be rectified. Again she described how she had found the emerging stories of suffering 'heartbreaking'. By this point her contrition was becoming rather familiar.

Sarah O'Connor, whom I spoke to a lot over those weeks, said she thought it was a bit late for Rudd to find all this heartbreaking, and wondered if what broke her heart was really the anger of the Commonwealth heads of government and the fury of voters.

Rudd continued to apologise. 'These people worked here for decades. In many cases, they helped to establish the National Health Service. They paid their taxes and enriched our culture. They are British in all but legal status,' she said. She admitted that new government policies designed to combat illegal immigration had 'had an unintended, and sometimes devastating, impact on people from the Windrush generation, who are here legally, but who have struggled to get the documentation to prove their status'.

She added, 'The burden of proof on some of the Windrush generation to evidence their legal rights was too much on the individual. Now we are working with this group in a much more proactive and personal way in order to help them.' She gave details of how the Windrush Taskforce would be staffed by fifty experienced case workers.

'This should never have been allowed to happen,' she said. It was a curious thing to say – suggesting that she had merely been a bystander observing the disaster, rather than the person in charge of the department. She didn't explain how it was that she had allowed it to happen or why ministers had been so unforgivably slow to respond to numerous, detailed, disturbing accounts from those affected by Home Office mistakes. It was a difficult position to be in, since answering that question would have required her to attack her predecessor and current boss, Theresa May.

Instead she devoted some time to a wearisome buck-passing exercise, listing tough Labour initiatives aimed at tackling illegal immigration – missing the point that the key injustice of the Windrush disaster was that people who were in the UK entirely legally had been repeatedly hit by the department's actions.

Crucially, she stated that 'everyone that arrived in the UK before 1973 . . . was given settlement rights and [was] not required to get any specific documentation to prove these rights'.[1] For the past five years, Home Office staff had been rejecting numerous applications by Windrush victims who had spent months, sometimes years, trying to gather documentary proof that they were in the UK before 1973. Rudd was now acknowledging, almost in passing, that none of this was required.

'It is abundantly clear that everyone considers people who came in the Windrush generation to be British. But under the current rules this is not the case,' she said. It is worth noting that this had not been abundantly clear in the least to Home Office staff in the new toughened environment.

Rudd told me later that as the scale of the problem became

clearer, the weekend after the Commonwealth heads of govern-ment summit she wrote in her diary: 'There's a good chance I might have to resign. We'll see.'

On Wednesday 25 April, when she appeared in front of the Home Affairs Select Committee to explain how so many peo-ple could have been so badly treated by the government for so long with no action being taken, she told MPs that she had been shocked by the Home Office's treatment of Paulette Wilson and others. 'Obviously I join everybody in saying how tragic it was to watch some of those cases and how committed I am to making sure that I put it right.' (There was something quite vexing about her prefixing this statement with the word 'obviously', when actu-ally there had been no evidence of her finding this tragic until she was required to by the spiralling scandal.)

Sarah O'Connor, Hubert Howard and Anthony Bryan were sitting behind her in the committee room, in the space reserved for members of the public. Sarah was particularly anxious about her worsening financial situation, the result of her being unable to work, and was frustrated that Rudd still seemed to be unaware of the real extent of the problem. Hubert remembers how con-sumed with worry Sarah seemed that day. 'I thought things were bad for me, but looking at Sarah, she was desperate.' They were unimpressed with what they heard.

Rudd continued: 'I bitterly, deeply regret that I did not see it as more than individual cases that had gone wrong and that needed addressing. I did not see it as a systemic issue until very recently.'

MPs were brutal in their questioning. They told Rudd that hos-tile environment policies were not pushing illegal immigrants out of the country, but simply driving them underground, further from the reach of Immigration Enforcement teams. Picking up on her earlier comments that the Home Office had lost touch with indi-viduals, one MP said: 'Did you make it less human? Was it you as

Home Secretary who made it less human?' Rudd sidestepped the questions and tried again to take a conciliatory approach, promising: 'I think that what this has revealed is that the Home Office needs to have a more human face.'

Not long into the session, Rudd was thrown off course by a question put to her by Yvette Cooper, the Labour MP who chaired the committee. 'Targets for removals. When were they set?'

'We do not have targets for removals,' she replied with easy confidence.

With this swift answer, Rudd brought an end to her career as Home Secretary.

In an earlier evidence session, Lucy Moreton, head of the Immigration Service Union, had given detailed responses on the question of Home Office targets for the number of people to be removed ('removal' being the technical term for deportation, if the individual concerned does not have a criminal record). Clearly this was critical to understanding why people like Paulette had been detained and prepared to be sent out of the country, without ever having been properly questioned and without having had a chance to describe their situation to a case worker. If teams were working towards removal targets, then that would make wrongful removals more likely.

Moreton had explained how the announcement of the net migration target had triggered more challenging objectives across the Home Office. Each region within Immigration Enforcement had a removal target to meet, she said.

Rudd's denial seemed to indicate either that she was incompetent, unaware of how her own department worked, or that she was being dishonest about what was happening. Neither interpretation of her answer boded well for her.

Cooper continued to press the point. She had been told by Home Office staff that local managers, under pressure to meet targets, would instruct staff to go looking for those people who would be simplest to remove, the 'low-hanging fruit'. People like Paulette Wilson were easy prey. 'How much are staff going to be under pressure simply to get someone into detention in order to deport them because of the targets?'

Rudd managed to push on through the rest of the questioning, and tried to put the whole issue behind her by concluding boldly: 'I am acknowledging that the Home Office needs to make changes and that cultural change is going to start here.'

But at this late stage, promises of change were not enough. Such was the level of media interest that as Rudd was denying the existence of targets, Moreton was being interviewed outside parliament by Sky News. The targets certainly existed, Moreton said. 'I'm somewhat bemused by why the Home Secretary would not be aware of that.'

Moreton told me that as Rudd was giving evidence, colleagues were sending her selfies taken by staff in front of their targets boards. The targets were usually displayed in offices – not quite like five-year plans in the Soviet Union ('We're not that organised in the Home Office,' she said), but printed on glossy paper, professionally produced, sometimes laminated, pinned up on the wall.

'All civil servants have to produce evidence that they are doing meaningful work to get their money – that's how the civil service works. You have a target from last year, and then you put it up a bit . . .' she said.

The targets were created for teams rather than for single employees, to avoid putting pressure on individuals to do the wrong thing, she said. But she said she thought there could be a link between the treatment of Paulette Wilson and Anthony Bryan and the introduction of targets. 'It's part of the culture of the organisation.'

Rudd was forced back to parliament the following day, Thursday 26 April, to make her third statement in ten days on what had gone wrong. This time it felt like there had been a strategic decision to shift the conversation to illegal immigration. The more frequently Conservative MPs could press their concerns about illegal immigration, the more swiftly the debate could be moved away from the actual issue.

The Home Office press team had begun to include this more aggressive line in their responses to my inquiries: 'It is wilfully misleading to conflate the situation experienced by people from the Windrush generation with measures in place to tackle illegal immigration and protect the UK taxpayer. It is clearly essential that we continue to take action against people who are here illegally.' It was an odd line to take because the situation experienced by everyone who had come forward was the direct consequence of ill-thought-through policies designed to tackle illegal immigration.

David Lammy was irritated by the attempt to change the subject. 'This is not about illegal immigration. This is about British citizens, and frankly it is deeply offensive to conflate the Windrush generation with illegal immigrants to try to distract from the Windrush crisis. This is about a hostile environment policy that blurs the line between illegal immigrants and people who are here legally, and are even British citizens. This is about a hostile environment not just for illegal immigrants but for anybody who looks like they could be an immigrant.'

Rudd finally admitted that the Home Office had set local targets for removals, but she insisted, 'I have never agreed that there should be specific removal targets and I would never support a policy that puts targets ahead of people.'

Unfortunately for Rudd, one of my colleagues at the *Guardian*, the investigations editor Nick Hopkins, had been given copies of a number of documents that suggested she had been very enthusiastic about deportation as a tool. In a private memo to Theresa May sent in early 2017 she had set out an 'ambitious' plan to increase removals and focus officials on 'arresting, detaining and forcibly removing illegal migrants', while 'ruthlessly' prioritising Home Office resources to ensure that her plans were achieved. The public should know that the immigration system had 'teeth', she wrote.

Rudd's attempts to distance herself from the brutality of the Home Office's actions were undermined by this leak, which made no mention of the possible human cost of getting things wrong. A second memo leaked to the *Guardian*, sent to Rudd and other senior ministers in June 2017, revealed that that the department was making progress on the 'path towards the 10% increased performance on enforced returns, which we promised the home secretary earlier this year'. This memo had been sent at around the time that Paulette Wilson's file was handed to the removals team.

Rudd tweeted that she 'wasn't aware of specific removal targets', adding: 'I accept I should have been and I'm sorry I wasn't.' Home Office sources meanwhile told Hopkins that Immigration Enforcement had been working to reach a target of 12,800 enforced returns for 2017–18.

Shadow Home Secretary Diane Abbott was dismissive about the discussion of whether or not the Home Secretary should have known about deportation targets or should have been better advised. 'They didn't want to admit to targets because that gives a clue as to why they might have been deporting an old woman,' she told me. 'Every dog on the street knows that the Home Office has targets.'

On Sunday 29 April the *Guardian* published in full Amber Rudd's letter to the prime minister outlining her ambitions for the Immigration Enforcement team, revealing that she herself had set an 'ambitious but deliverable' target for an increase in the enforced deportation of immigrants. Later that evening she resigned.

I had a call at home just after 10 p.m. from Nick Hopkins, telling me the news. I felt ambivalent; Rudd hadn't handled the crisis well but she wasn't the person responsible for the mess, and she seemed to be resigning on a technicality rather than admitting she had to step down because she had been very negligent and her department had behaved atrociously on her watch.

The Windrush people I spoke to that night said Rudd's departure had shifted attention from the person really responsible for the problem, Theresa May. Anthony Bryan said he 'nearly fell over' with shock when he heard the news. 'I feel like I helped bring down the Home Secretary. I wouldn't say I am pleased; I feel sorry for her in a sense because it looks like she is taking the punishment for Theresa May,' he said.

A colleague emailed quickly to say: 'That is some scalp.' But I wasn't inclined to celebrate. I worried that her departure would let the government off the hook, allowing ministers to signal that the crisis had been dealt with, a head had rolled and everyone should now move on.

HOSTILE BECOMES COMPLIANT

On the day of his appointment, Sajid Javid, the new Home Secretary, spoke earnestly about how he had been particularly affected by the scandal, as the child of immigrants. 'When I heard that people who were long-standing pillars of their communities were being impacted for simply not having the right documents to prove their legal status in the UK, I thought that that could be my mum, my brother, my uncle or even me.'

He promised 'a fair and humane' immigration policy that 'welcomes and celebrates people who are here legally'. He detached himself from Theresa May's aggressive vocabulary. 'Let me say that hostile is not a term that I am going to use. It is a compliant environment. I do not like the term hostile. The terminology is incorrect and that phrase is unhelpful, and its use does not represent our values as a country.'

This commitment was generally welcomed, although immigration experts looked hard at his statements and concluded that while he was changing the words he used, there was no sign of a change of direction. Compliance was unquestionably a less unpleasant notion than hostility, but if the government intended to continue making people comply with immigration rules by rendering them homeless, pushing them out of their jobs, denying them NHS treatment and detaining them, then introducing a compliant immigration environment meant precisely the same as creating a hostile environment.

The government was desperate to placate the British Caribbean community of over half a million, enraged by what had happened. The prime minister held a party at Downing Street to celebrate the seventieth anniversary of the arrival of the *Empire Windrush*. A fund of £500,000 was suddenly found, to set up annual Windrush Day celebrations honouring migrants from the Caribbean. The day would allow people to 'honour the enormous contribution' of those who arrived on the ship, a government press release announced, 'ensuring that we all celebrate the diversity of Britain's history'. This seemed a crude attempt to buy back favour. A compensation scheme was also set up.

There was some indication that elements of hostile environment policy were shifting. The Home Office suspended the controversial immigration checks it had begun on thousands of bank accounts. Banks had been meant to conduct quarterly checks on 70 million UK current accounts; if an account was believed to be held by an illegal immigrant, then the Home Office could instruct the bank to close it down and freeze assets. But amid growing uncertainty about the accuracy of their methods for determining who was illegal and who wasn't, officials said they needed to stop these checks to make sure that people living in the UK lawfully did not have their accounts frozen. Officials also said they would temporarily suspend the requirement for the tax authorities, HMRC, the benefits agency, the Department for Work and Pensions and the Driving and Vehicle Licensing Agency to share data with the Home Office – a significant element of the hostile environment introduced in 2014.

The government also suspended arrangements under which the NHS handed patients' details to the Home Office. In the previous year, NHS Digital, the health service's statistical arm, had shared three thousand patients' details (provided at GP and hospital appointments) with the Home Office for immigration status checks. This suspension was an important step towards dismantling part of the hostile environment.

Meanwhile, police chiefs said they would stop automatically

passing on information about victims of crime who were suspected of being in the country illegally to deportation authorities. As a result of the Windrush crisis, officers were told they were no longer automatically allowed to check the police national computer to see if someone had leave to remain in the UK. Some police officers were relieved. 'We had an inappropriate relationship with immigration enforcement whereby, by proxy, we were helping to kick people out of the country,'[1] said Shaun Sawyer, the National Police Chiefs Council Lead on Modern Slavery.

But the core hostile environment measures remained in place, and there was no discussion of repealing elements of the 2014 and 2016 Immigration Acts. The checks landlords were required to make on whether individuals have the right to rent and the large fines for employers who hire anyone unable to prove their right to be here remain in place, with no suggestion that the policy will change; NHS charging policies for people who were considered non-resident also remain. Many of the official statements seemed to make it clear that the language had changed but not the substance of policy. Once the immediate political crisis on Windrush subsided, the government returned to a defensive position, arguing that all it had ever wanted to do was to crack down on illegal immigrants – and applauding the policies it had introduced to do that – glossing over the fundamental fact that its systems were extremely bad at distinguishing exactly who those people were.

*

In the weeks which followed the political crisis, I noticed a startling change in tone from the Home Office press office. Phone calls suddenly became unaccountably warm, full of enthusiastic promises to help. I was so surprised by this shift that I noted one exchange in the margins of my notepad.

'How are you?' (This inquiry was already an unusual way to begin the conversation.)

'Fine,' I replied.

'That's fantastic! What can we do to help?'

I gave details of a mundane request for information.

'We'll get our special cases team to look at this as soon as we can! All the best, Amelia!' This level of friendliness was unprecedented and disconcerting. 'I'll get back to you as soon as possible!'

During this period of rapprochement with the Home Office I asked officials if I could go with Hubert Howard to Lunar House in Croydon to sit in on his meeting with the Windrush Taskforce, where he hoped finally to be given a document proving that he was in the UK legally.

Unexpectedly, permission was given, so in early May I met Hubert on the pavement outside Lunar House, and we entered the building together, where we were faced with two doors. On the left-hand side was the regular entrance, used by most people trying to sort out their immigration status, which led through to a busy waiting room; I couldn't see much inside, but some women with pushchairs were going in this way. On the right-hand side a door marked 'Appointments for Premium Service Customers' led to a calm, empty waiting room for people who were able to pay for a fast-track service. A Home Office security guard, standing in between the two entrances, found Hubert on a list of about twenty-five Windrush Taskforce appointments, with a big asterisk by his name. I asked if the asterisk was a coded reminder that he was accompanied by a journalist, but the guard just laughed and directed us to the Premium Service entrance, which had (I imagine) the same serene atmosphere that you might encounter in a first-class airport lounge, except for the fierce signs warning that staff would not tolerate verbal or physical abuse.

People on both sides of the ground-floor dividing wall seemed to end up in the same place, after going through the same airport-style security checks; it's just that those who were paying (or accompanied by journalists) had a less frazzling experience as they waited. It felt like a very depressing snapshot of a two-tier Britain.

It was a difficult day for Hubert, who had spent much of the past thirteen years trying to persuade the authorities that he was in the UK legally, having arrived from Jamaica in 1960 at the age of three. His repeated attempts to obtain a British passport had been rejected. He had lost a good job with the Peabody Trust and been denied benefits, leaving him with no money to live on. He had been unable to travel to visit his mother in Jamaica before she died. The frustrations and emotions he had been dealing with for years were pushed, newly raw, back to the surface; from the moment we entered the building he was doing his best to rein in a simmering sense of fury and despair.

After a wait of no more than a minute we were taken upstairs, to a second waiting room, before being led almost immediately to sit across a desk from a pointedly friendly Home Office employee in his early thirties (no piece of Perspex separating us) who took the package of documents that Hubert had brought, and carefully examined his mother's original British passport, on which he travelled to the UK. The opening pages showed that the blue-covered passport was issued by the colonial government of the day in Jamaica. It described the bearer as a 'British subject: Citizen of the United Kingdom and Colonies', and it noted that Hubert travelled to the UK in 1960; his name had been written on the page after his mother's photograph, and the document contained an entry stamp confirming that they were both given indefinite leave to remain on arriving in Britain.

The official reassured him that since he had the passport, there would be no difficulty in granting him the driving licence-sized biometric document registering that he was living legally in the

UK, and proving that he had the right to work and to access the NHS and other state services.

'Don't worry. We want to grant; we don't want to refuse. If we can't prove it all today, we will work with you to prove it another way,' he said, at pains to sound affable.

For Hubert, finally having the chance to sit down with an official after so many years felt like a critical opportunity to understand how the Home Office had been allowed to turn his life upside down. He had brought a long list of questions, to remind himself what he needed to ask, so he might finally get some clarity.

He pointed out that the Home Office had already seen all these documents. He asked why his previous attempts to regularise his status had been rejected.

'Don't worry. We have been hearing that from a lot of other people.'

Some of his documents had never been returned to him by Capita, he said; would they be returned now? He also asked why the Home Office had repeatedly addressed letters to him as Hubert Leslie (his middle name) and had failed to correct this administrative error whenever he pointed it out. The official said it was hard for him to answer those questions, but acknowledged that a number of other Windrush victims had raised this issue too.

'Am I going to get an apology?'

'Obviously mistakes have been made. We are trying . . . I am certainly sorry for any problems you have had,' the staff member said.

The official tried to be reassuring, told Hubert again not to worry, and said that no amount of documentation was too small; staff would liaise with tax offices (something that had never previously been done) in order to cross-check records. Hubert said he had no shortage of documents and pulled out a photocopy of his primary-school class register from the 1960s (happily obtained before the school shut down and became an academy, when records were destroyed), which he had previously submitted as part of a thick dossier of evidence proving that he had lived in the UK continuously for over half a century.

He had tried to explain to the Home Office in 2008 that he was here legally, and again in 2011. 'What happened to my files? Every time I called they said they didn't know about my files, they didn't know anything about me,' he said, barely managing to control his dismay and incredulity at the extraordinary change in official attitude towards him.

The official kept his eyes lowered and said he couldn't answer. 'I am just filling in the records.'

Hubert was shocked at the ease with which everything was happening. He couldn't understand why something that was so simple to fix had been impossible when he had applied for naturalisation in 2014.

'I can't tell you what went wrong with the previous application. There have definitely been mistakes. What we're doing now is trying to make it right.'

Hubert was shepherded to a corridor where there were fourteen booths behind grey curtains, each with a camera, and a device for scanning fingerprints. After a short break, during which we went to eat spaghetti in a cafe around the corner, we returned to hear what the Home Office had concluded. A second smiling Windrush Taskforce employee said everything was now in order.

'We have been able to confirm your right to remain without restrictions in the UK. I am pleased to say that we have been able to issue you with a No Time Limit document,' she said. 'What we are doing with our Windrush customers is we are expediting the production of biometric cards.' (I bristled at the weird use of the word 'customer' in this context.) 'You will receive one of them in the next three to four days by courier.' If Hubert showed the card to anyone, she added, they would know that he was 'perfectly legal in the UK. You can access work, public services, housing.'

'I've been dealing with this for thirteen years,' Hubert said, looking crushed as he thanked her and got ready to leave.

'You are very welcome. Have a safe journey home. Really nice to meet you,' she replied, bombarding him with more smiles.

The speed with which it was all sorted out was devastating and Hubert was suddenly in tears as he left the building.

The exit from Lunar House opens on to a side street to the right of the building, through a small concrete alleyway, offering applicants who have been lucky enough to be granted UK residency a very bleak snapshot of the country that is now legally theirs. Everything is grey, the NCP car park across the road, the dirty, dull walls, peeling paint, the soaring concrete buildings, the unhealthy pigeons, the damp pavement splattered with dirty bits of gum. There is nothing uplifting about this view of a country in which so many have invested all their future hopes and ambitions. It looks like a total dump. This is one of the ugliest corners of Britain, and you could forgive anyone emerging from the Home Office's automatic glass doors, finally British, for having a flash of buyers' remorse as they survey this unwelcoming vision.

'Thirteen years. This has been painful for me. It has been painful for all the people around me,' he said, as we walked out. 'It has been a struggle and it's destroyed my life.' He abandoned his attempt to hold in his emotions and wept. 'I feel let down; I feel terrible; I don't see how an organisation calling itself the Home Office can treat people like this; I don't understand how the government can treat people like this.' I felt miserably ill equipped to respond, standing in the alleyway, with my notebook and a dictaphone, unable to say anything helpful to a heartbroken sixty-one-year-old, unexpectedly crying in the street.

The *Guardian*'s photographer was hovering to take a picture that we had anticipated would be an upbeat image of someone whose problems were beginning to be resolved. Although the interview had resulted in a promise that documents were coming, it didn't feel like a moment for celebration. I felt it wasn't fair to expect Hubert to be photographed until he was a bit more composed, so I waited, listening to him explain all his complicated feelings. The photograph published in the newspaper the following day shows him standing in front of Lunar House looking under intense strain; it is not a portrait of a happy man.

'I feel relief that it is over, but I'm very, very angry that I had to go through all this. It has completely ruined my life. I couldn't do anything. Buying clothes was a problem. Friends had to buy them for me. I couldn't afford them. I'm someone who has always worked and paid taxes – from the 1970s until 2012.'

He calculated that he might be owed £25,000 a year in lost earnings for five years (a total of £125,000), before the wasted time and the hurt to his mother, who died without his support, were included in the equation. 'The worst thing that has happened to me in my entire life was that my mother passed away, and I wasn't with her. She was a grafter. She worked in factories, she saved to bring me over. She did everything for me. I haven't been by her graveside.'

WHAT GOOD IS AN APOLOGY WHEN YOU'RE DEAD?

For some people, the government's apologies and promises came too late.

Throughout the summer of 2018 I was regularly in touch with Sarah O'Connor, who often rang to tell me how she was getting on with her application to the Windrush Taskforce and to give me details of her slow progress towards extracting herself from all the problems that had spiralled from being designated an illegal immigrant. Her reliable mix of articulate anger and bleak humour meant I was always very happy to hear from her.

She addressed a Windrush event in the House of Commons in early May, organised by David Lammy, attended by Immigration Minister Caroline Nokes, as well as Jeremy Corbyn and Diane Abbott. In her speech she explained how traumatic her experiences had been.

'I've been here for fifty-one years, I've worked for thirty-odd years and got told that I'm an immigrant, I'm not entitled to anything,' she told the meeting, entirely unflustered at speaking in front of such a large audience. 'When all this happened to me and I was told I was an immigrant, I wouldn't cry in front of the Jobcentre, I went home and broke down. I was only six when I came over here. How was I supposed to know all of these laws? It just breaks me. The government and parliament need to sit down and sort something out. Aren't we all British? Why do we have to go through all this rigmarole and hardship and pain?'

Sylvester Marshall also addressed the same meeting, managing to get himself to the House of Commons just a few hours after his first radiotherapy session. Anthony Bryan was there too, and

Paulette Wilson and her daughter Natalie came from Wolver-hampton for the event. Paulette enjoyed revisiting the Commons, searching for the canteen where she used to work. We had supper in the Strangers' Dining Room, with her MP Emma Reynolds; Paulette met a colleague from decades earlier. It was a really positive occasion, and there is a lovely photograph of Sarah smiling, standing next to Anthony, Paulette, and Sylvester, on the green outside Westminster, where everyone looks much more relaxed than they had done when I met them first to talk about their immigration difficulties.

Over those months, Sarah emerged as one of the most vocal and forthright of the victims, and was happy to appear on television explaining how the government needed to do more to help people like her, who were still feeling the financial and practical consequences of the Home Office mess. I travelled on the tube back with her after a Windrush event in the summer, eating popcorn and talking about children; Sarah told me about her granddaughter and gave me helpful parenting advice.

In July she underwent a ceremony to become a British citizen and a few days later she sent me a cheerful photograph of herself wearing a beautiful electric-blue dress on one of the hottest days of the summer's heatwave, next to her daughter Stephanie, holding up a certificate of naturalisation headed with the British crest. She seemed much happier than on any of the four or five occasions I had met her over the previous few months.

'It went OK. Daughters were very proud but I had mixed feelings about it,' she emailed me. She didn't entirely feel it was right that she had had to go through a formal process to satisfy officials that she really was British, when she had actually been British since arriving as a child.

A few weeks later I had another email from her, with bad news. 'Just when I think things are going good for me something just hits me again and I feel like giving up,' she wrote. Her landlord had told her that he wanted to evict her, partly in response to arrears accrued over the period when she was forbidden to work. She would have to move out by the start of October and had not yet found anywhere to go. She had been unable to get a new job, despite having papers now formally granting her the right to work, and this was complicating the search for somewhere to live. 'Every place I am looking at wants people who are working.' I said I was sorry she was facing another major problem, and forwarded her the details of a Windrush Taskforce meeting she might want to attend, where she could discuss these issues and hear about plans for a compensation scheme.

She wasn't at the meeting, but the following week I had an email from Stephanie. 'Unfortunately my mum passed away last night. I wanted to let you know. I'm glad she got her citizenship before she died.' Sarah was fifty-seven and not expecting to die; doctors said her death was caused by high blood pressure. When I met her first in March, she had told me the stress of her situation was making her ill.

Her MP, Labour's Margaret Hodge, paid tribute to her optimism. 'She had been through hell. She was forced to sell her clothes and her car. She showed a really positive, brave resilience in the face of terrible circumstances.' Hodge wrote a furious letter to Sajid Javid stating that Sarah had fallen into extreme financial hardship as a result of the Home Office's decision to question her immigration status.

Stephanie said the immigration problems her mother faced had a huge impact on her. When she began to speak publicly as a campaigner for the Windrush cause, she had started to feel re-energised. 'Mum was such a fighter,' Stephanie said; but she had lost all hope again once her landlord began the process of evicting her. The events of the last year of her life took their toll.

'She felt like she wasn't getting anywhere, and she was deflated. I was trying to keep her upbeat; she said she just wanted to give up.'

I had hoped to go to Sarah's citizenship ceremony in the summer, but it fell during the school holidays and I wasn't able to juggle things to get there. Instead I met her family at her funeral in September. It was heartbreaking.

A fortnight after she died, a clip from a *Guardian* interview with Sarah from April was shown to Theresa May during the BBC's Sunday morning politics show hosted by Andrew Marr. In the interview Sarah dismissed the slew of apologies issued by the government. 'An apology is all good and well . . . [but] an apology doesn't help the things that the Windrush people have gone through.'

What was the prime minister's message to her family? Marr asked.

'Well, I hear what Sarah said about apologies, but I can only apologise for what she went through and for what her family have gone through,' Theresa May said, struggling lamely for something to say.

'Are you actually apologising for the policy?' Marr asked.

'The policy . . . the purpose of the policy, it was to ensure – and we maintained the compliant environment policy – the purpose of the policy is to ensure that those people who are here illegally are identified and appropriate action is taken. I apologise for the fact that some people who should not have been caught up in that were caught up in that, with, in some cases, as we've just seen, tragic results.'

It was clear that the prime minister had no intention of apologising for the policy – hostile or compliant.

———

Two months before she died, Sarah said that one of the worst things about being caught up in the Windrush nightmare was the way it reminded her of the racism she experienced in the 1970s. She found it depressing that Britain seemed to be reverting to a more intolerant era, one that she had hoped had been left behind. 'I grew up when the National Front was about, and that was a really bad time. As the years went on, I thought that had been stamped out, but reading everyone's stories, it feels like it has become a hostile country again. It's all wrong.'

She pinpointed the hostile environment as responsible for the resurgence of xenophobic attitudes. 'The Home Office attitude has been: send them back. But unfortunately we are British. This has ignited the fire of racism again.'

That feeling was echoed by many of those hit by the scandal. Elwaldo Romeo, who moved from Antigua to London when he was four, and who got a letter from the Home Office fifty-nine years later telling him he was in the UK illegally and offering him 'help and support on returning home voluntarily', said layers of racism lay behind the scandal. 'It makes me cross when I think what my ancestors went through. Antigua was a breeding colony for slaves. When slavery was abolished, no one looked after the slaves; they had no land of their own; they were destitute in the Caribbean. They couldn't go back to Africa, because they were no longer Africans. They were British subjects. That's where my anger sets in. I was born British. Then I get a letter saying: you are no longer British. So what am I? How can you lose something that was given to you?'

Anthony Bryan was uncomfortable about analysing the cause of his detention, but also concluded that racism had to lie beneath his treatment. 'Why has this affected so many black people? I don't want to play the race card. After fifty years here, I would like to feel that it isn't racism, but it's very hard not to conclude that it was.'

Clearly there was no government master plan to deliberately target older people of West Indian origin, but the Windrush scandal is a textbook example of institutional racism. In his report on the flawed investigations into the murder of the black teenager Stephen Lawrence in 1993, the judge Sir William Macpherson defined institutional racism as something that could be seen in 'attitudes and behaviour which amount to discrimination through unwitting prejudice, ignorance, thoughtlessness, and racist stereotyping which disadvantage minority ethnic people'. At the very least, there was much government thoughtlessness and ignorance in the development of the hostile environment and in the failure to deal with its effects.

Even when the issue grabbed national headlines and the government apologised, most politicians presented it simply as a bureaucratic fiasco, swerving any uncomfortable deeper analysis. This felt odd. The hostile environment policies aimed to push unwanted foreigners out of the country; the Windrush scandal showed that people without white skin were more frequently classified as foreigners and wrongly penalised by the new measures. It raised much bigger, disturbing questions about racial discrimination.

Labour MP David Lammy notes that in parts of the country people still believe that 'being English is being of white Anglo-Saxon stock'. He also sensed a worrying return to a time of troubled race relations. 'There were times when I thought we were making progress as a country. Despite the murder of Stephen Lawrence, despite the riots and deaths in police custody, I held on to that positive view. But I think that Windrush has rattled black and ethnic minority communities. It feels like we have stepped back into the early 1970s; it's frightening,' he told me.

Why were politicians so unresponsive to the warnings that minorities were likely to be adversely affected by the hostile environment policies? Black voices are still rarely heard in public debate, the race equality think tank the Runnymede Trust points out, and yet they remain the group most likely to experience discrimination. In 2018, 47 per cent of black children were growing up in poverty (compared to 28 per cent of white children). There are few, if any, influential national or even local institutions that represent black people, or that focus on racial discrimination. A Conservative government is likely to be less engaged: few constituencies with large numbers of black voters are held by Conservative ministers; around 85–90 per cent of black people vote for the Labour party. Immigration legislation is exempt from race relations legislation and disproportionately affects ethnic minorities. The introduction of the hostile environment made the effect more pronounced.

Arthur Torrington, of the Windrush Foundation, who has been campaigning for twenty-three years to persuade the government to recognise the legacy of the pioneers who arrived on the *Empire Windrush*, told me the crisis reflected deep-rooted prejudices. 'They ignored so many warnings, from the High Commissioners, from campaigners. It was only when public pressure was on them that they apologised. The government still hasn't accepted its own institutional racism; it's a legacy of empire which still hasn't been rooted out.'

The anger felt by Barbados High Commissioner Guy Hewitt at the unfolding crisis was fuelled by a sense that Britain has a serious problem with institutional racism. He believes that the country needs to go through the truth and reconciliation processes undergone in Germany and South Africa before it can move forward. People need to speak more truthfully about how 'colonisation, slavery and the subcontinent really built up the resources of Britain', he said in his speech at the Windrush event at the House of Commons in May. British people needed to be reminded about the 'unholy trinity of colonisation, sugar and slavery in the West Indies'.

It was the plantation economies, producing sugar, then called 'white gold', that financed the Industrial Revolution in England and expanded capitalism worldwide. The University College London concluded that as many as one-fifth of wealthy Victorian Britons derived all or part of their fortunes from the slave economy. The compensation paid to them at emancipation, representing 40 per cent of the Treasury's annual budget (equating to around £16.5 billion in today's terms) was so large that it wasn't paid off until 2015. Regrettably, the call by the Caribbean for reparations for the deprivation caused by colonisation has seemingly fallen on deaf ears in the UK and across Europe.

'The UK is still not at ease with race. Colonial history is still not taught here. The modern global Britain, with a multicultural society, is still an aspiration rather than a reality,' he told me.

This backdrop of ingrained racist attitudes goes some way to explaining why the issue remained hidden for so long. 'It comes back to who has a voice,' David Lammy said.

———

How do you begin a conversation with someone whom you've helped tip out of their job? I was mildly uncomfortable about interviewing Amber Rudd five months after she resigned, in the (very) brief period before she was rehabilitated and reappointed by the prime minister as a cabinet minister. It felt awkward making small talk in the queue for coffee in the House of Commons. Rudd, however, was briskly professional. We went into one of parliament's newer offices along a quiet, carpeted corridor, through a small room occupied by two assistants, into another small office, overlooking a building site with scaffolding sheathed in ugly greying white plastic. While it wasn't exactly poky, it had none of the grandeur that a secretary of state's office would have; in the snakes and ladders of political offices, this room represented a rapid slide down.

She seemed determined to be open in her reflections on what had gone wrong, but halfway through our conversation I began to wonder how clearly she understood the inevitable consequences of the hostile environment that she had presided over.

The crisis was 'one of the most painful parts of my life', she began, before stopping herself to add: 'I don't want to sound, nor do I feel, too self-indulgent. Although it was a painful period for me, it was a lot more painful for everyone involved . . . I don't want to come over as too "poor me".'

She had been aware of the stories in the *Guardian*, but admitted she had developed a hardness in her approach to reading about controversial Home Office decisions. 'You do take a slightly more cynical view than is perhaps healthy,' she said. 'Mistakes are made sometimes, but there are also individuals who make mistakes. I suppose as a result of that you develop a slightly thicker skin.' Nevertheless, she said she regretted not acting sooner. 'I do look back and think: why didn't I see what was happening earlier? I should have done more.'

But she had had other things on her mind throughout 2017, responding to the five terrorist attacks that had been launched in London and Manchester. The Home Office is one of the most challenging ministerial roles. The Home Secretary is responsible for tackling terrorism, cutting crime and controlling immigration. The minister needs to be simultaneously on top of crime statistics, violent extremism and the ethics of everything from digital surveillance and CCTV cameras to the retention of DNA samples. The Home Secretary is also in charge of the nation's police force and its fire brigades, as well as the security services. It is such a wide remit that it is widely accepted to be one of the most dangerous jobs in government; career-ruining time bombs are ticking away in every corner of the building.

'It is a big job, being Home Secretary,' she acknowledged, and laughed wryly. 'I wish I had immersed myself more fully in what was going on with immigration enforcement. What can I say?'

Rudd was even contacted for help by one of her constituents who was a classic Windrush victim, a Jamaican-born man in his fifties, who had divorced his wife, lost all his documentation and was struggling to get benefits. She had a couple of face-to-face meetings with him in late 2017, and with the help of constituency case workers, managed to arrange papers for him. 'It took a bit of time. I thought: that's a bit odd . . .' But she was mistakenly reassured by the resolution of his situation, and did not see it as being the result of her special intervention as Home Secretary. 'I guess that gave me a false sense of comfort, that although people in this cohort would have been encountering a difficulty, the right adjustments were being made.'

In response to further articles published in the *Guardian* at the start of 2018, which increasingly suggested that the problems were part of a pattern, Rudd asked officials to look into the situation. Her special adviser spoke to Hugh Ind, the Home Office's Head of Immigration Enforcement, to ask if he thought there was an issue. According to a note from the special adviser to Rudd, summarising the conversation, Ind said: 'No'. 'They had examined their records and thought there were at most 200 people who might be in a difficult position evidencing their Windrush status and highlighted specific safeguards they'd put in place to ensure no one from the Windrush generation would end up in detention again,' the note said.

The Immigration Minister, Caroline Nokes, had only been moved into the job in January 2018 and was unaware of the problems. 'I had three Immigration Ministers in two years,' Rudd said; 'one of the learnings I would take from this is that the Immigration Minister is an incredibly senior job and we need to make sure that people stay in it for longer.'

Despite her determination not to sound sorry for herself, it was clear that she felt wounded. She said she felt badly let down by the Home Office staff, who themselves had failed to grasp the extent of the Windrush problem and had failed to brief her properly on what they knew. She consulted the deputy permanent secretary in the Home Office, Patsy Wilkinson, on how the department was dealing with the most vulnerable people. 'As Home Secretary I wanted to make sure that I could have confidence that our hostile or compliant environment wasn't putting people on the streets and I got reassurance that we had sufficient safeguards put in place that that wouldn't happen.'

I was startled by this. It sounded as if she still didn't see that the hostile environment was constructed precisely to have that outcome. If you are classified as an illegal immigrant, told you are not allowed to work and given no access to state benefits, you are very likely to end up on the streets. Most homeless hostels won't house you, because they rely on state funding, and the state does not fund shelters for people here illegally.

Windrush people were routinely being made homeless, I pointed out. 'The difficulty with asking for reassurance that the hostile environment is not putting people on the streets is that it is designed to put people on the streets,' I said. Wasn't that the whole point of the policy?

'At the core of it is this reasonable view that illegal migrants should not be here and that you have to have a system whereby they are encouraged to leave; because you cannot deport everybody – the business of deportation is hard,' she said. 'The problem with the Windrush people is that they should never have been labelled as illegal immigrants.'

The government still needed to make sure it did 'the compassionate thing for anyone who's here', she added. 'I'd say that somebody and it's probably the Immigration Minister (and I'm not passing the buck, I wish I had done it) should probe more deeply whether we are looking after people who are vulnerable at the bottom of the chain.'

I felt she didn't fully understand the logical conclusion of the hostile environment policies, which is that if you are deliberately trying to make life hard for people, then life is inevitably going to become hard for the most vulnerable at the bottom of the chain, and that's not the moment to start thinking about being compassionate. The system was not meant to be compassionate. There was an uncomfortable silence in her tidy, clutter-free office.

Was it particularly difficult working for Theresa May, I asked (moving on), defending policies that her predecessor, and now boss, had put through and having to work towards the tens of thousands net migration target? 'I'm not going to discuss that,' she said. 'I supported these policies at the time in government. So I don't think so.'

She had been taken aback by the level of support for the victims of Home Office policy. 'I did think it was interesting that the whole country rose up in outrage at the idea of the Windrush generation not being treated well – which I thought showed that the public at large have a fair view about immigration – that people who come here, wherever they come from, shouldn't be treated badly.'

The events around the catastrophic Home Affairs Select Committee hearing still loomed large in her reflections on what went wrong. To anyone outside Westminster this seems like such a side issue – the real problem was that the Windrush crisis was making life impossible for thousands of people who should have been recognised as British citizens. The question of what the Home Secretary did or didn't mean to say about deportation targets, and what advice she was given by her staff, seems very insignificant by comparison. But she felt her advisers had let her down in the week of the crisis; she attributed this lack of support to the criticisms she had made of her own department in her first apology to the House of Commons.

The implication that it was their behaviour which was at fault, rather than the policies they were obliged to implement, may have annoyed Home Office staff, she conceded. 'I don't know if it's true that that led to some of the leaks against me because they were so irritated with me for having said that. Clearly they were irritated with me.'

Anticipating that the question of targets might come up, she had checked before she went to appear at the Home Affairs Select Committee and had been told that there were none. In the hours after that excruciatingly difficult session where she had said confidently that there were no deportation targets, she returned to her office and called up the Director General of the Home Office; he told her, again, that there were none. 'Everyone around me was confused. I got Hugh Ind on the speakerphone and I said: "What is going on? Do we, or do we not have targets?" It was one of those moments where you're told one thing and you start probing and slowly it unravels. So I probed him and it turned out that effectively we didn't currently have targets but we used to; it was all very weaselly.'

From the outside this all feels rather academic because Rudd herself was talking with enthusiasm about achieving a 10 per cent increase in deportations, which sounds awfully like a target. Part of the problem was the slipperiness around the vocabulary, and the willingness of Rudd and her officials to view notions like targets, aspirations, ambitions, goals and objectives as very different things, while to most people they seem remarkably similar concepts.

But she was still feeling very bruised. Reading an internal investigation into the advice given to her by civil servants in the days leading up to her resignation 'was like reading a horror story of my life'.

Throughout the crisis she had also repeated that she was confident that no one had wrongly been deported, because that's what officials had told her. She found it 'outrageous' that a week after she was told by Home Office staff that it was unlikely that there had been any deportations among the Windrush cohort, the new

Home Secretary, Sajid Javid, was informed that there had been at least sixty-three. Of these, thirty-two had been deported because of a criminal conviction (the seriousness of which was not set out), while thirty-one were either enforced removals because individuals had been classified as here illegally, or 'voluntary returns'.

'I think they were telling me something that was untrue,' she said. 'I think nobody had a proper grip on immigration enforcement.'

Might Paulette Wilson have been pushed through the system towards deportation because of targets? 'No. I still find it absolutely extraordinary and outrageous that someone could be treated like that,' she said, formulating the sentence in a curious way that distanced herself from the outrageous treatment, as if she were an independent observer, someone with no connection to the department responsible.

Rudd said she had gradually realised that, aside from the question of removals targets, the scale of what had gone wrong meant she would need to resign.

'I spent two days agonising about it over the weekend. I felt this sick feeling throughout those days about what was going to be the right thing to do; it felt conclusive to me by the end of the day on Sunday that I clearly should have known that there were targets and I had clearly sort of been caught on what looked to people like a lie – which was upsetting for me because it wasn't a lie; it was a mistake I made which definitely seemed to show I didn't know what was going on,' she said. 'I thought this was the right thing to do, to resign, so I called the prime minister.'

It felt 'very upsetting. But I slept well for the first time on Sunday night.' She felt she had been permanently changed by what happened, claiming that in future she would be more sensitive to the individuals on the receiving end of policy decisions. 'The thing about a senior job in politics is that you rarely see the actual individuals because you are operating at such a high level. But when the individuals bubble up like that into such a dramatic evidence of a policy going wrong, I don't think it's anything you ever forget. I think all ministers who experience that will be a bit better next time.'

It will be interesting to see whether the memory of the experience does have an enduring effect, or whether there is a return of the unhealthy cynicism which she said afflicts senior politicians.

I left the conversation convinced that Rudd was genuinely sorry for the hardship that people had suffered, but suspecting she was just as sorry about the way she had been treated by her colleagues and the briefly catastrophic impact that the scandal had had on her career.

Sajid Javid conceded later that 164 people had been wrongly detained for removal and that number was likely to rise further. The government had mistakenly removed at least 83 people from the country. The Home Office would release no details about those who had been sent out of the country in error. The Caribbean High Commissioners had no information on their identities. It was clear that it would be easier to search for them by travelling to Jamaica.

DEPORTATION

Visitors to the British High Commission in Kingston are invited to place their umbrellas in long, transparent plastic bags, to prevent rain water from dripping on to the floors of the building. 'Good day!' a notice to visitors reads. 'Kindly wrap up your umbrella.'

I made my way to the building in a low mood on the last day of a dispiriting week-long tour of Jamaica, every day spent interviewing people made destitute and desperate, separated for years from their families in the UK by flawed British policies.

It had taken weeks of emailing the Foreign Office and Home Office press offices to persuade them to let me meet the British High Commissioner. They had finally agreed, but in a way which was only partially useful, writing to say that they were 'happy to offer an off the record, background briefing' with Asif Ahmad, the British High Commissioner to Jamaica. This meant I was allowed to meet him and ask him questions, but it would not necessarily be possible to write much about the answers he gave, and certainly not to reveal that any interesting information he divulged had come from the head of the British diplomatic team in Jamaica.

There was a fifteen-minute wait in the main reception inside the High Commission's fortress-like compound before I was taken to his office, so I passed the time walking around the room, inspecting the unhappy-looking potted plants, admiring the black polished stone floors, the British and Jamaican flags and the plaque laid by Harold Wilson in 1975 marking the opening of the building, and watching the BBC news playing on a television screwed to the wall, before noticing the umbrella bags.

I had never seen a disposable umbrella bag before. There was something unexpectedly upsetting about this punctilious concern that raindrops should be prevented from entering the building. For years, High Commission staff had been steadfastly ignoring pleas for help from dozens of elderly people stranded in Jamaica, cut off from their families – some hungry, penniless and homeless – and desperate for advice on how to return home. Yet here inside the building, UK staff were getting on with their jobs, broadly oblivious to the suffering experienced by Windrush victims, but meticulously focusing on the small stuff, ensuring, with absurd British precision, that wet umbrellas should be sheathed in specially designed plastic bags. I felt a burst of fury towards British officialdom with its callous indifference to the things that really matter and its ridiculous obsession with things that don't. By the time I was called in to see the High Commissioner, I was feeling mutinous towards all the staff working there, with their stupid plastic umbrella bags.

The High Commission building is designed to be impenetrable. Visitors' cars inch forward towards the building's gates over two rows of silver bollards that sink into the ground to allow you to enter, before rising again to prevent other vehicles from following you inside the compound. Before you can edge across the second set of submerged bollards, a security guard checks the vehicle and puts his head to the window to ask: 'You're not carrying any firearms, are you?' The low embassy building is surrounded by royal poinciana trees, with their beautiful red blossoms and feathery leaves. To get to the High Commissioner's office, visitors have to pass through another internal glass door, accessed by typing in a security code. A sign notes reassuringly that today the British High Commission alert state is normal. It's clear that for destitute Windrush victims, this simply is not a place where you could ever imagine being able to pop by to get some advice on how to resolve a complicated and painful immigration issue.

Before I left England, I had watched a short film made by the High Commission for the benefit of people about to be deported. Removing someone from their home and deporting them to a country on the other side of the world is one of the most brutal acts that the state can inflict on an individual, so it takes a remarkably brazen bit of PR spin to repackage deportation as an exciting exotic travel opportunity. This is the contortion attempted in the 'Coming Home to Jamaica Guide' – an exceptionally disingenuous piece of propaganda.

Intended to be shown to inmates in Britain's immigration detention centres ahead of a flight home, the film is made in the upbeat, enticing style of a daytime television holiday programme, where viewers are tantalised with visions of a distant, glamorous resort they are unlikely ever to visit. 'Every year a large number of Jamaicans find themselves repatriated to their home country against their wishes,' a bright voice says, as the film begins and images of an avenue of palm trees and sparkling blue seas flash up on the screen. 'We can only imagine their feelings as they peer out the aircraft window on the final approach to a land they may have only spent a small portion of their lives in – a sense of wonder at the vibrant, beautiful colours of both land and sea . . .' Images of children playing by the beach appear. 'The challenge of resuming a life in Jamaica after an absence of twenty or thirty years can be daunting. But the challenge can be met!' The British officials who commissioned the film seem determined to present the experience of deportation as nothing more than a pesky hurdle to be overcome.

The cheerful presenter acknowledges that there may be 'apprehension' but adds the jaunty reassurance that 'Help is at hand!', as if the practicalities of being deported are just some of the routine and minor headaches associated with international travel.

The film goes on to offer helpful travel tips for what is being branded as an unexpected, slightly inconveniently timed holiday. 'Jamaica! The most vibrant little country in the world,' the voice-over continues relentlessly, across an image of people laughing and high-fiving over a table where they are playing dominoes in the sunshine – glossing over the painful reality that those watching the film are about to be dumped, against their will, in an unfamiliar country, where they may have no friends, no family and nowhere to stay. 'You will find that people are welcoming and colourful and our dynamic culture is always adding new elements!' (What new elements?)

Free accommodation is promised for the newly arrived deport-ees, and the camera flashes to a long pastel-blue corridor with eighteen or so wooden doors into what appear to be windowless cupboards with beds in them, each smaller than a British prison cell, barely room to wheel a suitcase in. 'Free short-term accommo-dation! Three meals a day!'

The camera doesn't linger long on another shelter in Montego Bay, the Refuge of Hope, operated by the Open Heart Charitable Mission, which sits behind high, looped barbed wire, and which looks a lot like a shed (painted an upbeat egg-yolk yellow). 'We provide emergency accommodation!'

Produced by High Commission staff in conjunction with some-thing called the Rehabilitation and Reintegration Programme, the film attempts to offer some happy success stories of returning resi-dents. A woman is interviewed as she paints the outside of her house a beautiful, optimistic bright orange. 'It is not easy, but you can do it!' she says encouragingly. A man who has set up a courier service business is filmed standing by the ocean, resting on a glossy blue bike, palm leaves gently fluttering in the sea breeze behind him. Deportation, he acknowledges, 'was rather embarrassing. That stigma is going to be there. It is best if you try to overcome it.'

Despite its determination to be upbeat, the film somehow exudes a melancholy hopelessness.

A booklet has been published to go alongside it, full of advice about how to settle back into life in Jamaica. Mental health is highlighted as a key area of concern.

Most people adjust fairly well but some people may experience mental health problems. Signs to watch out for are: difficulty in sleeping, or sleeping too much, feeling sad . . . having no interest in the pleasures of life, loss of appetite, difficulty in concentrating or making decisions, feelings of hopelessness or helplessness, thoughts that life is not worth living, suicidal thoughts.

The booklet suggests that if a deported person begins to experience mental health problems, they should 'develop a healthy lifestyle: eat well, manage stress, get adequate sleep and exercise'. Particularly weird is a checklist of dos and don'ts, which advises that returnees should, for their own safety, conceal their Britishness and adopt a Jamaican accent: 'Try to be "Jamaican" – use local accents and dialect (overseas accents can attract unwanted attention).' There is a strange implicit acknowledgement here that these returnees are in fact more British than Jamaican, if they have to assume the local dialect. People should also 'try to find lodgings in areas that are considered safe', the guide suggests – which prompts the question: exactly how many people go out of their way to find lodgings in areas that are considered unsafe?

———

I'm not sure how grateful Vernon Vanriel would have been for a helpful tip from the Foreign Office to look for lodgings in an area considered safe. When I met him towards the beginning of the trip in the coastal town of Savanna-la-Mar in western Jamaica, he was living in an abandoned roadside grocery shack, with no electricity, no running water, no glass in the windows, and a flimsy plywood door that allowed the torrential rain to seep in while we spoke. Since he had previously spent time sleeping rough on the streets in Jamaica, this was (despite its obvious shortcomings) a relatively acceptable place to be living at the age of sixty-two, and he felt grateful to the shack's owner who allowed him to stay there. Like most people fighting off destitution, he didn't have the luxury of considering whether or not his lodgings were in a safe area.

I'm also not sure how easy it would have been for him to adopt a Jamaican accent, given how utterly his voice had been moulded by his Tottenham upbringing. When he opened his mouth, I was transported immediately from the palm trees and the oppressive Caribbean heat back to the pubs and sports clubs of the Seven Sisters Road. Something about his turn of phrase (with its wheezy traces of Sid James in a 1960s *Carry On* film) was unmistakably steeped in North London, which is where he arrived in April 1962 at the age of six and where he lived for forty-three years.

'England is the best country to live in – no ifs and buts, kill me stone dead and I won't change my mind,' he said, startlingly British idioms and touchingly faded expressions from the 1970s streaming out, his voice crackly and croaky from tobacco. After months of isolation, Vernon was delighted to meet people from London. 'I'll tell you a little story . . . moving us to England was the best thing my father ever did in his life, God bless him for that; I loved London, I loved the British people from my heart, body and soul.'

I had travelled to Jamaica with the *Guardian*'s photographer David Levene in the late summer of 2018, after the political crisis had subsided, to try to find some of the dozens of people whom the government had finally admitted it had either removed or refused re-entry to Britain. It was a very sad trip; despite the Foreign Office's attempts to sell deportation or forced relocation as an exciting life opportunity, it was clear that for the vast majority it was a life-shattering event.

It was very hard to find Windrush people who had been forcibly removed from Britain. The British government refused to make public any details of the people it admitted it had wrongly despatched back to the Caribbean; the Caribbean High Commissioners in London had no details of who they were; the charities who resettled deportees were unable to point to people of the right age who had been forced to return. The news organisations in Jamaica were curiously unengaged with this issue – perhaps partly down to a widely felt anger at the British government's fondness for deporting people to Jamaica, and partly to a common misperception that most deportees were violent criminals and consequently deserved scant sympathy.

The Jamaican Foreign Ministry was struggling to track down deportees from Britain; the stigma of deportation or forced removal was so profound that many people had never even explained to their closest families the reason they were back in Jamaica. Officials were scouring the island, going to remote villages in search of those who had been wrongly returned.

It was easier to find people who had been refused re-entry to England after a stay in Jamaica, whose Britishness had been removed without them realising it, leaving them stranded. These were among the eighty-three individuals the Home Office was trying to contact; officials had recognised that they had a responsibility to do what they could to repair these people's lives, but most of them were still waiting for help, three months after the UK government's acknowledgement of official culpability. Decisions to refuse re-entry had been made for decades, under Labour as well as Conservative administrations, because unclear immigration status was often picked up at passport control; the frequency of removals increased with the introduction of the hostile environment.

Vernon had been one of Britain's best boxers in the 1970s and 1980s, and had fought sell-out matches at the Royal Albert Hall. I'd seen an old boxing photograph of him online the night before we met, after David Lammy's office had sent me his mobile phone number and explained that he was in a dire situation. He was almost unrecognisable. I was shocked at how thin and unwell he had become. He was also extremely hungry. There was no food in his wooden shack, and he was happy to eat some crisps and nuts that we had bought in a petrol station on our way. (Feeling depressed by your situation? The Foreign Office's 'Coming Home to Jamaica Guide' advises you to 'eat well'. This is not easy when you have no money.)

He radiated an unusual combination of cheerfulness and abject desperation, after thirteen years spent trying to return to the country where he grew up and lived for most of his life. 'If I ever end up accidentally going to hell, I'll be well prepared for it from the experience I have had here,' he said, laughing but bleakly serious at the same time. 'I have deteriorated to something unrecognisable.'

I felt very troubled by the sight of his home; he had two or three items of his own clothing, a pair of shorts and some T-shirts, folded on the shelves, alongside a couple of half-empty boiled sweet jars, two bottles of artificial almond flavouring and a cash register, the last remnants of the abandoned shop. There was a camp bed behind a plywood partition, but no other furniture. Tiny ants or some other barely visible mite-like insects swarmed over the surfaces, on to my laptop as I typed while we talked, and over the toothbrush and the small piece of soap balanced on a ledge. A couple of candle stubs had been melted to the wooden counter to light the room at night. 'There's nothing good about it here. I've got no toilet, no bathroom, no kitchen, no electricity, no furniture. It gets excruciatingly hot,' he said. 'I deserve a medal. I'm in here by myself twenty-four hours a day.'

In the baking midday heat, we listened to Vernon's account of arriving in London as a child. Jamaica was still a British colony when he left in April 1962, with his mother, Myrtle, an older brother, Cecil, and three older sisters, Icylin, Lynette and Blossom, to join their father who had already gone to work in London. No visas were required to move from Jamaica to the UK; they travelled on his mother's passport, the same blue-black British passport which would have been issued to people in England. It stated that they were British subjects. Sitting on a wooden stool by the counter of the empty grocery stall, observed by six stray dogs at the doorway, he said he hadn't found the move from Jamaica particularly disruptive. 'There was a bit of racism but if I made a fuss about racism I would be a wicked man, it wasn't that severe.' After leaving school he trained as an electrician, and set up his own business, VJ Electrics, when he was in his early twenties. At the same time, his boxing career was flourishing and he turned professional in 1976, trained by Terry Lawless, the same coach who worked with Frank Bruno. 'I was number two in Britain in 1983–4; number nine in Commonwealth and fourteen in Europe. Looking back in hindsight I did tremendously well.'

Among the few possessions he had managed to hang on to through thirteen years of moving around Jamaica, living at times on the streets, were his boxing gloves in a Lonsdale training bag and a file of newspaper cuttings from his boxing heyday. The headlines from 1983 read: 'Vanriel beats the Brighton Rock'; 'Speedy Vernon'; 'No charity as Vanriel hammers him in six'. As we looked through the papers, the weather shifted dramatically and a thunderstorm broke, turning the street outside into a river of muddy water. At the height of his boxing career, he was known as Vernon 'the Entertainer' Vanriel. He remembered sitting in his dressing room at the Royal Albert Hall, waiting to walk to the ring, and hearing fans singing his name. He sang the chant for us, in his frail, husky voice, to the tune of the Welsh hymn 'Bread of Heaven', as the torrential rain beat against the corrugated iron roof of the hut. 'Vernon Vanriel, Vernon Vanriel. We'll support you ever more. We'll support you ever more.'

'They were singing, and I wasn't even in the ring yet. The atmosphere was electrifying.' It was an unforgettable conversation, interrupted when Vernon nipped out on a bicycle, splashing through the flooded street, to get some meat scraps from a roadside stall around the corner to feed the stray dogs. He managed to evoke the drama and the disappointments of a decades-old boxing career, in his Jamaican hut, thousands of miles from the Royal Albert Hall. It seemed less painful to talk about that than his difficulties trying to return home to his family.

His life in London became very unsettled in the 1980 and 1990s. His boxing career ended when he began to suffer from depression, and his family life was complicated. In 2005 he went to Jamaica to spend some time with his son who was living there. He travelled on a Jamaican passport, because it was quicker and cheaper to apply for than a British one. 'I never thought of myself as Jamaican, but getting a British passport was problematic and expensive and I didn't have the money,' he said. When he wanted to return to his family in the UK two years later in 2007, the British High Commission refused him a visa.

Changes introduced in the 1988 Immigration Act meant that people who had indefinite leave to remain in the UK (which Vernon had, as a result of his pre-1973 arrival) but who spent more than two years abroad lost their entitlement to return. For years the British High Commission in Jamaica had held a very firm line on refusing to let British long-term residents return home if they had misplaced their passport with the stamp showing indefinite leave to remain or if they had spent more than two years out of the country. Vernon hadn't been aware of the changing rules. 'I was in such a state of confusion. I don't think I've ever recovered,' he said.

He tried to rebuild a career as a boxing trainer in Jamaica, and successfully coached one athlete to the finals of the Jamaican boxing championships, but recurrent ill health made it impossible to continue. Since he had stopped working he had found it hard to survive in a country he had left when he was six.

'When I first came here I had a few bob in my pocket, looking the part, if I say so myself. When I got a kid to the boxing finals, I was almost like a king. But as I have faded it has become harder. Jamaican people are funny; if you're doing well, they are with you, they support you. They stop you and talk to you. If you're not doing well they treat you with scorn. Now people walk past me purposefully turning their heads; they think I'm not worthy. Nobody wants to know you when you're down and out.'

He lost touch with his son and was visiting local churches to get free meals. Because Jamaica has no free healthcare, and because he was near destitute, he was unable to get consistent treatment for his heart and lung problems. A doctor in Savanna-la-Mar wrote on his behalf to the British High Commission, pleading with them to allow him to return home; Vernon found a copy of the letter, stored alongside his boxing articles. 'In summary Mr Vanriel has a chronic lung condition and now a severe heart condition and will now need specialist follow up, which he can hardly afford now, if not for the support of his family living in the UK. I am hoping that this information can further assist him in returning to the UK where he has lived and worked for most of his life. Yours respectfully, Dr Vincent Chisholm.' The letter appeared to have had no impact.

Vernon was trying to maintain contact with the Windrush Taskforce in the UK, calling whenever he was able to charge his phone and get credit. His elder sister, Lynette, recently retired as a nurse in North London, was sending him money from her pension.

Vernon was visibly willing himself to stay positive, battling not to feel despondent about the long wait for a decision on his case. 'I'm not bitter or angry in any way. Sometimes in life everything happens for a reason. I don't want to say anything derogatory. I love London; obviously it has some shortcomings – they could have treated immigrants better. They have done wrong but they have also done a lot of good.' He was upbeat about the British education system, and about the National Health Service. He felt he had been given a good start in England. 'I learned the boxing, the electrical work and how to be a human being.'

———

The staunch refusal of the British High Commission to help stranded British residents get back to their families was disturbing. I kept thinking about a terrible story of a fiftieth birthday party that ended catastrophically, which an immigration lawyer had told me about earlier in the year, and which displayed British officials in an exceptionally bad light.

Joe Robinson had come to Britain aged six and spent forty-four years in Northampton, bringing up a family, working as a youth worker and a hospital porter. He had never been back to Jamaica, so his children organised a surprise holiday in an all-inclusive resort for his fiftieth birthday in 2009. A big party of eleven members of the extended family (including his elderly father, who was also returning to Jamaica for the first time) went with him for the celebrations. They all had a wonderful time, but after ten days when it was time to go home Joe was not allowed to board the plane back to England. Because he had never previously been abroad, his children had organised a Jamaican passport for him before they left, but there was no indefinite leave to remain stamp in the document, so no one at the check-in counter at Kingston airport was prepared to believe that he was actually British. What should have been a routine bit of confusion at the border, easily cleared up by diplomats at the High Commission, became a life-changing disaster because British officials refused to help. Joe was stuck in Jamaica for twenty-one months after his birthday party.

The rest of the family were obliged to leave him behind in Kingston. It took his children almost two years to unravel the situation. They instructed two law firms, at great expense, to no avail, before finding an expert immigration lawyer in Wales who was able to help.

'The British High Commission would not assist him at all because he was not a citizen; the Jamaican government had little or no interest in him,' Hilary Brown, the lawyer told me. She gathered extensive tax records, medical files, family testimonies, National Insurance payments, dental records, school documents, to prove a lifetime in the UK, and only then was he allowed to return home. 'There was a lack of empathy on the part of the British High Commission, and a refusal to do any checks on his behalf. They just said: "You prove it." Imagine how hard that is – you're away from all your documents, you can't access anything, and the High Commission won't help you at all.' In her experience, Home Office staff rarely go out of their way to find information that might help an applicant, but will regularly do behind-the-scenes research for information that can be used to attack a claimant's credibility. 'It would have been very easy for a Home Office worker to find evidence that he had lived in the UK for decades, but there's so often an attitude that says: "I couldn't care less," or "I don't have the time or energy to unpick this."'

Joe couldn't stay on indefinitely at the expensive hotel where his birthday party had been held, so he scrabbled around to find cheap hostels, relying on his family to send money to support him. Often he had no idea where his next meal was coming from. The family spent around £26,000 on legal bills. When he finally got home in 2011, he was told he owed £4,500 for unpaid rent and council tax. He was taken to court and evicted from his flat. He spent years sleeping on relatives' sofas and was only rehoused by the council seven years later when his case attracted attention during the Windrush crisis.

Every time I think about his treatment I feel amazed and furious. What does it say about the Foreign Office that they declined to help him? It requires a remarkable, unflinching bureaucratic insensitivity to refuse to help a man whose surprise birthday party has ended so cataclysmically. Would officials have left a white tourist who had lost a passport similarly stranded?

———

'Alright, my dear,' Vernon said, as we left him a few hours later, a diminished, lonely figure in the empty street outside the ant-infested shop. 'Stay in touch.'

There is always an awkward moment as a journalist, particularly working abroad in economically struggling countries, when you finish an interview, say goodbye, step into an air-conditioned car and drive away, back to a hotel with electricity and food, leaving the person you've interviewed in the same unhappy situation, to reflect on the uncomfortable experience of having handed over their entire life story for unknown readers of a distant publication to skim through.

In order not to feel too bad about the departure, you have to have an unshakeable faith in the capacity of journalism to have a positive impact. Sometimes this faith is misplaced, and the act of reporting on a problem has no clear results. But in Vernon's case something constructive did happen within days of our visit. Not long after I alerted the Home Office to the fact that I was writing about him and requested a comment on his situation, Vernon rang to say that he had been called by the British High Commission, who wanted to check his address so they could courier him a passport from Kingston. The passport arrived by car later that day. A few days after that, an airline ticket to London (first class, British Airways, marked with the astonishing price of £2,261) was couriered to him. His passport application was already being processed by the time we met him, but media attention appeared to trigger a sudden, rapid acceleration.

'It was absolutely miraculous,' he said, when he called to pass on the good news. He was already making plans for his return to London. 'The first thing I want to do is go straight to my mother's grave, and then to see my sisters. I feel rejuvenated, that's the word.'

David and I continued to search for people who had been deported or denied the chance to return home. We drove along the unfamiliar highways, eyes prickly with jet lag, my ears buzzing from exhaustion after late nights working in the badly lit hotel room, where peculiar dank smells rose up from the thick carpet when the air conditioning was switched off. I stared at the sights, wide-eyed, noticing everything, but not understanding much, processing the strangeness of a new country.

I was particularly struck by the endlessly bossy public information signs, many of them rhyming, painted on billboards and placed at intervals along the road. 'Stay Alive – Don't Drink Alcohol and Drive'. 'Protect Your Head – Don't End Up Dead'. 'A Blocked Drain Is a Stain'. 'Safety Begins with S But Starts with U'. 'Eat More Fish This Lent!' 'Drive with Care – We Love Our Children'.

The slogans jangled and looped in my tired brain, jumbled up with advertisements for unfamiliar Jamaican products: 'Life's Just More Fun with Honey Bun'. From the road, we observed the elaborate metal security grilles fitted over verandahs to keep criminals out (mostly installed in the past decade as violent crime in Jamaica has risen) – some of them in the shape of spiders' webs, some made in the shape of peacocks' tails, an apparent attempt to beautify the inherently ugly business of fencing in your home against burglars. We met deported British citizens in Mandeville, a town in central Jamaica favoured by many people returning from the UK because of its cooler climate, which returnees said helped to stave off homesickness. English accents can be heard on the streets here, but the loneliness of forced exile was impossible to stifle.

I was fascinated by all the inconsequential things that seem interesting when you arrive somewhere new, in the first few days before your eyes glaze over and nothing seems remarkable any more: people selling dustpans and brushes at the traffic lights; a derelict roadside hut, enticingly signed 'Giddy House Bar – exotic dancing'; a beautiful black goat, its legs tucked beneath its body, sitting on the steps of a shop; street sellers trading bras, displayed on the fence of a Methodist church; a huge rusting bauxite plant; the Constant Smiles dentist; the Windy Air Conditioning and Fans company (possibly the best name imaginable for an air-conditioning firm).

There were parts of Kingston where Daniel, who drove us for a week, refused to let us get out because he was worried about security, explaining the problem of rising gun crime. We were in no position to argue. I was disorientated by a short work trip here. I couldn't imagine how people despatched back here permanently after a lifetime in the UK would feel.

———

In Kingston, outrage about the British government's treatment of some long-term residents remained strong. Pausing for a moment near the seafront, listening to vintage reggae being played for a 1940s nostalgic music event, we met Herbie Miller, director of the Jamaican Music Museum, who said the behaviour of UK officials had been unforgivable. 'To see how the British government treated people who grew up in England who came home for a funeral or a vacation or a wedding, and were suddenly told: you're an illegal immigrant . . . These people worked in your hospitals, your transport systems, they took low-paid menial jobs. It hurts because these people spent their life there, they went as little kids, and then they are put through this anguish. Britain should be ashamed of itself.'

Barrister Bert Samuels, who sits on the National Council of Reparations campaigning for the UK government to pay compensation to the descendants of slaves in Jamaica, said the Windrush scandal was closely connected to the call for reparations for the slave trade. 'The legacy of slavery is why we are so impoverished and why so many of us have had to leave Jamaica for greener pastures, to send remittances home. We were British subjects until 1962. We fought in two world wars, we sent our soldiers who shed their blood for Britain. Then all of a sudden it became a policy that we had to apply for a visa to go to a country that used us for three centuries. We felt discarded. It is widely accepted in Jamaica that Britain has used us and refused us.'

During a visit to Jamaica in 2015, David Cameron dismissed discussions about slavery, commenting breezily that he wanted to 'move on from this painful legacy'. Diplomatic ties were badly damaged during that trip, when Cameron offered an unexpected gift from Britain to Jamaica: £25 million to build a prison so he could deport some of the six hundred Jamaican national prisoners who were held in British jails. It was resented as a very peculiar and misplaced gesture from the UK government, particularly at a time when Jamaican politicians wanted to talk about why Britain was not willing to consider paying reparations for its role in the slave trade, rather than how they could help Britain to rid itself of hundreds of unwanted criminals who were expensive to maintain. The offer to gift Jamaica a prison was rejected.

I travelled to the University of the West Indies Kingston campus to meet sixty-eight-year-old Ken Morgan, whose British passport had been confiscated twenty-five years earlier in the mid-1990s, when he tried to return to the UK after a family funeral. There had been another torrential rainstorm just before we met, and the smell of hot rain evaporating off the asphalt rose up to the balcony where we sat reflecting on why the British authorities had been allowed to ignore the problems of stuck Windrush citizens so long. Ken had arrived in London at the age of nine, as a British subject in 1959, before Jamaica became independent, but later was unable to persuade staff at the British High Commission that he was British and should be allowed to return home. For a while he was destitute on the streets of Kingston, but felt too ashamed to return to Clarendon, the central Jamaican parish where some of his family still lived. Convention dictates that you should return home from emigration to the UK or US rich, with resources to build an impressive retirement residence, not penniless and without prospects.

An official behind a glass barrier at the High Commission refused to view Ken as a British subject in need of consular assistance. He also refused to return his confiscated passport, was unmoved by the dire situation Ken found himself in, and told him: 'Mr Morgan, that was never a proper British passport.'

Well educated in London, where he had attended a grammar school and had later worked as an English teacher, Ken decided he was not going to be ground down by this catastrophic turn of events.

'The shocking thing is that without a British passport, the world still turns, the sun still shines, the rain still falls,' he said, laughing. He got a job as a graphic designer at the university, met his wife there, brought up a daughter, and gradually, over the course of twenty-five years, rebuilt a happy existence in Jamaica. He had had periods of feeling profound fury towards the British authorities, but these had passed. 'I cursed all these British, everybody, everything, but you cannot harbour all that inside yourself.' But he had felt profoundly disturbed to realise in recent months that so many other people had been similarly treated. 'All these lives have been ruined but you can't focus on that. You can only control the things you can control. You have to roll your sleeves up and get on with life.'

After decades of being rebuffed and ignored by Britain's representatives in Jamaica, trying in vain to get someone to listen to him, he noted with wry pleasure the sudden onslaught of phone calls he began to get from the High Commission shortly after the scandal became public in April. 'I got a ton of calls.' He thinks he was called around twenty times in the space of a fortnight. An official helped him fill out the necessary forms and a ten-year visa (which would normally have cost £798) was delivered by courier to his home within twenty-four hours, free of charge. He was amazed at the speed. 'Nothing happens that fast in Jamaica.'

He remained upset that no one at the High Commission had invited him inside the building to apologise for what had happened. 'A lunch or a breakfast, or something . . . It doesn't have to be anything fancy. At least they could say: the government is concerned about you. To this day they haven't done that. I'm a British citizen. The treatment we're getting does not feel first class.'

———

As I searched for some of the eighty-three people whom the British government had removed to the Caribbean, or who had returned 'voluntarily' after being sent enforcement notices, I expected to find individuals who had been placed on one of the notorious deportation charter flights and discarded in Jamaica, but the reality was more complicated. The vast majority of people who had fallen victim to the Home Office's tough immigration policies were those who had found themselves stuck in the wrong country and unable to return; we only met one person who had been formally deported.

Probably the most upsetting and difficult encounter we had in Jamaica was with Colin Smith (not his real name), aged fifty-eight, who was homeless when we met him, sometimes spending the night in a derelict, roofless police station, sleeping on a bit of cardboard amid piles of rubble, broken glass and rotting rafters.

His deportation in June 2013 on a British Airways flight from London had left him unemployed and destitute in a country where he knew almost no one, permanently separated from his girlfriend and teenage stepdaughters who live in Kent. He had been convicted of a relatively minor offence related to the 2011 London riots and sentenced to fourteen months in prison; he also had some drug convictions, dating back a few years. This meant he was one of the Windrush-age deportees whom the new Home Secretary Sajid Javid excluded from his count of those wrongly removed from the UK. Javid had decided to make a 'purposeful distinction between criminal and other cases'. It was a depressingly populist stance. The public had been overwhelmingly outraged by the treatment of the Windrush generation. But, judging that this popular sympathy would be limited to those felt to be deserving, the Home Secretary was not inclined to stand up for anyone less easily portrayed as desirable.

In their endless apologies for the debacle, the government repeatedly stressed that they were particularly sorry about what had happened because the Windrush generation had contributed so much to Britain. In apologising for their mistakes, ministers cast those affected as deserving migrants who had laboured hard in the NHS and on the buses, had paid their taxes and behaved impeccably. The subtext was clear: of course they were British, these good, tax-paying, law-abiding, hard-working people. So what did that mean for the people whose records were less immaculate? Immigration lawyers argued that a pre-1973 arrival meant a right to remain in the UK, regardless of convictions, but the government seemed at pains to wash its hands of anyone with a criminal record.

Colin (who asked for his real name not to be printed because he was embarrassed about his criminal record) had tried to kill himself twice in the immigration detention centre while he awaited deportation, so he was accompanied on the British Airways flight by two medical assistants as well as two guards. He was medicated and handcuffed on the journey, the handcuffs only removed briefly to allow him to eat. 'I felt ashamed. I thought that other people were looking at me.' He was driven straight from the airport in Jamaica to a mental hospital and left there.

He described Kingston as a very violent place and said he had witnessed a number of murders while living on the streets. 'They have deported me to a place which is a war zone.' Daily life was extremely hard. 'I don't know where I'm going to sleep tonight. I don't have stable meals, I sleep in very disgusting places, old buildings, abandoned shops and houses.'

We met at the National Organisation for Deported Migrants, next to the derelict police station where he had been sleeping. Oswald Dawkins, who runs the charity, was trying to help him to make an application to the British High Commission to return to the UK, but his ability to provide any evidence of his life in Britain was hampered by the fact that since being deported he had lost his flat in London, and the contents had been thrown away. During five years of homelessness in Kingston, his London address book had been lost, and with it the contact details of all the people who might have been able to help verify his story of his life in the UK.

As a child in the UK, Colin remembers being abused in the streets. 'I was called black monkey, asked if I came on the banana boat, and told go back home,' he said. Back in Jamaica he had been similarly abused as an alien. 'I've been called names – deportee, foreign. I've been threatened. I often feel frightened.'

Some days before we met, Colin had had a phone call from someone at the Windrush Taskforce asking him where he would stay if he returned to the UK and if he had enough money for a fare back. 'She was very nice. She kept using the term: "There is light at the end of the tunnel,"' he said. But he had heard nothing since and was uncertain about whether he would be given permission to return. 'Sometimes I want to go down to the sea and jump in and never come out,' he said. 'I committed a crime, yes, but I served my time, I've paid my due. I shouldn't have been sent here.'

He had a look of real desperation, asking as he got ready to leave: 'What do you think? Do you think they will focus on the criminal conviction?' It might be easy for the Home Secretary to make a 'purposeful distinction' between those people he wanted to help and those he didn't care about, but the intensity of unhappiness felt the same among all the people I met. The government had arbitrarily decided that people like Colin were not worthy of sympathy, but permanent separation from your home hurts regardless of whether you've got a criminal record or not.

———

I recounted some of these stories to the High Commissioner, when I was finally led through to his office.

Given the restrictions imposed by the Foreign Office press office, I'm not sure what can be written about the actual conversation, except to say that my fury subsided a little in the face of someone who I felt really did seem to want to help try to unravel this mess. Asif Ahmad said that as the son of immigrants to Britain, he (like Sajid Javid) felt lucky that he and his family had escaped this problem. He had been appointed only a few months before the issue began to be written about in the media, and his understanding of the situation came from news reports in the UK rather than information from staff in Kingston.

He agreed that I could report information from the conversation with the vague attribution 'diplomats say', which is a standard (if a little unhelpful) journalistic convention when Foreign Office staff want to say something beyond the anodyne phrases of ribbon-cutting events, or something that hasn't been carefully vetted by a media team. So . . . diplomats indicated that the whole crisis had been a shock to the system and had led to a soul-searching discussion among ambassadors and High Commissioners in their annual heads of mission meeting that summer, where they examined their responsibility to challenge ministerial decisions and reminded each other of the importance of speaking out when there was a recognition that a policy was causing problems. Within the High Commission in Kingston, there was a feeling of real empathy for those people who had quite innocently left the UK to visit Jamaica, who had no reason to believe they would get stuck.

Given that there was this feeling of sympathy for those affected, I was puzzled by how it was that officials had not noticed a problem which had been occurring on such a large scale. How was it that so many elderly people had been coming to the High Commission for years in desperate need of help, and never getting it? If there was such empathy from staff, how come the problem had never been relayed back to London as an issue that required urgent attention?

Diplomats suggested that this was perhaps partly the consequence of an outsourcing decision. Historically, all embassies had had internal visa sections, and in the past there would have been queues of people waiting outside to make a visa application. Some years ago, however, decision-making was moved from Kingston to New York and then later to Croydon. An external company – Visa

Facilitation Services – became responsible in Jamaica for taking applicants' fingerprints and other biometric details. Three people inside the High Commission were employed to stick visas into the passports before returning them to Visa Facilitation Services to be sent back to applicants; this was now the only involvement of the High Commission in the visa-granting process. Workers inside the High Commission no longer had a live caseload of immigration cases; as a result, diplomats became further removed from the people who were hoping to travel to the UK, and were less likely to have heard directly about these problems.

This is clearly not the full story. Windrush people in need of help had tried to seek advice from staff inside the building and had consistently been turned away. It's hard to avoid concluding that there must have been an element of racism in those decisions.

Some months later I had a second, much more open conversation with the High Commissioner by telephone. He acknowledged that the treatment of Joe Robinson, stuck for twenty-one months after his fiftieth birthday holiday in Jamaica, had been 'horrendous'. 'Everybody got into this process mindset that said if you can't produce the documents you cannot get through.' Staff were 'dealing with people as though they were commodities and case numbers rather than individuals and human beings', he said. When officials are responsible for enforcing hard-edged government policy they can sometimes 'dehumanise' the process, so they can deal with it without having to worry about it too much, he said. 'It is human nature if you are doing things that are unpleasant to somehow remove them from your own conscience.'

During a large staff meeting Foreign and Home Office employees had had a frank discussion about how they got into a 'situation where obvious cases of injustice were being overlooked'. After this internal dialogue, staff were encouraged to be careful to retain an innate curiosity and empathy when doing their job, and not be afraid to question decisions they felt might be wrong, he said. 'Even if we are making decisions that are correct, we need to understand that there are human beings and lives behind this.' With the government's ongoing commitment to maintaining a tough approach to immigration, this would be hard, Ahmed acknowledged. 'These are things that are not quite compatible with the compliant environment the Home Secretary wants to achieve.'

There was a desire to celebrate the Windrush generation within the High Commission. Aware that the building's Trafalgar Road address, and Trafalgar House and Nelson House official residences, sent out unfortunate colonial messages to visitors, officials had decided to rename a part of the green space outside the High Commission building as Windrush Gardens. Perhaps one day Ken Morgan will be invited through the fortress gates to see it.

POSTSCRIPT

The Windrush scandal wasn't a mistake. It was the direct consequence of a harsh set of policies designed to bring down immigration numbers by ejecting people from Britain, and by making life intolerable for anyone without documents. Conservative ministers would like us to remember this scandal as an unfortunate bureaucratic error for which they have apologised repeatedly. But this was a deliberate strategy. The only surprise was that people cared about the victims, at which point ministers were forced to declare that they too cared.

They put on an impressive show of remorse and for a while I was taken in.

A few days before she resigned, Amber Rudd declared that 'cultural change is going to start here'. The Director of the Home Office, Philip Rutnam, said he had been appalled by reading accounts of people let down so badly by his staff, adding: 'In my thirty-odd years of public service, I've never seen an episode like this.'[1] Immigration Minister Caroline Nokes said a new approach was needed, admitting: 'Too often the discussions around immigration are steered by the tabloid press.' In turn, Sajid Javid acknowledged something had gone 'massively' wrong within the department and said he would introduce a fairer, more compassionate era at the Home Office.

Listening to the repeated promises that everything would be different and so much better, it was hard not to feel exuberant. I really thought that things were going to change. The Home Office was going to be reformed, officials would be more sensitive to the lives of the people they were processing, Britain would become a more welcoming place.

Almost a year on, at the time of writing, I have to admit I'm struggling to find much evidence of the new, compassionate Home Office. There's no sign of the cultural change which was meant to have started twelve months ago. The tabloid press continues to inspire immigration policy. With the sobering passage of time, these statements sound hollow. I feel foolish for wanting to believe them. I roll my eyes whenever I hear the government declaring (again) that it has dispensed with the notion of the hostile environment and has adopted instead a compliant immigration environment. None of the core legislation has been repealed, so who are they trying to fool with this empty rebranding?

At the beginning of March 2019 I met Sajid Javid for an early morning briefing on what he planned to do to put things right. This was another off-the-record conversation, where I was under instructions not to make notes or recordings; instead I had to sit still and listen, which I did – so dutifully that the motion-sensitive overhead lamps in his huge office kept turning themselves off, leaving just the dim wintry light from the street, until he waved his arms to turn them on again. Reform was coming, he said, but not quite yet; first he needed to hear the conclusions of the 'lessons learned' review he'd commissioned, which would be published at an unspecified later date. Compensation payments were coming, at some point later in the year.

By this point, only two people had been given money from an emergency hardship fund, set up belatedly nine months after the scandal erupted, to help those made homeless and pushed into financial crisis by the Home Office's mistakes. While they waited for compensation, some of those affected were getting eviction letters, unable to buy winter coats, still being pursued by bailiffs for thousands of pounds' worth of debt run up when they were prevented from working. Their situation remained dire, but the official response was curiously relaxed.

In Kingston, I had thought Ken Morgan was being unduly cynical when he said he didn't expect change any time soon. 'The British know that we are old people, we're not young and sprightly. They'll just drag this out until we die,' he told me. But the Home Office subsequently admitted that of the 164 people who were wrongly detained or removed from the country, at least nineteen had died before officials were able to contact them to apologise; another twenty-seven could not be traced.

Dozens of parliamentary debates and committee hearings have been held in an attempt to understand what went wrong. Four excoriating official reports[2] have already been published by parliamentary committees and Whitehall bodies, identifying the root problems and clearly pinpointing what needs to be done. But the Home Secretary seemed to be in no particular rush to act. He was still promising reform at some vague point in the future, just as he had been almost a year earlier. There was nothing tangible to grab hold of. My remaining optimism flickered out with the overhead lighting.

The official deputed to escort me out at the end of the meeting remarked that the scandal had shaken everyone in the building. 'This has been a difficult time for the Home Office. We're all still getting to grips with it. Don't write that down.' It seemed odd that an unnamed official should feel so nervous about making idle small talk in the lift, but then so many of the encounters I've had with the Home Office have been about controlling the message, trying to dictate what does and doesn't get written.

The widow of one of the Home Office's victims had recently shown me a letter she had been sent by the department in response to a request for help, printed on paper headed with a new logo: 'UK Visas and Immigration, Proud to be Supporting the Windrush Generation'. 'They're proud, are they? Jesus. And where's the support?' she wondered. Her husband had been sacked from his job with Tesco after fifty years in the UK, and had died, devastated, without discovering why he had been misclassified as illegal. The mismatch between the chirpy letterhead and the complete absence of assistance was shameless. I felt despondent at this new display of message management, masking bureaucratic inaction.

And yet I'm trying to restrain my scepticism about the government's response because the national shame felt over Windrush has triggered some significant changes.

The Windrush Taskforce, staffed by experienced Home Office employees, has so far taken over seven thousand calls from affected people. Over six thousand people have been granted papers confirming they are living legally in the UK, 4,200 of whom are now British citizens. This is a remarkable number – it means six thousand families no longer have someone worrying about their status, constantly scanning the horizon for Immigration Enforcement vans, concerned about the threat of deportation or loss of work or access to healthcare. That alone is a huge victory.

On 3 April 2019, Sajid Javid finally announced the compensation scheme. Officials expect to pay out between £200 million and £570 million in compensation to an estimated fifteen thousand people. It's impossible to know what the final figure will be because no one has any accurate data on how many people have been affected, and the Home Office acknowledges that the number could be as high as thirty thousand. Javid apologised again, saying with real feeling: 'We would not be the country we are today without the men and women who crossed oceans to come here legally, to make their homes, to work hard, to pay taxes and to raise their families, and we all know it, which is why the whole country was shocked by the unacceptable treatment experienced by some members of the Windrush generation. People who have built their lives in this country, people who have done so much for this country, people who have every right to be in this country were told they were not welcome. It was a terrible mistake.'

Wendy Williams, the Home Office employee leading the 'lessons learned' review, which will offer the government guidance about how to avoid such a catastrophe in the future, has met more than two hundred people to hear about the problems they experienced, and said listening to them had been harrowing. The Home Office had spent more than £6 million by December 2018 on its Windrush programme, employing around 175 members of staff.[3] There is a clear official desire to tidy up the mess.

Such was the unease about incentivised Home Office deportation targets that Javid said he would not be setting them again. He has also repeatedly refused to endorse the party's aspiration to reduce net migration to the tens of thousands, so it's likely that this pernicious goal, which has led to so many problems, will also be quietly abandoned.

Even without the core legislation being amended, some decisions being taken within the Home Office have changed as a result of the scandal. Newly nervous about wrongfully detaining or deporting people who are here legally, Home Office staff chose to detain and remove fewer people post-Windrush. The number of people locked up in immigration detention centres fell by an extraordinary 41 per cent between September 2017 and September 2018, by which point just 2,049 were being held (much lower than the total capacity for immigration detention of 3,800).[4] A Home Office document notes that the fall coincides with 'changes across the immigration system following Windrush'.

This was a surprising and positive development given that the UK's record on immigration detention has been one of the worst in Europe, particularly its attachment to indefinite detention, which has meant many detainees are held for months and sometimes years. The Home Office makes repeated mistakes with regard to the people it detains, and was forced to pay £21 million in compensation to 850 people wrongly held between 2012 and 2017.[5] Numerous studies have condemned our immigration detention system, criticising the excessive length of time for which people are held and the number who are detained completely unnecessarily. A 41 per cent[6] fall in the number of people in immigration detention post-Windrush is real cause for celebration. Similarly the number of enforced returns from the UK decreased by 18 per cent to 10,190 in the year to September 2018, compared with 12,380 the previous year, a drop officials attributed again to 'changes across the immigration system following Windrush'.

Once the voices of those whose lives were damaged by the hostile environment were finally heard, the Windrush crisis saw the whole country and its media united in dismay at what the government was doing. People who work in the immigration sector, in charities or as legal advisers, were amazed. There has never before been a Home Office crisis where the public have come together to condemn the government's excessively harsh behaviour; earlier outcries have always been fuelled by a sense that the government was not being tough enough on migrants. 'This scandal was different because people were saying: "Gosh, isn't our system horrible, doesn't it do really nasty things to people, how can we change it?" That's a huge shift,' said Steve Valdez-Symonds of Amnesty, who has been working as a lawyer and campaigner in the immigration sector for two decades.[7]

For once, the Windrush stories made people take the side of those who were classified as illegal immigrants, forcing them to scrutinise Britain's immigration system and to discover that there was much there they did not like. Previously only a small group of policy experts were aware of the hostile environment programme and understood the implications of ratcheting up immigration controls and obliging civilians to start acting as border guards. This pushed the issue to a much broader audience. Once it hit the headlines, anyone remotely engaged with the news was obliged to pay attention; many were dismayed by what they saw. It turned out that the British public was inclined to take a more decent approach on immigration controls than politicians had expected. For years Labour and the Conservatives had been racing to portray themselves as tough on immigration; now there was at least a question about whether this was politically essential. A new humanity had entered the debate.

'You have to take the wins when they come, because they don't often come,' said Satbir Singh, head of the Joint Council for the Welfare of Immigrants, stressing the significance of the response to Windrush. 'We have never before seen the public uniformly reject the mistreatment of migrants or people of colour. The pendulum of public opinion has always swung the other way towards more restrictive policies, tightening the screws. That's incredibly encouraging. The government saw that the politics of hostility don't sell any more, and that's a start.'

Despite the wearisome nature of the government's repeated protestations that it valued the contributions of the Windrush generation, it was nevertheless good to see finally some official recognition of the important role immigrants have played. Nationally, there were signs that hostility towards immigration was weakening. A British Social Attitudes survey published in July 2018 showed that just 17 per cent of British people thought that immigrants had a negative impact on the economy while only 23 per cent felt they had a negative impact on the country's cultural life, a sharp fall in negativity on immigration since 2011.[8] Given the degree to which the toxic Brexit campaign normalised xenophobia, this is a remarkable shift.

There is much here to feel positive about, but I'm torn.

It's clear that ministers now feel confident that the public's concern is moving on; Brexit has sucked attention from this and so much else. It is safe for politicians to make effusive, noisy promises of Home Office reform while simultaneously doing absolutely nothing. The efficiency with which ministers have deflated the crisis in the year since the scandal broke is as impressive as it is depressing.

Officials have worked hard to minimise what happened. The Windrush branding was initially useful as a shortcut to help people understand what was happening, but ultimately it became unhelpful because it radically diminished the scale of the problem, presenting it as something restricted to a small group.

The crisis represented a major failure within the Home Office to recognise that its policies were destroying the lives of thousands of people, from countries all over the world – India, Pakistan, Afghanistan, Nigeria, Zimbabwe, China – not just the Caribbean. But it suits the government to present what took place as a relatively small predicament affecting a niche group of retirement-age Caribbean people who had no papers.

The government only admitted there was a problem when it became absolutely impossible to continue denying it. Ministers still refuse to accept the link between what happened and the hostile environment policy decisions, finding it more convenient to present this as a bureaucratic error affecting a limited number of people. Their atonement has been pretty superficial.

Once they realised that they could no longer ignore the issue, the ministers were compelled by soaring public anger to act on Windrush, to some extent because those affected were so blameless. The coincidence of the crisis with the seventieth anniversary of the arrival of the *Empire Windrush* forced people to reflect on the positive role played by Caribbean immigrants to the UK – their role in the Second World War, in building the NHS and the transport system, as teachers and carers, as factory workers and in the construction industry. A group of people who for decades had faced racism and myriad obstacles to advancement were amazed suddenly to find themselves transformed overnight, fifty years after Enoch Powell's hate-filled speech, into national treasures, embraced by the media's right wing, respected and beloved.

Obviously they had English as their first (only) language; they were mostly Christian; many had been at primary school here, had found jobs and worked hard for decades. It was easy for the whole country to be united in horror at the government's treatment of them. The fact that many arrived before their own countries became independent, effectively moving within one country, dragged their treatment away from a debate about migration, because they weren't really immigrants anyway – they were people who had moved internally from one part of the dying empire to another.

So while there was a sudden upswell of affection for this group and a warm articulation of how much Britain owed to the Windrush generation, this hasn't evolved into the much bigger discussion we need about the debt we owe to immigrants more widely, or a more general debate about the positive impact of all immigration.

It's hard to predict how much further the public sympathy would go. What about Syrian asylum seekers who find themselves designated illegal immigrants? Many are pushed to near destitution, given poor housing, disbelieved by officials, made to feel profoundly unwelcome. Would a similar exposé of how badly they fare in the asylum system trigger equivalent outrage? What about grandparents from Pakistan whose application to extend a visit to see family in the UK gets lost, and who find themselves unexpectedly classified as illegals? What about an Indian masters student whose request to continue her studies is refused (due, her lawyers believe, to a bureaucratic mistake by Home Office staff) and who finds herself detained in an immigration removal centre? Every day these new examples of Home Office errors pour into my inbox. My colleague Gary Younge points out: 'It has yet to fully sink in that what was wrong for the Windrush generation is wrong for all immigrants.'

The problem goes much deeper than the group of Caribbean-born residents who were so badly affected. There are many more people in the UK who have a right to be here but who don't have a clear set of documents to prove it. But the promises from two Home Secretaries that things would change, and that a more humane and sensitive system was on its way, have been rapidly narrowed to mean that things would change for the relatively small group of Windrush victims, leaving the rest of the system to operate as normal.

In a searing report on the government's handling of the Windrush situation, the National Audit Office said officials had shown a 'lack of curiosity' and a 'lack of urgency' about the adverse impact of its hostile environment legislation on a much bigger group of non-Caribbean Commonwealth citizens, many of whom may also have experienced difficulties.[9] The National Audit Office is culturally a very dry body, careful with its language, but this report was uncharacteristically caustic – it criticised the Home Office's poor-quality data that wrongly classified people as illegal immigrants, the risky use of deportation targets, the failure to respond to numerous warnings that the policies would hurt people living here legally, and the department's refusal to widen the scope of its search for victims of its policies. There are numerous examples of the department doing 'as little, rather than as much, as possible to help and find people affected by its actions'.

Perhaps the most devastating conclusion from the National Audit Office was that there was no evidence that the hostile environment policies (ostensibly introduced to save taxpayers' money by curtailing access to services for those who were deemed ineligible) were going to cut costs in the slightest. Once you remove the urge to save money, what else was driving the hostile environment policies? Nothing but xenophobic, anti-immigrant conviction.

Even within the narrowly defined group of Caribbean-born Windrush people, we still don't know the true scale of what happened and we may never find out. The government is making no attempt to establish how many people wrongly lost their jobs or their homes, or have been denied benefits or access to healthcare. The Home Secretary has written only eighteen letters of apology to individuals who are believed to have suffered significant detriment because they were wrongly detained or deported; they have not been publicly identified, despite repeated requests, so a huge part of the scandal remains hidden. There have been no personal apologies to those who had their lives wrecked in other ways. Although the compensation fund sounds huge, the small print reveals a less generous picture, with a cap on £500 for legal bills and just a £1,000 lump payment for people like Joycelyn John who were pushed into 'voluntary' returns to unfamiliar countries.

A couple of senior officials have been shuffled off into other jobs, but no one has been sacked for wrongly detaining or deporting legal citizens. Those responsible have escaped punishment.

Meanwhile the Home Office remains obsessed with tackling illegal immigration, whipping up an alarming, distorted public perception of illegal migrants. In reality, most aren't the menacing figures of popular imagination, but have been shunted from legality to illegality by a technicality of the bureaucratic process: overstayers, people whose visas have expired, who may be in work, and those who are attempting to progress through the complex, protracted procedure of regularising their status. There are an estimated 120,000 children born in the UK who have no British citizenship, who are caught up in a similar fight for status. No one is arguing for open borders, or for officials to turn a blind eye to the arrival of immigrants without the correct visas, but the Home Office focus on illegality is wildly disproportionate to the problem, and sours the whole system.

And there is mounting nervousness about how the same department will manage to register the 3.5 million EU nationals who will need formal confirmation of their status in the UK after Brexit. This will be the first key test of whether the Home Office has learned any lessons. Officials have said that as a consequence of Windrush, they will be looking for reasons to grant immigration status to people from European countries who have been living in the UK for five years, rather than searching for reasons to refuse it (which might ordinarily have been the case). The Labour MP Yvette Cooper has warned it could become 'Windrush on steroids'.

Immigration case workers who sit at the frontline of all this say nothing has changed. Staff at advice charities continue to complain about soaring fees, delays, inflexible decision-making, inexperienced Home Office workers who don't understand the issues they are expected to handle, impossibly complex systems for remedying problems, life-changing bureaucratic errors, lost documents, routine misspelling of names with dire consequences. There has been no clear instruction from the top requiring workers to adopt a more humane approach and there's still no sign that compassion has entered the department's vocabulary.

*

For the past eighteen months I've been struggling to understand what caused the scandal and why its catastrophic effects were ignored for so long. It's very clear now what caused the problem; confronting why it stayed so hidden is a more difficult exercise. So many people were affected in very serious ways, over a long period of time, and yet politicians and the media paid scant attention. No one really noticed. Why not?

The Conservative government did its best to create a climate in which these problems would stay hidden. First, crucially, there was the inspired government strategy to dismantle all the places where people could go to seek help, just as life was being made harder for them.

The Conservatives' passion for austerity provided a justification – cutting legal aid for immigration measures was necessary to save money, they said. But it also eased the process of cutting net migration because migrants could no longer challenge Home Office decisions. For good measure, a number of appeal routes against Home Office decisions were withdrawn.

There was a parallel removal of state funding for the network of grassroots race equality organisations that had flourished from the 1970s to the 1990s. The race equality campaigner Simon Woolley showed me the gaping stretch of office space at Operation Black Vote's headquarters which had been filled with fifteen members of staff until the funding was cut and the headcount dropped to four. 'They didn't want detractors; they pulled the money,' he said. Meanwhile, the introduction of fees for employment tribunals meant claims for race discrimination dropped by 58 per cent.[10]

The trend is echoed across the sector. Citizens Advice services have been cut; the Equalities and Human Rights Commission has shrunk to a fraction of its original size. For a while David Cameron had the audacity to suggest that his cosy notion of the Big Society could pick up the slack. Sure, the knowledge and expertise built up over decades in legal advice centres and anti-discrimination organisations would go, but it would be replaced by well-meaning neighbours happy to help out. The state needed to shrink, but society would fill the void. What problem can't be solved by a church hall coffee morning?

The idea was delusional. What actually happened was that people with desperate, life-changing problems simply had nowhere to turn.

As the state became more hostile towards immigrants, cuts to disability payments, the freezing of benefits and a punitive process of welfare reform were creating a parallel hostile environment for anyone who had previously relied on state support. Within the

Department for Work and Pensions, individual discretion and face-to-face contact were being replaced by tickbox processes. Those affected were also being frightened into compliance by a harsh sanctioning system. Cuts to advice centres and legal support conveniently prevented victims from getting redress and muted their capacity to complain.

Some people with immigration problems visited their MP for help, but in every constituency caseloads were expanding wildly, taking up the slack created by the shrinking of the advice sector. Most MPs were faced with such a broad and complex spectrum of immigration issues that they weren't able to spot a trend.

The collapse of the local newspaper industry meant that there was no outlet where victims of Home Office mistakes could describe their difficulties. There aren't many local media organisations which are sufficiently well resourced to allow reporters to spend time looking at immigration issues, which are never straightforward. Without journalists on the ground all over the country, problems remain hidden.

Even within well-resourced media organisations, there isn't always the desire to focus on such bleak issues. Over this period of slashed government budgets, there has been such an array of examples of state-sanctioned cruelty to choose from that it can be hard to push issues on to the front page. I've spent years writing about the human consequences of cuts to benefits bills, the lives destroyed by withdrawal of disability benefits. Sometimes it feels like there's been a gradual hardening in the face of all these difficulties. We've become desensitised to the painful human cost of this determination to save money by rolling back the state. The collateral victims of the austerity programme are visible all around us – the homeless, those unable to work, and the unwelcomed migrants. There has been a gradual withering of empathy.

The Home Office's decision to classify thousands of British

residents as illegal immigrants came as Britain experienced a frenzy of Brexit-fuelled anti-immigrant hysteria. The stigma attached to being an illegal immigrant is so strong that it's not surprising that those who were wrongly targeted were so nervous about telling anyone, even family members, about the letters they were getting from Immigration Enforcement. Some blamed themselves, concluding that perhaps it was somehow their own fault that they had become illegal.

And of course the Home Office's actions were inflicted on a group of people who had been so messed around by the police and other state bodies for decades that many of the victims were not as surprised by their treatment as others might have been. Most already had low expectations of the state; this merely confirmed that they were right in their assumptions.

All of this happened in a country where routine racism remains a persistent reality. The High Court recently ruled that the flagship hostile environment policy, the right to rent scheme requiring landlords to check the immigration status of tenants, is racially discriminatory. The Home Office shrugged and said it would appeal the ruling.

If you're British-born, white, with a British-sounding surname, you won't ever face the hostile environment. Landlords aren't checking white people's papers. Because Britain remains a society in which discrimination is rife, those affected by the hostile environment tend not to be people who are able to get their voices heard. The scandal spotlighted who matters and who doesn't matter. Questionable deportations to the Caribbean and elsewhere have been happening for decades, but they were accepted as unremarkable examples of routine Home Office barbarity. The families of those removed felt unable to challenge the decisions, and they rarely made the news.

Despite the government's apologies, the episode doesn't look like it marks a turning point for the better in British history. It seems more like a reminder that the country has not developed into a happy post-racist nation, as is sometimes suggested. No one now would dare claim that the state has become a fair, colour-blind institution. Windrush is the one-word retort to such complacency.

The historian David Olusoga said the Home Office scandal shattered the myth of the Windrush generation as the symbol of a newly inclusive Britain, which was so powerfully evoked in the opening ceremony of the 2012 Olympic Games. 'We wanted to believe that myth so much: the plucky group of 492 people who came here to rebuild the nation, who faced racism, but we got there in the end and a new multicoloured, rainbow, diverse nation was proof of that. We look to history for warm baths to feel comfortable about our past. Facts struggle when they are up against myths that are so potent,' he said. The revelations of Home Office behaviour exposed the 'falsehood of British harmony'. He told me he found it 'difficult to imagine that this would have been tolerated had these people been white'.

Arten Llazari, the head of the Refugee and Migrant Centre in Wolverhampton, the charity that helped Paulette, spent years trying without success to get the media and politicians to pay attention to what was happening. 'These people were acceptable collateral damage; with very few exceptions, they happened to be black. We don't think we're racist any more, but we are. Nobody gave a toss.'

I'm left feeling disheartened by the efficiency with which the government has introduced mechanisms to bully and intimidate its own citizens. Who wants to live in a country where Immigration Enforcement vans circle the streets with menacing intent? How did we become that country?

Still I can't entirely suppress a sense that something positive has happened. In the past year, I've begun feeling hopeful again about the power of journalism to force change. In many ways, writing about these cases has been easy because the core injustice was so straightforward and shocking. I kept going, fuelled by a simple feeling of outrage.

The ability to feel outrage is a powerful tool. In order for the Windrush events to become a scandal, there had to be an understanding that this was not how things should be, that this was not the way the state should behave. Which is to say, in order to feel outraged about what happened, you needed to have a strong belief in the responsibility of the state to behave differently, in a fair and just manner towards everyone.

Often when I was interviewing people, I was disconcerted by their resigned acceptance of the lousy treatment they had received. For some, after a lifetime in Britain, discovering that the state was not on their side was not an enormous surprise. They didn't see their treatment as particularly scandalous, it was simply the same unpleasant, unjust behaviour meted out by a country that has not always been as welcoming as it should. I don't want to say that I have a wide-eyed or naïve expectation that the state will always behave well, but having not been so ground down by officialdom, I was more able to shake off cynicism and believe that things can be better.

Occasionally, I have felt out of my depth, plunged into a world that I was unfamiliar with. Sometimes I would get messages on Twitter noting accusingly, 'We don't want white voices writing about black issues.' It's hard to know how to respond. I understand the sensitivities; I'm aware that I look at the issue with my own unhelpful unconscious bias. It's true that the *Guardian*'s newsroom has for years not been diverse enough; that's changing. But fundamentally, reporters have to be able to tackle all subjects.

The challenges of the past year have made me think hard about how I do my job. There is a perception of what it means to be an investigative journalist, framed by the idea that it is a hard-nosed and macho calling, usually about uncovering corruption in the international arms industry, about espionage and data analysis. Reporting on people's lives and their problems doesn't automatically fit into that bracket. Sometimes colleagues talk slightly dismissively about human interest stories, as if they're a lighter category of news reporting, there for entertainment and relief from the meatier core sections of a publication. But here, the whole investigation emerged from writing about people's lives, amplifying their voices, helping readers to understand that real people were being affected in terrible ways, exposing the human consequences of policy decisions. That approach helped build a consensus that what was happening was really wrong – both among readers and among politicians.

When the issue finally seized mainstream attention in April 2018, the Windrush scandal revealed that most Britons don't want to live in a country that takes pride in being hostile towards vulnerable and marginalised people. This also makes me feel hopeful. We may not be having the full debate on immigration yet, or a radical reassessment of our national attitudes towards migrants, but it feels like that conversation is something that might be possible in the future.

Hearing from those affected about how they are gradually getting back on track has been generally positive. Some remain broken by their experiences, heavily in debt and traumatised, but most are inching towards rebuilding their lives. Every week or so I have a call from someone I've met in the past year, telling me their citizenship papers have come through, or their passport has arrived, allowing them to travel. Recently I've had a message from someone I've never met, saying: 'Thanks. I am back in Jamaica for the first time in fifty years.'

I've been to several town hall Windrush meetings, where I've watched people queue up to take a microphone and recount, often in tears, the difficulties they have experienced. Sometimes there is a discussion of ways that the government could make amends. More than once the idea of sending new vans to areas of high immigration has been suggested, marked this time with the words: 'You are welcome here'. At the end of March 2019 I went to Northampton to a welcome home party for eighty-three-year-old Ivan Anglin, one of the people I'd met in Jamaica. The last time I'd seen him, he seemed dejected and lonely as he waited to hear if he was going to be allowed to return to the UK after a long stretch of enforced exile following deportation. Back in England the contrast could not have been more stark. He was surrounded by his daughters, nine grandchildren and so many great-grandchildren that he had begun to lose track. It was an incredibly happy occasion.

Paulette Wilson was granted indefinite leave to remain in January 2018, a month after the *Guardian* first highlighted her case. She became a British citizen in the summer. A few weeks later, she received a letter of apology from Sajid Javid, who told her he was 'truly sorry'. 'As you had arrived in Britain before 1973 and had remained here continuously, you had every right to be here and should not have been subject to detention. Moreover, in its handling of your case, the Department should have demonstrated more flexibility, common sense and empathy.' Paulette's whole demeanour has changed. She is no longer knocking at her daughter's door in the middle of the night, begging to be allowed to sleep in her bed, terrified that Immigration Enforcement officers are going to come and take her away. She has returned to her voluntary job cooking meals for the homeless (no longer reliant herself on the food). She remains more puzzled than angry about the government's treatment of her. 'I've never done anything wrong; how could I be an illegal?'

Anthony Bryan got British citizenship in July 2018 and has been re-employed by his old boss. That summer he travelled back to

Jamaica for the first time in fifty years, with his partner, Janet, and spent several weeks with his mother at the home she had retired to, in the same hilltop village where he spent the first eight years of his life. He emailed me photographs of himself sitting in the family home next to his mother, looking uncomfortably hot and very happy. He also had a letter of apology from Sajid Javid, who wrote: 'I fully acknowledge that the Department did not allow for the difficulty you faced in proving your arrival date.' He is still trying to clear the debts that piled up during his enforced time off work, including legal fees, and has the occasional sleepless night worrying about how he is going to repay everything he owes. 'I'm still angry with the government, but to protect myself I try to defuse the anger, listening to music. It's hard.'

I waited for Sylvester Marshall outside Lunar House in May 2018 while he was interviewed about his status. He emerged, delighted, holding a piece of paper confirming that he was not an illegal immigrant. For the first time in years, he said he no longer felt frightened walking down the street. 'I've always been looking over my shoulder to see if there's any police; I worried that they will pick me up, ask for papers and deport me. Now I can relax.' But he was upset by the imbalance between the number of years he had wasted trying to persuade immigration officials he was not lying and the speed with which things had been resolved in the space of an hour. He has finished his cancer radiotherapy and is feeling much better. He hates to dwell on what might have happened if his case hadn't been suddenly, swiftly sorted at the height of the political crisis in April 2018. 'I don't know where I would be now. Either deported to Jamaica, or living homeless, somewhere in the bushes in London. I try not to think about it. Maybe I'd be six foot under, dead and gone.'

Michael Braithwaite got his papers unexpectedly within days of a call to the Home Office alerting them that his story was going to be covered in the media. Once news of his treatment appeared in the *Guardian*, he was offered his old teaching assistant job back by the head teacher who had sacked him. For the moment he does not feel up to returning, although he is helping other children with special needs in another school in a more part-time role. 'This has been a hard road for me,' he said. But he is happy with his own role in pushing the scandal on to the political agenda. A play has been written about his experiences; he is beginning to feel cheerful enough to return to playing his guitar and writing music.

Winston Robinson found the period after losing his job as an ambulance driver profoundly unsettling. He felt depressed and lonely. 'So I sought solace with a younger woman.' As a result, much to his surprise, he now has a two-year-old daughter and five-month-old twins and is extremely happy, if rather sleep-deprived and overwhelmed, to have these new responsibilities at the age of sixty-one. He has been talking with his former employers about getting his job back. 'I am soldiering on.'

Hubert Howard was issued with a biometric residency card shortly after his appointment at Lunar House, but later in the summer his application for British citizenship was rejected. Despite the fact that he has lived in Britain since he was three, a recent low-level criminal conviction (which he says was the result of a misunderstanding, and for which he received a suspended sentence) meant he did not pass the Home Office's good character test. He was heartbroken. He has been offered a job back with Peabody housing association but is not currently well enough to work. His former employers have written a character reference which he hopes to use to challenge the citizenship refusal. 'Hubert has great integrity, is a passionate and loyal person and has a warm and friendly disposition,' the letter reads. 'He was well-respected, reliable, hardworking and diligent in his duties.' So far this has not persuaded the Home Office to reconsider. Hubert remains heavily in debt as a result of losing his job after officials registered him as an illegal immigrant, and day-to-day life remains challenging. 'I've been knocking my head against a brick wall for years. It makes me feel like I am crazy. I've been here since 1960. It's not like I'm a dangerous person. I feel I can't take any more.'

Trevor Johnson's case was only resolved after one of his sisters posted a picture of him on Facebook and an eighty-one-year-old retired dinner lady from his primary school recognised him and got in touch, providing the evidence that the Home Office required. He has become increasingly angry as the scale of the scandal emerged. 'I'm still scared, still worried – that's what it has done to me. I've turned into someone who is fretting all the time. I've been here for forty-odd years, I loved it here, I still love it. But I've lost faith.'

Vernon Vanriel returned to the UK in September 2018 and is living with his sister, finally getting medical treatment and, at the time of writing, hoping to be rehoused. He is sad that he wasted thirteen years, one month and ten days trapped in Jamaica. 'No amount of compensation will eradicate the pain that I've felt.' In December 2018 he appeared in front of a House of Commons committee, leaving MPs visibly distressed by his description of what he went through. 'To find that I was refused entry to the country that I grew up in and that I loved so dearly was just mind-blowing to me,' he told them. More than once he cried as he explained what he had been through. Despite everything, he is delighted to be home and is beginning to rebuild his life. Vernon hopes that once he is in better health he will be able to pursue his ambitions as a boxing coach. He has already begun training a few young boxers and is hoping eventually to set up his own training club, which he plans to call the Windrush VIBE Boxing Academy (VIBE stands for Vernon's International Boxing Excellence). 'I've got my life back; I'm doing boxing which is what my heart desires. I hope to be back on top of the world again.'

Ken Morgan returned to London in the autumn of 2018 to sort out his paperwork. He was amazed by the transformation of the city that had occurred in the two decades he had spent away. He ate fish and chips in Walthamstow on his first day back and said it felt good to be home.

Colin Smith remains homeless in Kingston, still waiting to see if the Windrush Taskforce will help him get back to his family.

Joycelyn John saw news of the scandal breaking in Grenada and realised that she had been wrongly forced into self-deportation. Her brother called the Windrush Taskforce and she was issued with an air ticket back to England in July 2018. 'A bit of me was ecstatic, a bit of me was angry that no one had listened to me in the first place.' She was rehoused in September, but the flat she moved into was entirely empty and council officials didn't think to provide any furniture or a fridge or oven. Friends gave her a bed and some chairs, but it was months before she was able to get a fridge. She too received a letter of apology from the Home Secretary. 'I wish to assure you that the Home Office is making sure lessons have been learned,' Javid wrote, adding (with the useful assistance of the copy and paste functions) the same reference to his own background that each letter of apology ends with. 'People of the Windrush generation who came to Britain from the Commonwealth, as my parents did, have helped make this country what it is today. The experiences faced by you and others have been completely unacceptable.' She cried when she read the letter. 'They ruined my life completely. I came back to nothing, had to start rebuilding my life from scratch at the age of fifty-eight. So many years of my life have gone down the pan.' Although her right to live in the UK has been confirmed, she hasn't got a passport yet because she can't afford the fee and she remains frightened. 'I'm still looking over my shoulder all the time; I'm still a nervous wreck.'

I listen to these stories and I feel such shame at hearing what these people have been through, and at the realisation that Britain could treat its citizens so badly. But I want to be hopeful that the memory of the Windrush scandal will linger and ensure that such extremes of institutional cruelty are never allowed to be repeated.

AFTERWORD

On 19 March 2020 the 275-page Windrush Lessons Learned Review was published, analysing the causes of the disaster and setting out thirty recommendations the government needed to adopt if it was to ensure that the scandal could never be repeated. The report, commissioned by Sajid Javid when he was Home Secretary, is forensically researched. Over the course of eighteen months, forty-six Home Office employees worked alongside Wendy Williams, the semi-independent official appointed to lead the review. They spoke to around 450 Home Office staff, government officials and politicians and to some 270 people affected by the scandal. Williams said her conversations with victims had been humbling and heartbreaking. Her team sifted through 69,000 official documents: briefing notes to ministers, letters, emails and reports. The review's conclusions are hard-hitting and broadly chime with the conclusions I came to as I wrote this book.

Williams found that the Home Office demonstrated an 'ignorance and thoughtlessness' towards the issue of race and the history of the Windrush generation consistent with elements of institutional racism. Warnings were repeatedly ignored. The scandal was 'foreseeable and avoidable' and came about in part because of 'officials' poor understanding of Britain's colonial history'. The Windrush generation's history had been 'institutionally forgotten'. A 'culture of disbelief and carelessness' had spread through the Home Office, which had become so defensive after years of controversy that junior officials felt unable to flag their concerns to senior staff.

A politically driven immigration policy had inured the department to the mounting evidence of harm being done. There was a 'target-dominated' culture within the Immigration Enforcement teams, and low-quality decision-making was prevalent. An official admitted that staff would pick easy targets, 'low-hanging fruit', for deportation. Williams encountered a lack of empathy for individuals and was disturbed by the use of 'dehumanising jargon'. Some members of staff displayed an 'irrational and unreasonable' approach to applicants. The entire culture of the department needed to be changed, she said, to 'recognise that migration and wider Home Office policy is about people and, whatever its objective, should be rooted in humanity'.

The stories she collected from people who lost their immigration status were familiar and yet still profoundly upsetting. A former serviceman told Williams that although he had served in the UK armed forces, he had no documentation and 'had become so frightened of not being allowed back into the country that, for years, he'd refused his wife's requests for a holiday, telling her instead that he was afraid of flying'.

Williams was clearly disturbed by the ongoing difficulties experienced by those affected, despite multiple apologies from politicians. She wrote:

I met people who were, even after receiving their documents from the Home Office, in severe financial and personal difficulties. Some were unable to find work after time away from the job market. Others were in temporary accommodation, having to live with families or facing eviction because of unpaid bills. Some were in serious debt. Many of the people affected had experienced a sense of loss and devastation that had fundamentally affected their ability to cope and undermined their sense of identity and feelings of self-worth.

She expressed frustration that ministers and senior officials still did not appear to accept the full extent of the injustice done: 'Many gave the impression that the situation was unforeseen, unforeseeable and therefore unavoidable. Whereas, the evidence clearly shows that the sequence of events which culminated in the scandal, while unforeseen, was both foreseeable and avoidable.'

The timing of the report's publication was unfortunate. Alarm about the looming Covid-19 pandemic was mounting. The streets of London were already deserted and there was an atmosphere of post-apocalyptic desolation on the tube when I travelled to the press launch in Westminster. It was the last time I used public transport for months. Four days later, Britain went into lockdown and for a while this damning review looked destined to be forgotten.

The new Home Secretary, Priti Patel, responded to the report with more slightly qualified apologies, a familiar mixture of contrition and pointed, party-political attempts to shift some of the blame onto Labour. 'On behalf of this and successive governments, I am truly sorry for the actions that spanned decades,' she said. She acknowledged that 'lives were ruined and families were torn apart' and that people had 'suffered terrible injustices' as a result of 'being made to feel unwelcome in their own country. They have described their experiences as unthinkable and unimaginable.'

By now three Home Secretaries and two prime ministers had expressed remorse about what happened, and everyone involved was getting severe apology fatigue, particularly given the agonisingly slow pace of progress towards paying out compensation. Figures released after the compensation scheme had been in operation for a year (and two years after the government first apologised and promised to right the wrongs done to the Windrush generation) showed that just £360,000 had been paid out to sixty people; only 5 per cent of those who had applied had received any money. Around 254 cases had been languishing on officials' desks without a decision for over a year. At least five people had died after applying for compensation but before receiving it.

If the government was so sorry, 'why have we still got Windrush people living in dustbins and airports?' asked Elwaldo Romeo, who in 2017 had been told to return to Antigua, the country he left aged four, fifty-nine years earlier. It was a good question. I was still spending a lot of time meeting people who were struggling to extract themselves from Windrush-related difficulties. Some people, like Gbolagade Ibukun-Oluwa, fifty-nine, who became homeless after being classified as an illegal immigrant (despite having lived and worked in the UK for forty years), were still waiting for citizenship. Several nights a week Gbolagade slept in his wheelchair in Heathrow Terminal 4, trying to sort out his papers whenever he could get enough money to put credit on his phone. Others were still waiting for compensation, including Anthony Williams, fifty-six, a former soldier, who arrived in Birmingham from Jamaica in 1971 aged seven and went to primary and secondary school before joining the army and serving with the Royal Artillery for thirteen years. Williams had been designated an illegal immigrant in 2013 and sacked from his job. He spent five years destitute, able neither to work or claim unemployment benefit. He had no money to heat his flat and spent most of the time in winter keeping warm at the local library. Mostly he ate 35p tins of sardines and pasta. He was unable to register for a doctor's appointment and when he got a tooth infection he was also unable to visit a dentist. The infection spread, and first all his top teeth fell out, then most of his lower teeth. He was so frightened that Immigration Enforcement officers would visit him to arrest him and take him to a removal centre that he disconnected the intercom in his flat and never answered the door. Williams applied for compensation as soon as the scheme was launched. Fourteen months later he was still waiting for a decision, still living with the financial consequences of five years of enforced unemployment in a flat that he was unable to afford to furnish properly.

'I gave the youngest part of my life to the queen and country, and I've been treated like a piece of crap by the government and the Ministry of Defence. The worst thing is when politicians say they are sorry, and they understand what we went through. They don't understand. They've weakened that word, sorry,' he told me. 'I was so broke that I didn't buy a bed for this flat until last year. I still don't have carpets or curtains because I can't afford them, and I don't use the heating. I had to sell my computer and my bike. It was really humiliating.'

On 22 June 2020, ministers tried to make the second annual Windrush Day a celebratory occasion. The day was funded with the £500,000 annual grant, announced by Theresa May as one of her gestures of remorse; events marking how 'Caribbean communities have changed our lives for the better' were announced by the Communities Minister, with cookery, dance, poetry and music events scheduled (mostly online only because of the continuing Covid-19 restrictions); an *Empire Windrush* colouring-in poster was printed. But news coverage was dominated by reports about the mounting fury of those who were still waiting for compensation. Paulette Wilson, Anthony Bryan, Elwaldo Romeo, Michael Braithwaite and Glenda Caesar (who was sacked from her job as an administrator for a GP surgery and pushed into destitution after the Home Office refused to believe she was in the UK legally, despite the fact that she had arrived in 1961 from Dominica, aged six months) went to Downing Street to deliver a petition signed by 130,000 people, calling on the government to speed up compensation payments and implement all thirty of the recommendations in the Williams review. Williams went on television and warned that there was a 'grave risk' of a repeat Windrush-style scandal happening if the government did not adopt her suggested measures in full.

Weeks of Black Lives Matter protests following the killing of George Floyd by police in Minnesota had made the government anxious to appear to be doing the right thing on race-related issues. A new cross-government commission into all aspects of racial inequality was set up, followed a few days later by the launch of a new cross-government working group on Windrush to help 'address the challenges faced by the Windrush generation and their descendants'. These announcements of further working groups and commissions merely prompted further fury from those affected, who pointed out that in the preceding twenty-four months there had been extensive investigations about what to do, and that now was the time for action.

Facing a new surge of negative media coverage on Windrush, Priti Patel unexpectedly returned to the dispatch box in Westminster the day after Windrush Day and told MPs that she would be accepting all thirty of Wendy Williams's recommendations. We still don't know if and how this will actually materialise (and it is hard not to feel a little sceptical given the piles of commitments that have yet to be actually implemented) but taken at face value, this is an incredibly positive development. Still, this felt like a moment of vindication. If the measures are to be adopted in full, then this will have to mean comprehensive reform of the Home Office, with officials accepting that 'systemic and cultural change is necessary' and ministers obliged to come up with a new Home Office mission statement based on 'fairness, humanity, openness, diversity and inclusion'.

Potentially most significant is the seventh recommendation, which requires the government to undertake a 'full review and evaluation of the hostile/compliant environment policy and measures – individually and cumulatively'. This review would analyse whether the measures are 'effective and proportionate in meeting their stated aim, given the risks inherent in the policy'. While news of a further review makes the heart slightly sink, this will be the first time the totality of the hostile environment measures have been scrutinised; previous piecemeal assessments have indicated that they don't save money and they don't work, so it's plausible that this could trigger reform.

All Home Office staff will be required to learn about Britain's colonial history, the history of inward and outward migration and the history of black Britons, so that they fully understand the legacy of empire. One senior official had revealed to Williams that staff didn't really have a clue about the interplay between the colonial system and immigration legislation, remarking:

One of the notable things . . . about when Windrush broke was [that] we all had to go and educate ourselves about historic legislation . . . No one knew off the top of their head what the 1971 Act said, what the rules [were] about British colonies that got independence and what happened to people from those colonies . . . all of that was thirty, forty years ago. Well, it's still live – it still matters – but nobody had thought about that for a very long period of time.

Williams recommended a migrants' commissioner must be appointed, 'responsible for speaking up for migrants'. New emphasis should be put on making sure Home Office staff are able to tell superiors about problems and that senior civil servants are able to be 'candid' in their advice to ministers.

The full scale of the scandal remains unknown and Williams said she was aware that some people were still not coming forward to sort out their status because they still feared arrest by Immigration Enforcement teams; she ruled that further work should be undertaken by seeking out other people affected, particularly from non-Caribbean countries.

Williams was criticised for stepping back from finding that the Home Office was institutionally racist, a finding apparently included in earlier drafts of the report, but nevertheless there are a number of significant findings on the issue of race. She highlights the lack of ethnic diversity at senior levels in the Home Office. Black, Asian and minority ethnic staff are predominantly concentrated in the lower grades, and in 2018 made up 26.14 per cent and 26.33 per cent of the two lowest grades respectively, but only 7.18 per cent of the senior civil service roles. 'The Windrush scandal was in part able to happen because of the public's and officials' poor understanding of Britain's colonial history,' she wrote. 'I think it is unfortunate that most of the policymakers were white and most of the people involved were black,' a senior official told her. She was underwhelmed about civil servants' understanding of the nature of racism. 'There seems to be a misconception that racism is confined to decisions made with racist motivations . . . This is a misunderstanding of both the law and racism generally.' She notes that the Home Office failed to track 'the racial impact of its policies and decisions'.

When talking to civil servants she noted that:

Some showed ignorance and a lack of understanding of the root causes and a lack of acceptance of the full extent of the injustice done. In addition, some of those that I interviewed when asked about the perception that race might have played a role in the scandal were unimpressively unreflective, focusing on direct discrimination in the form of discriminatory motivation and showing little awareness of the possibility of indirect discrimination or the way in which race, immigration and nationality intersect.

She concluded that 'race clearly played a part in what occurred'; with that in mind, she recommended that the Home Office needs to set up a race advisory board, to inform policymaking and to improve the make-up of the department itself.

Bits of the report are very revealing about what was happening behind the scenes when I was making regular calls to the Home Office press office, trying to understand why people were being treated so badly. An internal email from the Immigration and Borders Secretariat to the press office warned that staff would need to 'think carefully about how to respond' to the first inquiries about why Paulette Wilson and Anthony Bryan had been detained. Internal emails reveal how, in response to *Guardian* requests for comment on individual cases, the Home Office was slowly 'beginning to recognise that the problems being brought to their attention by the media represented a pattern; they were "joining the dots" about this being a more widespread problem'. The *Guardian* was 'uncovering a series of cases with a pattern that could no longer be interpreted as unique or a "one-off". One member of staff at the Home Office told us it was becoming clear there by the end of 2017 that there was "something about Commonwealth cases",' Williams wrote. In February, there was a flurry of internal communications, discussing how to respond to the *Guardian*'s queries and Home Office staff were told to put the 'emphasis on the responsibility of the individual to prove their status'.

This chimes with a familiar desire by officials to blame the individuals affected for their difficulties. Officials told Williams: 'It was the fault of the people caught up in it that they didn't get evidence of their status and when they tried to, they didn't provide the right documentation.' But her research reveals that although there were attempts to get the Windrush cohort to register for citizenship in the 1980s, there was a parallel imperative not to 'stimulate a flood of inquiries'. 'Publicity leaflets from the time also explained that there would be no consequences if people chose not to register at that time. It is therefore unsurprising that some did not register,' she noted. A leaflet from the time stated: 'If you have the right to register but you don't want to, you do not have to. Your other rights in the United Kingdom will not change in any way. You will not lose your entitlement to social benefits, such as health services, housing, welfare and pension rights, by not registering. Your position under immigration law is not changed.'

But the desire to shove the blame on the victims persisted; this may have been partly because of the growing detachment between staff and the people whose files they were processing. A senior official told Williams he had become uneasy at the way caseworkers had 'never met a migrant and somehow lived in a kind of bubble where the most important thing was how many files you got through'.

Some staff members told her that the pressure they felt as a result of 'throughput targets' – numbers of decisions they were expected to make each day – meant there was no time to exercise proper judgement. 'This, and the fact that they never met the people face to face, had led to them suspending "common sense".' The process was viewed by many as a 'tick-box exercise' focused on rules, not ethics. On reflection, some admitted that the standard of proof on people to be able to establish their immigration status was extremely high and commented that they would struggle themselves to provide that degree of evidence of their own residence in the UK. They also acknowledged that the Home Office gave applicants minimal help, 'often referring people to the gov.uk website, which staff themselves said they struggled to understand or navigate'. Williams recommended that the immigration system should make it possible for staff to increase direct contact with applicants where appropriate.

She noted some frustration from civil servants, who in their own defence pointed out that some of the injustices were fuelled by the still prevalent conviction that the British public really wants the government to operate a tough immigration system. One senior official told her:

People have a humane and compassionate attitude to individuals, who are in some cases at the sharp end of the immigration system. And yet when they look at the immigration system as a whole, say it isn't tough enough. And so . . . there is that sort of tension, I think, within the public consciousness as well. And successive Home Secretaries of successive governments have wrestled with that.

Another said: 'It's a politically hugely contentious environment. One half of the population never thinks you're doing enough and the other thinks you're doing too much.'

Despite all the apologies and promises, I'm not convinced that politicians and officials have really learned the lessons of Windrush yet. There are still signs that action is primarily motivated by PR damage-limitation concerns. Here is just one example. An excellent film was written about Anthony Bryan's experience by his younger brother Stephen Thompson. When pre-broadcast media revealed in May 2020 that Anthony was facing serious financial problems because he was still waiting for compensation to be paid for the five weeks he spent in immigration detention and the years of forced unemployment, he was suddenly unexpectedly contacted by Home Office staff and offered an interim payment. He was also informed that Priti Patel would like to talk to him by phone, and staff suggested that her office would call him an hour before the programme was broadcast. An email from her office said that the Home Secretary 'feels it vitally important to hear directly from affected members of the community, such as Mr Bryan'. Anthony suspected that the Home Secretary's sudden desire to talk to him had more to do with the programme airing than any real urge to hear what he had to say, and declined the call.

Officials still fail to understand that swift payment of compensation is vital – not simply as a gesture of recognition that victims have been gravely harmed, but more crucially because most of those affected are still in a dire financial position as a direct consequence of the Home Office's original mistakes. Some people are still receiving eviction notices; others are still in debt, unable to pay off loans they took out when they were forced into unemployment and denied benefits, or unable to return money borrowed from friends for legal bills and food.

Stephen Thompson said the delays in paying compensation had hit Anthony and his family hard. 'My brother is naturally the forgiving and accepting type; he doesn't do embittered. But the unfortunate reality is that the longer this goes on and the longer the government drags its heels over the next stage, it will be hard for him to stay that way. There has been a slow, steady erosion of his desire to see the good in everything,' he said. 'He is trying to be patient, but the truth is that they are in very, very bad straits financially. He feels let down.'

Very few of the people I've met and written about here have received full compensation, and only a handful have received interim payments. The daughter of one of those who has waited over a year for any response to a claim said the process of applying for compensation had been exhausting: 'They seem to have forgotten that those affected have done nothing wrong.'

In February I attended an emotional meeting in Manchester where claimants told the Home Office official in charge of the compensation scheme, Daniel Hobbs, about the difficulties they were experiencing. Because their original problems stemmed from the department demanding they provide unrealistic quantities of documentary evidence proving they had lived in the UK for decades, many felt it was dispiriting to be asked to provide impossible levels of documentary proof again in order to apply for compensation. One man was asked to provide payslips from the bar job he did in the 1990s, but pointed out that because he was given only forty-eight hours to pack up his life before deportation to Jamaica (a country he had left thirty-five years earlier), he had lost all his records. And besides, who has kept their payslips from the 1990s?

It is hard to understand what the delay is about, but as I type I'm watching Patel out of the corner of my eye being questioned again by the Home Affairs Select Committee about the compensation scheme. She apologises again about Windrush being a 'stain' on the department, agrees the delays are 'unacceptable' and announces that eleven new members of staff will be starting work from Monday to help process the claims. So perhaps that may finally help. Fingers crossed.

In the meantime, generous *Guardian* readers and philanthropists have stepped in, horrified by the ongoing ill-treatment of this group of people, offering to pay for dental treatment, funerals, furniture, housing costs, legal bills – which is both inspiring and incredibly frustrating, since those affected shouldn't still have to be reliant on charity.

By now over 12,000 people have received documentation confirming that they are (and always were) here legally, 5,900 of whom were granted citizenship. But for some people this process has been very slow. Hubert Howard became very ill in the summer of 2019 and was still fighting for citizenship as he lay dying in an intensive care bed. He was finally granted it three weeks before he died (fifty-nine years after arriving in the UK from Jamaica aged three). His friend Tyrone McGibbon described Howard as 'one of the nicest people you could meet. But recently we didn't see that side of him so much. He was stressed out because of what he was going through for the past few years. The Windrush saga made him ill – the non-stop pressure. There is only so much people can take before they can't take any more. It was just too much for him in the end.' Jashwa Moses, a reggae musician who had arrived in Britain in the 1960s aged twelve, died shortly after securing citizenship in 2019 but before receiving compensation, so he was unable to make a long-planned trip back to Jamaica.

Richard Stewart, seventy-four, died in 2019 without receiving compensation or a personal apology from the government. He had been waiting for his case to be resolved so that he could travel back to Jamaica for the first time in half a century and visit his mother's grave. In 1955, aged ten, he moved from Jamaica to England as a British subject to join his parents and played county cricket as a fast bowler for Middlesex in the 1960s. In 2012 he was told he was in the UK illegally. His son, Wesley Stewart, said the cause of death was unknown, but noted that his father had become stressed and depressed during the protracted process of attempting to sort out his paperwork. 'It was upsetting for him; he said he had been in the country for longer than David Cameron had been alive, but he worried about whether he was going to get deported.'

I dread opening more emails with bad news, but they continue to come. In March, the daughter of Briggs Levi Maynard, ninety-one, who arrived in Britain from Barbados in 1957 to take up a job as a bus conductor, emailed to say her father had died from Covid-19. He had experienced various difficulties because of his lack of documentation, including being told by airport staff that he would not be able to return home after a holiday because he did not have UK residency (despite the fact he had lived here for sixty years). When he died he still had not received British citizenship. The mystifying administrative slowness feels hugely unfair.

In July, just as I was finishing writing this, I had a call from Natalie Barnes, telling me her mother, Paulette Wilson, had died, unexpectedly and prematurely, at the age of sixty-four. Tributes flooded in from politicians and campaigners to a woman whose voice had been so pivotal in exposing this scandal. It was Paulette's brave decision to talk about her treatment by the Home Office that encouraged so many people to come forward to describe how they had been similarly mistreated. Without her determination to speak out, it is likely that the problems experienced by the Windrush cohort would have remained a complicated, little-understood immigration problem. Natalie said her mother had received compensation for wrongful detention, but had been left depressed and exhausted by the experiences of the last few years. When I last met her outside Downing Street, she said she was weary of all the apologies and had hoped two years ago that there would be a swifter resolution of everyone's difficulties. 'The word "sorry" can roll off anyone's tongue easily, but we don't want more apologies,' she said.

Ministers owe it to the memory of Paulette and all the others who have died prematurely, stressed and distressed by their experiences, to make sure that real reform of the Home Office actually happens and that the compensation process is speeded up so that the remaining victims are still alive to receive the justice they deserve.

ACKNOWLEDGEMENTS

This account of the Windrush scandal is inevitably written from my perspective as a journalist discovering something disturbing, grasping to understand it and writing about it. But long before I realised what was going on, this was an issue that those affected and their families, lawyers and immigration case workers had tried to highlight. They were all incredibly generous with their time as I raced to catch up with what they already knew.

Mostly I want to thank those affected by this scandal, and their families, who took the brave decision to talk in public about their difficulties. Paulette Wilson and Natalie Barnes; Anthony Bryan, Janet McKay and Lucille Thompson; Hubert Howard; Renford McIntyre; Judy Griffith; Glenda Caesar; Jeffrey M; Tyrone McGibbon; Huthley S; Sentina Bristol; Rachelle and Elwaldo Romeo; Stephanie and Sarah O'Connor; Michael Braithwaite; Cardlin, Trevor, Desmond and Icyline Johnson; Ewen Herbert Small; Noel Smith; Tony Perry; Lydden Lewis; George Poleon; Winston Robinson; Joycelyn John; Edward Bromfield; Bevis Smith; Gladstone Wilson; Samantha Cooper; George Lee; Donald Thompson; 'Colin Smith'; Ivan and Patricia Anglin; Vernon Vanriel; Richard Stewart; Winston Walker; Margaret O'Brien; Sylvester Marshall; Nick Broderick; and Ken Morgan. Although we've mostly been talking about things going wrong, it has been a real pleasure meeting and interviewing them.

A group of people worked hard to force the government to recognise its Windrush failings ahead of the Commonwealth summit in April 2018. Guy Hewitt, Barbados High Commissioner to London; Dr Kevin Isaac, St Kitts and Nevis High Commissioner to London; Seth George Ramocan, Jamaican High Commissioner to London, and the nine other Caribbean High Commissioners; David Lammy MP and his tireless parliamentary assistant Jack McKenna who worked on this 24/7 for a number of weeks; Omar Khan, Director of the Runnymede Trust, and Kimberly McIntosh; Satbir Singh, Chief Executive of the Joint Council for the Welfare of Immigrants, and his colleagues Chai Patel and Denise Meredith; the energetic campaigner Patrick Vernon; Lord Herman Ouseley.

A huge number of people helped me as I wrote about this. At the Refugee and Migrant Centre in Wolverhampton, Arten Llazari, Heather Thomas and Daniel Ashwell. At Praxis, Laura Stahnke, Sally Daghlian, Bethan Lant and Chloe Robinson. Despite the funding cuts, there are still many lawyers prepared to take on complex immigration cases, doing the work pro bono or for reduced fees. You'd be lucky to find yourself represented by Jacqueline McKenzie of McKenzie Beute and Pope, who has been helping people extract themselves from this situation for a number of years; or Paulette Wilson's lawyer, James Wilson at JM Wilson Solicitors, who has done a lot of pro bono work for Windrush and other people with immigration difficulties; or Jeremy Bloom, with Duncan Lewis, who helped Sylvester Marshall; or Connie Sozi, with Deighton Pierce Glyn. I'm grateful to Adrian Berry of Garden Court Chambers for helping me to begin to understand some of the history of immigration and nationality law and equally to Frances Webber, of the Institute of Race Relations. Martin Forde QC took on the difficult and largely thankless task of drawing up a compensation scheme; he was dedicated in travelling around the country over the course of a year to talk to those affected to understand what help was needed, and was kind enough to spend time in explaining his conclusions.

The *Guardian* has been very supportive. I'm particularly grateful to Alan Travis, the paper's former home affairs editor, who helped me enormously as I began to write about this, and continued to help, even after he left the organisation, explaining key aspects of the hostile environment over many early morning, post school-run cups of coffee; also to Gary Younge for being incredibly helpful and for some very thoughtful advice on how to write a book. None of these stories would have made it into the paper without the help of editors, particularly national editor Owen Gibson, and his colleagues Rebecca Allison and Archie Bland. The paper's editor Kath Viner and deputy Paul Johnson made sure the issue stayed on the front page. I really appreciate how calm, good-humoured and insightful they have all been. Investigations editor Nick Hopkins' work on Amber Rudd was critical; health correspondent Denis Campbell helped unpick the hostile environment's entry into the NHS. Thanks also to new home affairs correspondent Jamie Grierson and reporters Sarah Marsh and Josh Halliday; to communities editor Caroline Bannock, who spent weeks corresponding with hundreds of people who contacted the *Guardian* about their immigration status; to Jan Thompson and Brendan O'Grady, who helped during some of the more stressful aspects of the reporting; to Robert Hahn, Jim Hedge, Fiona Shields, David Teather, Kira Cochrane, John Stuttle, Angela Foster, Rob Fearn, Rob Evans, Amelia Hill, Jamie Wilson, Clare Margetson, Melissa Denes, John Stuttle, Ali Usman, Colin Blackstock, Michael Pugh, Dan Sabbagh, Luc Torres, Richard Nelsson, Jason Rodrigues, Su Haire, Sanaz Movahedi, Martyn Dore and Sarah Hewitt; to Hugh Muir for helpful advice; to Patrick Butler for the *Guardian*'s appeal which raised over £1.1 million for charities working on hostile environment and Windrush issues; to the huge unseen structure of subeditors, night editors, picture editors, lawyers and IT experts. I'm very lucky with my colleagues at the *Guardian* – huge thanks to all my friends in the building for many happy hours spent in the canteen.

I'm grateful to Dr Jane Garnett for sending an essential Windrush reading list and for a much-needed tutorial; and to David

Olusoga for sharing his thoughts on the mythic status of *Empire Windrush*. Also to Fiona Bawdon for her prescience; Rob McNeil and Madeleine Sumption at the Migration Advisory Committee in Oxford for revealing the possible scale of the problem; Simon Woolley of Operation Black Vote; Nimrod Ben-Cnaan of the Law Centres Network; Gus John; Paul Gilroy; Arthur Torrington of the Windrush Foundation; Alford Gardner; Hilary Brown; Lee Jasper; Lucy Moreton; Luke de Noronha; Natasha Shallice. There are a number of current and former Home Office employees whom I can't name – thank you. A number of Home Office press officers have been very helpful and I'm grateful to them.

James Pullen at Wylie has been very encouraging over a number of years; huge thanks to him and to Sarah Chalfant. Laura Hassan, my editor at Faber, has been lovely to work with, as has Fred Baty, who took over for the final edit. I've really appreciated their skill and enthusiasm. Thanks also to Lauren Nicoll in Faber's publicity department, designer Donna Payne, Kate Ward in pre-press, Jack Murphy in production and Eleanor Rees for vital copyediting.

My siblings Tabby, Nella and Tom have helped me enormously, as have my parents, David and Sue Gentleman. Finally, much love and thanks to Jo, Rose and William.

NOTES

Introduction

1 https://www.justiceinspectorates.gov.uk/hmiprisons/wp-content/uploads/sites/4/2016/07/Colnbrook-Web-2016.pdf

2 Paulette is uncertain about her date of arrival in the UK, and doesn't know how old she was. Her age on arrival is listed variously as ten and eleven in the Home Office files.

A Person with No Leave to Remain

1 https://publications.parliament.uk/pa/cm201719/cmselect/cmhaff/913/91306.htm#_idTextAnchor029

2 https://www.theguardian.com/uk-news/2018/jun/28/wrongful-detention-cost-21m-as-immigration-staff-chased-bonuses

3 Joy Gardner, a forty-year-old mature student, died in 1993 following an attempt by police and immigration officers to detain her and deport her to Jamaica. Her house was raided in London, and she was restrained with handcuffs and leather belts and gagged with 3.96 m of Elastoplast tape, which officers wrapped seven times around her head, according to a summary published by Amnesty. She fell into a coma and was pronounced dead four days later. Her five-year-old son witnessed some of the struggle between officers and his mother. Joy's mother, Myrna Simpson, had emigrated to Britain from Jamaica in 1961, and hoped to send for Joy once she was financially stable. By the time Joy arrived in 1987, immigration laws had changed and so she no longer had an automatic right to British citizenship. She overstayed her visa and was told by the Home Office that she should leave the country voluntarily or risk deportation. Her death brought public attention to the extreme methods used routinely in the execution of deportation orders.

Jimmy Mubenga, aged forty-six, died after being restrained by G4S guards on a British Airways flight in October 2010 while being deported to Angola. Several witnesses said he was held down in his seat for over half an hour and his cries that he could not breathe were ignored until they stopped. An inquest jury in 2011 held that the killing was unlawful.

Five Weeks' Detention and a Ticket to Jamaica

1 https://www.justiceinspectorates.gov.uk/hmiprisons/wp-content/uploads/sites/4/2015/08/The-Verne-web-2015.pdf
2 Anthony is referring to the 1971 Immigration Act, which was implemented in 1973.

£54,000

1 https://www.gov.uk/guidance/nhs-entitlements-migrant-health-guide#introduction
2 https://assets.publishing.service.gov.uk/government/uploads/system/uploads/attachment_data/file/590027/Cons_Response_cost_recovery.pdf
3 https://www.theguardian.com/commentisfree/2018/mar/12/doctor-nhs-care-government-albert-thompson

We Are Here Because You Were There

1 Under Section 4 of the Vagrancy Act 1824, police were able to stop and search people they considered to be acting suspiciously. This became informally known as the sus law (for 'suspected person'); it was often used against individuals police suspected of intent to commit an arrestable offence, and was disproportionately used against black communities. The sus law was repealed in August 1981, but was replaced in 1984 by new stop and search powers under the Police and Criminal Evidence Act.
2 David Olusoga, *Black and British: A Forgotten History* (Macmillan, 2016), p. 481
3 Mike Phillips and Trevor Phillips, *Windrush: The Irresistible Rise of Multi-racial Britain* (HarperCollins, 1998), p. 59
4 Phillips and Phillips, *Windrush*, p. 68
5 Phillips and Phillips, *Windrush*, p. 68
6 Olusoga, *Black and British*, p. 491
7 Kathleen Paul, *Whitewashing Britain: Race and Citizenship in the Postwar Era* (Cornell University Press, 1997), p. 90
8 Robert Winder, *Bloody Foreigners: The Story of Immigration to Britain* (Little, Brown, 2004), p. 331

9 Olusoga, *Black and British*, pp. 491–2

10 Quoted in Olusoga, *Black and British*, p. 492

11 Phillips and Phillips, *Windrush*, p. 69

12 Winder, *Bloody Foreigners*, p. 339

13 Phillips and Phillips, *Windrush*, p. 53

14 Paul, *Whitewashing Britain*, p. 117

15 Olusoga, *Black and British*, p. 495

16 Phillips and Phillips, *Windrush*, p. 75

17 Olusoga, *Black and British*, p. 498

18 David Dutton, Lucien Jenkins and Richard Kerridge, *The Making of Modern Britain* (Cambridge University Press, 2016), p. 23

19 Paul, *Whitewashing Britain*, p. 134

20 Edward Pilkington, *Beyond the Mother Country: West Indians and the Notting Hill White Riots* (IB Tauris, 1988), p. 38

21 Phillips and Phillips, *Windrush*, p. 97

22 Sam Selvon, *The Lonely Londoners* (Allan Wingate, 1956; Penguin, 2006), p. 21

23 Winder, *Bloody Foreigners*, p. 342

24 E. R. Braithwaite, *To Sir, with Love* (Bodley Head, 1959; Vintage Classics, 2005), p. 95

25 Braithwaite, *To Sir, with Love*, p. 38

26 Phillips and Phillips, *Windrush*, pp. 13–14

27 Andrea Levy, *Small Island* (Tinder Press, 2004), p. 142

28 Phillips and Phillips, *Windrush*, p. 131

29 Stephen Bourne, *War to Windrush: Black Women in Britain 1939–48* (Jacaranda, 2018), p. 103

30 Pilkington, *Beyond the Mother Country*, p. 32

31 Winder, *Bloody Foreigners*, p. 364

32 Winder, *Bloody Foreigners*, p. 363

33 Olusoga, *Black and British*, p. 512

34 Winder, *Bloody Foreigners*, p. 370

A Hostile Environment

1 https://www.theguardian.com/politics/2011/oct/06/clarke-condemns-may-attack-human-rights-act

2 https://www.theguardian.com/theguardian/2013/jul/12/sarah-teather-angry-voices-immigration

3 David Laws, *Coalition* (Biteback, 2016), p. 351

4 https://blogs.spectator.co.uk/2013/09/nigel-farages-speech-full-text-and-audio/

5 https://www.theguardian.com/uk-news/2013/nov/05/migration-target-useless-experts

6 Robert Ford and Matthew Goodwin, *Revolt on the Right: Explaining Support for the Radical Right in Britain* (Routledge, 2014), p. 269

7 https://www.whatdotheyknow.com/request/178455/response/453923/attach/html/3/FOI29596.pdf.html

8 The ideas developed in the Hostile Environment committee were embraced in the 2014 Immigration Act, which promised measures to 'make it more difficult for illegal migrants to live in the UK, encouraging them to depart.' The aim of the package of policies was to deter people without permission from entering the UK and to encourage those already here to leave voluntarily. The new legislation required landlords to check the immigration status of their tenants; the landlord faced a £3,000 fine if found to be renting to illegal immigrants. The act also required temporary migrants to make contributions to the NHS, in the form of a surcharge. Banks were required to check against a database of known immigration offenders before giving permission for an account to be opened. There were new checks on driving licence applicants to ensure illegal immigrants would not get licences. The Act made it easier to remove people who had no right to be in the country, limiting rights of appeal and access to bail. An exemption from deportation for long-term residents was removed, without any discussion. The existing fine imposed on employers for hiring anyone without papers was doubled to £20,000. The 2014 Act meant that public and private sector workers became part of the immigration enforcement team, despite having no expertise or training in immigration law. Separate legislation introduced restrictions on access to judicial reviews and new constraints on access to bail for people detained under immigration powers.

9 http://jcwi.org.uk/sites/default/files/MAX%20IB%20Briefing.pdf

10 https://www.theguardian.com/politics/2013/oct/10/immigration-bill-theresa-may-hostile-environment

11 https://www.freemovement.org.uk/hostile-environment-affect/

12 https://www.lag.org.uk/document-downloads/204756/chasing-status-if-not-british--then-what-am-i-

13 https://www.bbc.co.uk/news/uk-politics-20400747

14 https://www.amnesty.org.uk/files/Resources/AIUK%20to%20Home%20
Office%20Windrush%20Lessons%20Learned%20Review.pdf

15 https://www.libertyhumanrights.org.uk/sites/default/files/HE%20web.pdf

16 Russell Hargrave, Drawbridge Britain (Eyewear Publishing, 2018), p. 125

Frightening People to Leave

1 https://assets.publishing.service.gov.uk/government/uploads/system/
uploads/attachment_data/file/547391/Overstayers-Report_Dec_2014.pdf

2 https://www.theguardian.com/uk-news/2013/jul/26/go-home-ad-
campaign-court-challenge

3 https://www.ourmigrationstory.org.uk/uploads/Operation_Vaken_
Evaluation_Report.pdf

4 https://www.bloomberg.com/news/articles/2018-04-19/former-may-aide-s-
attempt-to-defend-her-undermined-by-email-leak

5 http://www.politics.co.uk/news/2017/11/28/woman-reports-rape-to-
police-and-is-arrested-on-immigration

Hunting for Proof

1 http://www.legislation.gov.uk/ukpga/1971/77/section/3/1995-03-
31?view=plain

2 The 1948 British Nationality Act theoretically granted all 800 million
subjects of the British Empire the right to enter the UK. It didn't
matter if you were born in Kingston, Jamaica or Kingston upon Thames,
from 1948 to 1962 colonial subjects and British citizens were legally
indistinguishable. Arrivals from British colonies came as British subjects,
sharing the same rights to come and go, and to stay as long as they liked,
as British subjects who were born in the UK. Anyone born in Britain or
in a British colony was identified as a citizen of the United Kingdom and
Colonies (CUKC) or a British subject.

Gradually, as British colonies, dependencies and protectorates
became independent, those new nations conferred their own
nationalities on their citizens. Those affected ceased to be citizens of the
UK and Colonies, but they continued to be Commonwealth citizens,
and were entitled, if they had been resident in the UK for twelve
months, to reregister as CUKCs.

But a number of more restrictive immigration laws reduced those rights, in 1962, 1968, 1971 and 1981. Politicians implementing the 1948 British Nationality Act did not anticipate large-scale non-white migration, and were taken aback by the arrival of hundreds of thousands of Caribbean migrants in the 1950s. In 1945, the UK had a non-white population of around thirty thousand. By 1962, around half a million migrants had arrived; opinion polling in 1958 showed majority support for stricter migration control. In 1962 and 1968, the government duly began to restrict the rights of Commonwealth citizens to move freely to the UK. Some of these changes were made to appease the public's racist concerns. The Commonwealth Immigrants Act 1968 awarded an unconditional right to live and work in the UK only to citizens of the United Kingdom and Colonies who had a father or a grandfather born in the UK (which was more likely to be the case for people living in predominantly white Commonwealth countries like Canada or Australia).

The 1971 Immigration Act further constrained Commonwealth citizens' right to enter the UK, ending large-scale immigration from those countries. But crucially it included a safeguard for Commonwealth citizens who had already settled in the UK, confirming their right to live there indefinitely. It was clear that all the so-called Windrush generation who arrived before 1 January 1973 (when the law came into force) had a legal right to remain, and were not required to get any specific documentation to prove that status. Unfortunately the Home Office did not keep a record of those people who had been granted indefinite leave to remain; there was no consistent record-keeping of those who entered the UK since 1948, since those entries had not been controlled.

In 1978, Margaret Thatcher (then leader of the opposition) was talking about immigration in now familiar language, remarking that people were feeling 'rather swamped' by immigrants. Further, increasingly restrictive legislation was developed and introduced. The British Nationality Act in 1981 required Commonwealth citizens who had settled in the UK to register to become British citizens. Although there was a national drive to encourage this in the early 1980s, the fact that so many Windrush people failed to take steps to register suggests it was ill explained or badly advertised. Paulette Wilson said she had no memory of a government campaign encouraging her to register. 'I did not watch a lot of TV in those days, so I didn't know about it.' Anthony Bryan had a dim awareness of it. 'I went to primary school and secondary school here. I didn't think they were talking to me.'

The arrival of biometric cards for some categories of non-EU foreign nationals in 2008 complicated things further for people without proof of their immigration status. Culturally, Britain remains uncomfortable with the idea of ID cards, and the coalition government scrapped Labour proposals for a comprehensive ID card system when they came into power in 2010. But the phasing in of biometric cards for foreigners in 2008 represented a significant step towards an ID card regime. There was something inherently discriminatory about the way the cards were limited to migrants. While many European countries have ID card systems, they are universal; the biometric cards system introduced a 'papers please' system for foreigners only.

A Political Explosion

1 https://hansard.parliament.uk/Commons/2018-04-23/debates/
AFC7E55B-9796-4FDA-8BB6-9EBDC7CCDAE2/Windrush

Hostile Becomes Compliant

1 https://www.theguardian.com/uk-news/2018/dec/07/police-to-stop-
passing-on-immigration-status-of-victims

Postscript

1 https://www.parliamentlive.tv/Event/Index/eec23ff6-50c0-4d07-9112-
65817db4bb65
2 https://www.parliament.uk/business/committees/committees-a-z/
commons-select/home-affairs-committee/news-parliament-2017/the-
windrush-generation-report-published-17-19/
3 https://www.parliament.uk/business/committees/committees-a-z/joint-
select/human-rights-committee/inquiries/parliament-2017/windrush-
generation-inquiry/
4 https://www.nao.org.uk/report/handling-of-the-windrush-situation/
5 https://www.parliament.uk/business/committees/committees-a-z/commons-
select/public-accounts-committee/inquiries/parliament-2017/inquiry19/
6 https://www.gov.uk/government/publications/windrush-lessons-learned-
review

7 https://assets.publishing.service.gov.uk/government/uploads/system/
   uploads/attachment_data/file/765280/Letter_to_Chair_Windrush_
   update_October_17-12-18.pdf
8 https://www.amnesty.org.uk/files/Resources/AIUK%20to%20Home%20
   Office%20Windrush%20Lessons%20Learned%20Review.pdf
9 https://www.theguardian.com/uk-news/2018/jun/28/wrongful-detention-
   cost-21m-as-immigration-staff-chased-bonuses
10 https://www.gov.uk/government/publications/immigration-statistics-
   year-ending-september-2018/how-many-people-are-detained-or-
   returned

INDEX

281; numbers wrongly detained or removed from country, 279; Paulette Wilson's file, 7, 34, 38, 223; PR concerns, 311; press office, 63, 87, 161, 185, 187, 189, 227–8, 251, 308; race advisory board, recommendation for, 308; reform of, 306, 308, 314; 'reign of terror', 126; removal process, 34; reporting centres, 19, 28–9, 31–3, 55–6, 167; response to Windrush scandal, 277–82, 286–8; staff blamed by Home Secretary, 244–5, 247–8; staff in immigration centres, 35; staff morale, 156, 158–60, 310; staff remoteness from individuals and their situations, 309–10; staff retraining, 306–7; targets for removals, 34–5, 173, 220–3, 246–7; tip-offs, 179–80; Valentine's Day tweet (2013), 179–80; voluntary returns scheme, 168–75; Windrush scandal, 1–3, 9–13, 193, 290–2; Windrush Taskforce, *see* Windrush Taskforce

hostile environment: Amber Rudd's position, 243–6; aspects suspended, 2–3, 226–7; background, 131, 136–7, 191–2, 286; change in Home Office culture, 158–60; concept, 3, 225, 278; concerns about, 131–5, 138; creation, 8, 117–19, 180, 257; 'deserving and undeserving' division, 190; discriminatory impact, 131–3, 142–4, 239–41, 291; effects of austerity measures, 289; implementation, 140, 155, 176; ministerial working group (MATBAPS), 122–9; outsourced to private sector, 166, 168; people affected by, 11–12, 172, 212–13, 286, 291; public opinion, 14, 282; requirement for documentary evidence, 151; responses to Windrush scandal, 202–4, 207, 216, 219, 222, 284; resurgence of xenophobic attitudes, 239–41, 286; review of, 306; right to rent scheme, 291; Sajid Javid's position, 225

Howard, Hubert: anger at treatment by Home Office, 67, 70, 232–3; application for British citizenship rejected,

297–8; arrival in England, 67, 229; biometric card, 229–30, 231–2, 297; citizenship granted, 313; classified as illegal immigrant, 67, 69; *Daily Mail* publication of his story, 202; debts, 69, 297–8; death, 313; denied benefits, 69, 229; employment, 67, 69, 229, 297; evidence of lifetime in UK, 70, 230–1; *Guardian* publication of his story, 73–4, 145; Home Affairs Select Committee, 219; meeting with author, 67, 72; mother's passport, 68, 229; naturalisation process, 68–9; prevented from visiting mother in Jamaica, 67, 229, 233; school friend of Anthony Bryan, 60; tax and National Insurance records, 70; told he had 'settled status', 69; Windrush Taskforce meeting, 228–33

Hunt, Jeremy, 83, 86, 123

Ibukun-Oluwa, Gbolagade, 304
immigration: public attitudes, 310
Immigration Acts: (1971), 9, 18, 19, 55, 69, 148, 182, 307; (1988), 260; (2014), 127, 131, 134, 227; (2016), 137, 227
Immigration and Borders Secretariat, 308
Immigration Enforcement: Anthony Bryan's case, 44, 45–6; 'dehumanising jargon', 302; Detention, Progression and Returns Command, 35–6; Gladstone Wilson's case, 167; Interventions and Sanctions Directorate, 130–1; letters, 291; 'low-hanging fruit', 302; Paulette Wilson's case, 33, 35–6, 295; raids, 213; relationship with schools, 125; removal targets, 220, 223; Returns Preparations Team, 33; Trevor Johnson's case, 175; vans, 43–4, 71, 118, 168, 170, 280, 292; teams, 3, 71, 125, 156, 219, 302, 304, 307; Windrush awareness, 244
Immigration Lawyers' Practitioners Association, 64, 132, 164
Immigration Service Union, 155, 170, 220
Immigration Unit, 43